"Business leaders need coaches just as much as baseball players do. Kate and Eddie's book will improve your own batting average at work. They give you the necessary tools to keep your organization competitive and agile. A must-read if you want to win your own World Series."

—Tom Werner, Chairman, Boston Red Sox

"This well researched book will help managers everywhere peer deep inside themselves and emerge with self-understanding, even revelations, that will make them more effective at work and in their lives. No one can walk away without insight; few will put it down without having been changed for the better."

—Chris Zook, Partner, Bain & Company; author of *Profit from the Core*

"Before I met Eddie, the notion of being 'vulnerable' was absurd. Yet taking the plunge was a major lifestyle change and a commitment to a whole new way of thinking, behaving, and acting—in short, a new way to live. If you care about the people around you, listen to Eddie!"

—George Nguyen, President, Eaton Heavy Duty Transmissions

"As businesses expand their reach, typical alpha male behavior can be a liability. With the powerful tools in this book, competitive, driven alpha males can learn to work more effectively across cultural and gender barriers, creating high-performing global teams."

—Hector de J. Ruiz, PhD, Chairman and CEO, Advanced Micro Devices, Inc.

"This book is filled with practical insights on how alpha males and alpha females can enhance their own personal strengths while also creating outstanding, high-impact teams."

—Mike George, President and CEO, QVC, Inc.

"Ludeman and Erlandson hit the mark by providing fresh insights and practical tools in an informative, useful book. It will help you will corral high-achieving, competitive leaders for the good of your organization."

—Major General Mary Saunders, United States Air Force (Ret.)

"Alpha males define the organizations we work in. This book helps us understand why alpha males manage themselves the way they do, and how we can all better navigate our way to shared success. It's a unique book, filled with practical advice, keen insight, scholarly references, and a fresh conceptual framework."

—Patrick Canavan, Senior Vice President, Global Governance, Motorola, Inc.

"I've seen firsthand how Ludeman and Erlandson's penetrating findings can change brute talent into leadership brilliance. The book offers this gift to the millions of us who desperately need it. You'll finally understand the real cause of your greatest successes and incomprehensible failures. Apply what you read and you'll move your game to a whole new level."

—Joseph Grenny, coauthor of the bestseller *Crucial Conversations*

"This book provides outstanding ideas for coaching superstars to manage behavior that can stifle a team's spirit. The tools for changing destructive alpha traits and the practical techniques for those who work with alphas will level the playing field and pave the way for raising your team's performance."

—Douglas Basler, President, United Conveyor Corporation

"Bold performance demands bold leaders. But too many A players confuse aggression for assertiveness and sheer stamina for supportiveness. Ludeman and Erlandson show how to turn off the anger and become a more effective leader."

—Pascal D. Forgione Jr., PhD, Superintendent, Austin Independent School District

"*Alpha Male Syndrome* has given us the tools to integrate alpha males into our organization while still protecting our culture. Instead of not hiring them, we can harness their competence and eliminate their negative impact."

—Tony Hsieh, CEO and Director, Zappos.com

"*Alpha Male Syndrome* illustrates the powerful impact an alpha can have on engaging the head, heart, and hands of the organization. It shows alphas how to channel their energy to build greater levels of followership, commitment, and trust. A must-read for anyone who wants to build a sustainable, high-performance culture."

—Peter Leddy, Senior Vice President of Human Resources, Invitrogen Corporation

"Nice work, Kate and Eddie! Your insights have put some order and structure into some of the more intangible laws of nature in the corporate world."

—Eric Stange, President, Defense and Homeland Security, Accenture

"Remember Spencer Tracy and Katharine Hepburn in *Guess Who's Coming to Dinner*? Kate and Eddie show us it's not about who's coming—but who's showing up—and the unintended consequences of our behavior on our professional and personal lives and effectiveness. Hugely valuable to me, my work, and my life!"

—Marc Mathieu, Senior Vice President, The Coca-Cola Company

Alpha Male Syndrome

Kate Ludeman
and Eddie Erlandson

Harvard Business School Press
Boston, Massachusetts

Copyright 2006 Kate Ludeman and Eddie Erlandson
All rights reserved
Printed in the United States of America
10 09 08 07 06   5 4 3 2 1

978-1-59139-913-1 (ISBN 13)

Library of Congress Cataloguing-in-Publication Data
Ludeman, Kate.
 Alpha male syndrome / Kate Ludeman and Eddie Erlandson.
   p. cm.
 ISBN 1-59139-913-0
 1. Executives–Psychology. 2. Managing your boss. 3. Executive
ability. 4. Leadership. I. Erlandson, Eddie. II. Title.
 HD38.2.L83 2006
 658.4'094–dc22
                    2006011145

The paper used in this publication meets the minimum requirements of the American National Standard for Information Sciences—Permanence of Paper for Printed Library Materials, ANSI Z39.48-1992.

We dedicate this book to the indomitable women executives we have been privileged to work with and learn from. We admire your wisdom, your curiosity, your perseverance, and your commitment to stand your ground and get the best from your alpha male colleagues. We salute your courage and tenacity.

Contents

Appendix B   **The Alpha Scale**   247

                Notes   253
                Index   259
                About the Authors   275

Acknowledgments

From conception to publication, the collaborative spirit that created this book encompassed more than the two of us. We want to express our deepest gratitude to the following people for their indispensable contributions.

To Phil Goldberg, for his ability to grasp and bring life to the concepts that guide our work; for his creative genius as a storyteller; for his strong sense of structure and his expert writing and editing; for being dependable at every step and unwavering in his commitment to produce a first-rate book; and for making the process of working together as pleasurable as it was productive.

To Gay and Katie Hendricks, who have shaped our professional thinking, expanded our capacity for joy and happiness, and helped us learn to work passionately without feeling drained.

To Melinda Merino, our editor at Harvard Business School Press, who saw the potential in the subject, and whose insights and persistence helped us clarify both our ideas and our presentation.

To Bonnie Solow, our agent, for her unfailing support and commitment to our work and for her impeccable attention to details.

To Louise O'Brien, the editor at the *Harvard Business Review* who collaborated with us on our article, "Coaching Alpha Males" (May 2004), for her creativity in putting a name to the work we do and helping us develop our personal brand.

To Winnie Shows, who helped us formulate both the HBR article and also the proposal that led to this book.

To Attila Seress and James Han, who did the statistical analysis and programming required to create a valid measurement for alpha strengths and risks.

To the Worth Ethic leadership team, especially Erin Miller and Catherine Ludeman-Hall, for keeping the business running while we took time off to work on the book. Special appreciation also goes to Tonnia Adair Gibbs, Dona Haber, Sheri Hickman, Lisa Upson, and Jodi Wibbels for their commitment and follow-through on all the details of this all-encompassing project. They probably know more about working with alphas than we do!

To each and every one of our clients, who have taught us more than they realize and who demonstrated their powerful leadership by their commitment to make needed changes; in doing so they profoundly affected their colleagues, their companies, and their families.

To those clients who so generously and willingly allowed us to share their stories so that others may share the benefit of their learning process. We are convinced that your openness is your greatest influence skill.

To our very special Dell clients for their commitment to building a great company and for allowing us to join them in this journey for eleven years.

To each other! We are blessed with the opportunity to partner in creativity and contribution, and at the same time enjoy a wonderful relationship and life together.

Foreword

Why can so many great leaders be so good and *so bad* at the same time?

People tend to repeat behavior that is followed by positive reinforcement. The more successful we become, the more positive reinforcement we receive and the more likely we are to think, "I am successful. This is how I behave. Therefore, I'm successful because I behave this way."

Wrong!

All of my coaching clients have achieved amazing levels of success, status, and recognition. Many are alpha males. And, as Kate and Eddie point out so clearly in this book, almost all those executives are successful because they do many things right—*in spite of* engaging in behavior that is clearly dysfunctional. *Alpha Male Syndrome* shows exactly why so many alpha males become successful and yet still need to change before they sabotage themselves and their companies. It also explains why it's a crazy idea for up-and-comers to blindly copy alpha males just because they've achieved a certain level of success.

Many alpha males are designated at a very young age as high-potential leaders. This anointment can quickly degenerate into the "golden boy" syndrome, in which they believe that they are endowed with godlike qualities and have no need to ever change. As they advance through their careers, puffed up by their achievements, they often fail to see the interpersonal derailers that are obvious to the rest of the world—and that will ultimately lead to their downfall. As Kate and Eddie note, "They don't realize that the skills that got them to the playoffs are not enough to take them all the way to the championship." In other words, they don't understand that what got them here won't get them *there*.

A recent study by Development Dimensions International (DDI) indicates that the average American worker spends 10 to 20 hours a month either complaining about upper management or listening to someone else complain. What a waste of productivity! Even worse, what a waste of people's lives. My guess is that a huge percentage of this whining is spent complaining about the dysfunctional alpha male behavior described in this book.

What I love most about this book is that it goes beyond helping you, the reader, *understand* the Alpha Male Syndrome. It shows you *what to do about it*. The authors state, "If you and you alone change, others will change." They then proceed to help you change your own behavior—and therefore your world—in two very important ways:

1. If you have to deal with alpha males (as almost all of us do), the book explains how to manage the relationship to achieve maximum results, instead of spending your workdays in a state of anxiety or wasting your time in useless whining.

2. If you are an alpha male (as many of the readers of this book are), it shows you how to look in the mirror and make positive changes in your own behavior.

So whether you work with alpha males or are an alpha yourself, this book helps you change nonproductive behaviors, increase performance, and improve your life!

As a reader, I have one caution. You may be tempted to think that this is a very fascinating book about the problems of *other people*. If you do, you'll miss the deeper value of what is being communicated. As you read *Alpha Male Syndrome*, look in the mirror. Reflect upon your own life and your own behavior. As Kate and Eddie suggest, begin your journey toward changing the world by changing yourself.

—*Marshall Goldsmith, leading executive coach and author of*
  What Got You Here Won't Get You There

Alpha Male Syndrome

The Good, the Bad, the Ugly

Human history is the story of alphas, those indispensable powerhouses who take charge, conquer new worlds, and move heaven and earth to make things happen. Whether heading a band of warriors, bringing a vital new product to market, guiding a team to glory, or steering a giant conglomerate, alphas are hardwired for achievement and eager to tackle challenges that others find intimidating. Along the way, they inspire awe and admiration—and sometimes fear and trembling. Wherever they are and whatever they do, they stand out from the crowd, usually leaving an indelible impression on those whose lives they touch.

The business world swarms with alpha males. Although there are no hard numbers to support this approximation, we estimate that alphas comprise about 75 percent of top executives. Some are larger-than-life legends who run giant companies; others lead in relative obscurity at the top of little-known firms or small departments. The healthy ones—well-balanced human beings in full command of their alpha strengths—are natural leaders who are trusted by colleagues, respected by competitors, revered by employees, and adored by Wall Street. But other alpha males are risks to their organizations—and sometimes to themselves. They get depicted in Dilbert cartoons, not management textbooks. Inspiring resentment instead of respect, and fear instead of trust, they create corporate soap operas that make life miserable for coworkers, create expensive problems for their companies, and derail fast-track careers—including their own. Why? Because their greatest strengths have turned into tragic flaws. Evidence of this alpha ambiguity can be seen on the covers of *Fortune* and *Forbes*, on the front pages of newspapers, on CNN and ESPN: alpha males leading the way to amazing accomplishments, earthshaking breakthroughs, and skyrocketing profits—and abusing power, bankrupting companies, and wearing handcuffs.

Like many natural resources, alphas are both indispensable to progress and potentially hazardous. The purpose of this book is to help individuals and organizations harness the immense power of alpha males while minimizing their potential downside. If you're an alpha yourself, you know how to transform the world around you; this book will help you transform yourself so you can work your magic even more effectively. You will learn how to leverage your innate assets and at the same time get the upper hand on your alpha liabilities before they create problems. If you run a team or an organization inhabited by alpha males, you will learn how to optimize their enormous productive capacity while keeping a lid on their tendency to turn teamwork into guerrilla warfare. If you work for alphas, you will learn how to take full advantage of their leadership gifts while protecting your health, integrity, and career from their potential abuses.

What Is an Alpha?

Alpha is the first letter of the Greek alphabet. In English, it has come to denote "the first of anything." In astronomy, for instance, alpha is the brightest star in a constellation. Animal researchers use the word to signify dominance, applying it to the leader of the pack, who is first in power and importance. That usage has been extended to human beings. An alpha is defined as "a person tending to assume a dominant role in social or professional situations, or thought to possess the qualities and confidence for leadership."[1]

As we use the term in our work, *alpha* signifies a powerful, authoritative personality type with a specific set of traits. Alphas are aggressive, results-driven achievers who insist on top performance from themselves and others. Courageous and self-confident, they are turned on by bold, innovative ideas and ambitious goals, and they pursue their objectives with tenacity and an urgent sense of mission. Their intense competitive drive keeps them focused on the gold—silver or bronze simply won't do—and they're always keeping score. Often charismatic figures who command attention, they exert influence even when they're low-key and inconspicuous.

Alphas are found at every level of the organizational chart. Whether they're at the forefront of a global corporation or stacking shelves in a retail store, they look for ways to increase their power and influence, dominating meetings, taking the lead on projects, and otherwise making their presence felt. Indeed, many a corporate bigwig started out as an alpha nobody who somehow stood out from the crowd. This does not mean that all good leaders are alphas, or that only alphas have what it takes to lead a group to victory. On the contrary, depending on the nature of the business and the organization, many leadership positions are better filled by men and women who are *not* alphas, and who achieve their goals with styles that better suit their personalities and circumstances. However, even those executives possess *some* alpha qualities, or else they simply could not lead, and they certainly could not lead alphas.

Those positive leadership qualities constitute one-half of the alpha syndrome. The other half consists of a package of not-so-positive symptoms that leads to everything from minor business problems to full-fledged organizational catastrophes and personal disasters. We'll get to those in a moment. But first, a question that has probably been on your mind since you picked up this book: why alpha *males*? In this age of powerful women in every field of human endeavor, what about alpha females?

Why Alpha *Males?*

Because of the popular image of the alpha male, with his powerful physical presence and tough-guy demeanor, we seldom hear the term *alpha female.* But a great many women in leadership positions do possess the fundamental traits that define alphas. One of them, in fact, is one of the authors of this book. We decided to focus on alpha *males* for two primary reasons.

First, there are more of them. In general, men are more likely than women to have alpha characteristics, and the business world contains many more alpha males than alpha females, especially in the top executive ranks. As consultants, we've noted this disparity in every company we've worked with, and, as you'll see later in this chapter, our observations were confirmed by research data. Studies on the infamous glass ceiling offer further evidence of the male-female ratio at the highest corporate levels. A survey by the Catalyst organization, for instance, found that while women hold 50.3 percent of all management and professional positions, only 7.9 percent of the top earners are in the *Fortune* 500, and only 1.4 percent of the CEOs are women.[2]

The second reason for focusing on alpha males is that a great deal of wreckage is caused by boys behaving badly. In our research, men scored much higher than women on measures of the alpha risk factors we're about to describe. What does this mean? In short, alpha females get angry, but they're seldom as belligerent as alpha males. They like to win, and they set aggressive goals for themselves and their teams, but they're not as intimidating or as authoritarian as their male counterparts. And while they can be fiercely competitive, they're less likely than alpha males to use ruthless tactics or to see peers and colleagues as rivals who have to be destroyed. Which is why you don't see *New Yorker* cartoons about domineering alpha females.

Throughout the book, we will call upon our personal observations and scientific studies to highlight the differences between male and female alphas. But our primary focus is on the male of the species, because it is there, in the testosterone zone, that the alpha syndrome appears in its most troublesome form.

How We Learned About Alpha Males

Our interest in the subject actually began with the work we had to do on ourselves. You see, we too are alphas. Our positive alpha traits had made both of us highly successful in our careers. But our alpha liabilities had kept us from living completely successful lives.

Even as a child, Kate exhibited the ambition and drive of an alpha female. She was also fascinated by the alpha males she encountered growing up in South Texas. In the first grade, she figured out how to beat the strongest boys at the game of red rover, using direct eye contact and a smile to break through their supercharged strength as she approached the line. Later, she found a way to entice alpha boys to attend a summer school she organized in her small town, and in the fourth grade she bit the wrist of a bully to get him to quit bothering her friends. In college, she was one of only eight girls among 4,000 engineering students, and she was the one to organize lab teams that consistently came in first.

When she turned to organizational development work in her 30s, Kate focused on coaching alpha males, often joking that she was an expert in transforming jerks into nice guys. Many of her clients were hard-hitting, super-driven executives who accomplished extraordinary results, but at a cost. Because they harassed and abused people, thinking it was the only way to drive success, they caused morale problems within their business units and sometimes embarrassed their companies.

Kate's business succeeded because she found a way to get through to these tough guys and help them become better leaders. There were two keys. First, her training as an engineer gave her a knack for turning soft information about human relationships into the metrics-oriented language that alpha males understand best. Using hard data, she spelled out the risks of their current behavior and the bottom-line benefits of changing, then gave them a way to measure their progress. The other key was that she used her skills as a psychologist and her alpha female tenacity to stand up to alpha bullies — not an easy thing for women to do. The combination of straight talk and data earned the respect of hard-headed alpha males, and has since helped more than a thousand executives accelerate the progress of their careers and their companies.

At age 29, Eddie was a surgical resident at the University of Michigan, holding down two outside jobs and trying to live a normal family life with his two young children. But that wasn't enough for an achievement-obsessed alpha. He decided to become a marathon runner. After 50 marathons, the 26-mile run wasn't enough of a challenge, so he took on *ultra* marathons, becoming so obsessed with each 100-mile race that he ignored medical advice and ended up with stress fractures and a broken leg. Later, he realized that the excessive zeal that blew out his knees has blown up many an alpha's business career.

As a vascular surgeon, he was building a growing medical group, taking on leadership positions at the hospital, coaching his son's Special Olympics basketball team to the state championship, and still running lengthy races. In seizing every opportunity to accomplish something new, he diverted needed attention from his family, children, and friends. When he became chief of staff, he learned how to use his own alpha strengths to corral the energy and egos of other alphas, who were waging turf wars at the hospital. He also learned valuable lessons from his patients: of the approximately 10,000 surgeries he performed, about 75 percent were on alpha males.

Watching these driven individuals defy medical advice to achieve their career goals only to end up in surgery, Eddie decided to change his approach to medicine. He developed the Life Lessons wellness program and later gave up his medical practice entirely, turning to leadership coaching to help hard-charging executives succeed without jeopardizing their health or their family lives.

Throughout our separate journeys, we were both forced to come to grips with our alpha tendencies. While Eddie's challenges as an alpha male were different from Kate's as an alpha female, in both cases the alpha upside led to great success and exciting lives, and the downside was revealed in career snags, high stress, and failed marriages. When we met, in 1999, we began to learn from each other's insights and to help each other smooth out the rougher edges of our alpha natures. Eventually, we got married and moved to California to live a quiet life by the ocean. But, like true alphas, we went too far. After a year of drastically reduced work levels, we lacked appropriate outlets for our healthy alpha achievement drives. So we built a consulting firm that specializes in helping alphas and their companies thrive.

Individually and together we have coached hundreds of alpha executives, including Michael Dell and Kevin Rollins, Dell's chairman and CEO, respectively; eBay CEO Meg Whitman; Boston Red Sox CEO Larry Lucchino; Vice Admiral Keith Lippert, director of the Defense Logistics Agency; and over 1,000 vice presidents and senior executives at companies like Abbott Labs, Adecco, AMD, Amgen, Bristol-Myers, Coca-Cola, Eaton, the Gap, General Electric, IBM, Intel, KLA-Tencor, Microsoft, and Motorola. Throughout this book you will find examples from our experiences at these companies, especially at Dell, where we've worked with Michael Dell and his executive team since 1995.[3] Early in the remarkable rise of the computer giant, the company's leaders created a culture that reinforced the best of alpha traits and minimized unhealthy alpha behavior.

In May 2004, we presented some of the lessons we derived from those experiences in a *Harvard Business Review* article titled "Coaching the Alpha Male." Readers responded so enthusiastically that we decided to expand our research and write this book. The main thrust of both the book and our ongoing consulting work is to help individuals and organizations leverage alpha strengths to maximize productivity, teamwork, and overall effectiveness. As you'll see, doing that requires more than simply building on those formidable alpha assets. It also means taking an unflinching look at how those very qualities can mutate into liabilities with the potential to destroy careers and spread like viruses to teams, divisions, and entire companies. The tools in this book will help you identify those deadly alpha risks and stop them in their tracks, just as they've helped the hundreds of leaders with whom we've worked.

The Alpha Male Syndrome

Make no mistake: the world needs alpha males. We could not do without their courageous leadership, their goal-driven focus, their unwavering sense of responsibility, and all the other qualities they bring to bear when they roll up their sleeves and take charge. At their best, alphas are world-beaters. When they are *not* at their best—when they are unaware, out of balance, or out of control—they create problems that diminish the value of their productive energy. And when they are at their worst, they go down in flames and drag their coworkers, their families, and their organizations with them. In fact, when alpha males self-destruct, we all suffer, because economic progress and social well-being depend on their strengths. In other words, the alpha upside is limitless, but the downside can be devastating. We call this complex set of characteristics the alpha male *syndrome* because it fits both the basic definition of the word—"a distinctive or characteristic pattern of behavior"—and its usual connotation of disease or dysfunction: "a complex of symptoms indicating the existence of an undesirable condition or quality."[4]

As portrayed in figure 1-1, the range of alpha male traits can be viewed as a continuum ranging from devastating dysfunction on one extreme to gloriously noble leadership on the other. In between are degrees of healthy and unhealthy behavior. On the exceptional end of the spectrum is history's pantheon of extraordinary alpha males, with distinguished statesmen, titans of industry and philanthropy, creative geniuses, courageous generals, and stalwart heads of families. Here you will find George Washington, Winston Churchill, and Martin Luther King Jr. At the opposite extreme is the Alpha Hall of Shame, with its rogues' gallery of tyrants, despots, white-collar criminals, notorious gangsters, and redneck brawlers. This is the home of Genghis Khan, Joseph Stalin, Saddam Hussein, and other brutes.

In the business world, of course, most alpha males inhabit the middle range. To one degree or another, they fluctuate between healthy and unhealthy alpha tendencies: their magnetic leadership commands respect, but their aggressive tactics create resistance, resentment, and

FIGURE 1-1

The alpha syndrome continuum

1	2	3	4	5	6	7	8	9	10
Dysfunctional			Unhealthy			Healthy			Exceptional

revenge; they are celebrated for their achievements but loathed for the carnage they leave in their wake; people stand in awe of their competence and can-do energy, but they often hate reporting to them or teaming with them. As Thomas A. Stewart, editor of the *Harvard Business Review*, said after meeting powerhouse CEOs Jack Welch and Andy Grove, "Geez, are they impressive and stimulating! I love to be *around* them—but am I glad I don't work *for* them!"[5]

At the dysfunctional end of the continuum, alpha anger is explosive, alpha competitiveness is ruthless, and alpha aggressiveness and urgency is in the red zone. As you move to the right, negative alpha behavior becomes less destructive, less volatile, and less frequent. Crossing into the healthy part of the spectrum, you start to see alpha strengths with fewer downside risks, and alpha males who are trusted and respected instead of feared and loathed. As you approach the exceptional leadership end, alpha strengths become awe-inspiring, and the alphas are revered as inspirational leaders.

One of Kate's mentors, Richard Farson, wrote in *Management of the Absurd* that "strengths can become weaknesses when we rely too much on them, carry them to exaggerated lengths, or apply them where they don't belong."[6] People with the virtue of persistence sometimes turn stubborn, for example, and brilliant analysts can think themselves into a corner. Buddhists call these weaknesses the "near enemies" of their corresponding virtues. The stronger the positive qualities, the more likely they are to erupt as negatives. That's what happens to a great many alpha males, and because they have inordinate influence, their pendulum swings can be ruinous.

The difference between alphas who soar and alphas who sink is most evident in the area of interpersonal relations. Take Michael Dell and Michael Eisner, two classic alpha males. Brilliant, driven, and aggressive, both aimed high at an early age, boldly followed their dreams, and achieved extraordinary success in businesses marked by innovation. In 1984, Dell, then a nineteen-year-old college student, started the company that bears his name, telling his mother he would one day surpass IBM. That same year, Eisner capped a meteoric Hollywood career by being named chairman and CEO of the Walt Disney Company. He quickly propelled Disney from the doldrums of the entertainment industry to the mother of brand names and the darling of Wall Street. Meanwhile, Dell became the youngest CEO ever to crack the *Fortune* 500. Fast forward to 2005. Dell is named America's Most Admired Company by *Fortune* magazine, while the vanquished IBM bows out of the PC business.[7] In the meantime, the sordid details of Eisner's hiring and firing of Michael Ovitz are dragged into public view, and a board revolt culminates in Eisner's loss of his chairmanship and resignation as CEO.

The arcs of these larger-than-life characters capture both the extraordinary strengths and the dangerous risks of the alpha male personality. Both men had all it takes to excel in business and leave a lasting mark on society: competence, creativity, astute judgment, abundant energy, daring vision, unflagging self-confidence, and more. But Dell leveraged his alpha assets to become a leader who makes everyone around him better, while alpha blind spots got the better of Eisner's prodigious ability.[8] In the last years of Eisner's reign, the atmosphere at Disney was reportedly marked by paranoia, backbiting, and civil war; the culture at Dell remains the most collaborative and collegial we've ever observed in a large corporation. By all accounts, the iron-fisted Eisner needed to subordinate the other alphas in his orbit; Dell recruited seasoned executives and eagerly learned from them. Eisner consolidated his power and hogged the credit; Dell, at the height of his success, handed the CEO position to Kevin Rollins and created an unusual power-sharing arrangement. Most of Dell's talented, enormously wealthy senior executives choose to stay with the company rather than retire or accept one of the many choice job offers that come their way. By contrast, a joke that made the rounds in Hollywood during the Eisner years had homeless people carrying signs reading, "Will work for Disney."

How Dysfunctional Alphas Damage Organizations

When we're invited into a company as consultants, it is usually at the request of a strong alpha leader who wants to make the organization better—and most of the complaints we hear are about alpha males who drive people crazy. Employees complain that autocratic alpha managers are abusive, and that micromanaging alphas waste their time and create logjams. Coworkers complain about alphas who are demanding, impatient, and unwilling to listen. Peers resent alphas who solo rather than collaborate, and who fight to get their way even when they're demonstrably wrong. Managers complain about alpha subordinates who are not team players. Senior executives complain that abrasive alpha managers demoralize their troops. And everyone complains that alphas think they're smarter than everyone else.

The gripes we hear have usually been part of the corporate milieu for some time, consuming employee time and energy. According to a survey by badbossology.com, sponsored by Development Dimensions International, "The majority of employees spend 10 hours or more a month complaining about or listening to others complain about bad bosses, while nearly one-third spend 20 or more hours."[9] In many cases, bringing us in is like calling 911—an emergency. Companies want sustainable results, and quite often alpha males make a powerful impact initially only to run into dead ends, creating expensive overhead in the form of turnover, declining motivation, emotional turmoil, and other productivity killers.

Of course, alpha males have complaints of their own: employees don't understand their directives, or don't move quickly enough, or need to be constantly monitored. Because they're naturally confident and self-directed, alphas have trouble relating to people who are hard to motivate or have a strong need to be appreciated. Some are more comfortable working with objects, systems, and ideas than with human beings; their attitude is captured in this droll remark by an alpha male manager: "My job would be a lot more fun if I didn't have to work with people."

When told that subordinates gripe about their intimidating ways, some alpha executives reply, "They should *thank* me!" In their minds, they're only doing what's necessary to make everyone more effective. If only people were accountable; if only they were willing to go the extra mile; if only they didn't drop the ball—then the alpha could lighten up. The laments sound reasonable, but in most cases their frustration is caused by their own leadership shortcomings, not the ineptitude of others. Ken DiPietro, a former senior vice president at a major high-tech company, spoke for most alpha males when he said, "No one who is sane intends to come off as mean-spirited or inflexible in communicating with staff, but you can get so caught up in your desired outcome that you forget the impact you're having on the team."[10]

The rewards and risks of alpha traits are enumerated in table 1-1, which summarizes the alpha male syndrome: the very strengths that

TABLE 1-1

The alpha syndrome: When strengths become liabilities

Alpha attribute	Value to organization	Risk to organization
Dominant, confident, takes charge	Decisive, courageous leader; gets people to take action and move forward	Doesn't develop strong leaders; intimidating; creates fear; stifles disagreement
Charismatic, magnetic leader who leads the way	Brings out the best in others; gets people to do more than they thought was possible	Manipulates to get his way; uses charm to lure people down *his* path
Aggressive, competitive	Determined to win; turns others into winners	Competes with peers; alienates colleagues; reluctant to give others credit
High achiever with a strong sense of mission	Action-oriented; produces results; energizes teams to reach impossible goals	Takes strong performance for granted; expects the impossible and fails to acknowledge what's required to achieve it
Bold, creative, innovative thinker	Dreams up ingenious ideas; solves intractable problems; sees further than others	Arrogant, stubborn, overly opinionated; imposes own views; closed to others' thinking
Persistent, tenacious, determined, steadfast	Has courage of convictions; always moves forward; willing to take unpopular stand to get results	Drives self and others to exhaustion; urgent, impatient; thinks rules don't apply to him
Strong appetite for newness and change	Values speed; drives people and organizations toward needed change and rapid growth	Overzealous; undervalues organizational alignment; launches into action before gathering support from others
Farsighted, sees what's possible	Recognizes gap between today's reality and tomorrow's potential	So focused on future that present and near term are neglected; loses sight of business viability
Sees what's missing	Proactively spots problems; adjusts, corrects, prevents things from getting worse	Can be critical and demeaning; fails to appreciate others' contributions; people feel demoralized

make alphas so effective become their downfall when they're overused, excessive, or misplaced.

With egregiously dysfunctional alphas, the cost can be even greater than stress disorders, ruined careers, and reduced productivity. If you hear about a scandal in the executive ranks, it's a good bet you'll find alpha males with runaway egos who think the rules don't apply to them. Like other alpha risks, this one stems from a strength: creative, passionate alpha males often shatter the constraints of conventional thinking and generate brilliant innovations; but the same disdain for limits can lead them over the edge of legality or propriety. The more grandiose the self-image, the bigger the overreach. "Looking back on it, I wasn't always right," said a high-tech entrepreneur who lost investors more than $20 million. "But I was never in doubt." That's classic alpha male hubris: supremely confident, they find a way to get what they want even if it means turning an audacious idea into an actionable offense.

If it's not money, it's sex. We've observed that many leaders who fit the dysfunctional alpha male typology fall prey to sexual predation, becoming womanizers who use conquest and control to assert their dominance. Their magnetic charisma and take-charge personalities can make them exceptionally attractive, creating temptations that challenge even the most loyal of spouses, and—as we've seen repeatedly—cause everyone from religious leaders to heads of state to throw caution to the wind.

Add to that the tendency for alphas to think they should have whatever they want, and you have a perfect setup for dramas that can ruin careers and families, weaken mighty leaders, and throw organizations into turmoil. The following comments are from 360° interviews with the colleagues of an alpha male just before the company was hit with a very public sexual harassment suit: "If you're not attractive, you don't feel valued. He couldn't care less about super-bright women unless they're pretty." "He tells sexual jokes, he's flirty, and he obsesses about breasts. Occasionally he's funny, but mostly he's inappropriate and unprofessional. Everyone is sure he's having affairs."

In sum, when properly channeled and controlled, the alpha male drive to reach the top is a boon to progress, but when the ethic of "Do what it takes to get results" is taken to extremes, it becomes a menace to both personal careers and corporate health.

The Hard Data on Alphas

Based on our long experience working with alphas in their natural environments, we designed an in-depth questionnaire that measures the extent to which an individual has alpha characteristics. As a comprehensive, scientific instrument, the assessment will not only tell you if you're an alpha, but it will also enumerate your particular alpha risk factors and indicate whether you would benefit from enhancing particular alpha traits. It also takes into account gender differences, providing somewhat different text for alpha males and alpha females. Taking the assessment before going on to chapter 2 can make a significant difference in your ability to get the most out of this book. See the box "The Alpha Assessment" for instructions. (For a quick snapshot of your alpha strengths and risks, use the brief checklist, "Are You an Alpha?" at the end of this chapter.)

The Alpha Assessment was developed over a series of three validation phases on a population of 1,507. The subjects all worked full time in the business world, many in high-ranking leadership positions: 1,484 were drawn from the readership of *Harvard Business Review*, and 123 more came from personal business contacts; 63.8 percent were male; the average age was 41.2 years. Ethnically and racially diverse (65.2 percent white, 3.2 percent African American, 20.8 percent Asian, 4.5 percent Latino, and 6.3 percent other), they hailed from an astonishing 106 nations and spanned hundreds of different industries, among them agriculture, telecommunications, high technology, real estate, education, oil, automotive, and finance and banking. More than three-quarters (77.5 percent) said they supervise other people.

In addition to helping us refine the assessment tool itself, the validation phase yielded some fascinating data about alphas. Here are the most salient results. (See appendix B for additional details; a comprehensive description and extensive data can be found at www.AlphaMaleSyndrome.com.)

Overall, alpha traits correlate with being male, with increasing levels of education, with low anxiety, with supervisory positions, and with type

The Alpha Assessment

Our Web site, www.AlphaMaleSyndrome.com, contains additional tools, exercises, and ideas to supplement the information in this book. Whether you're looking for ways to better manage your own alpha tendencies or those of the alphas in your life, you'll derive value from the extra material.

To find out whether or not you're an alpha, go to www.AlphaMaleSyndrome/assessment for access to our Alpha Assessment. (The test is designed for both men and women.) It takes only 15 minutes to complete, and the results are automatically and instantaneously tabulated. The in-depth personalized report, like the sample in Appendix A, will tell you not only whether you're an alpha, but also the type of alpha you are (see chapter 2) and the degree to which your alpha tendencies show up as assets or liabilities. You'll also receive specific advice for enhancing your particular alpha strengths and minimizing your alpha risks. If you're *not* an alpha, the report will give you personalized tips for developing alpha strengths that might significantly boost your career.

A personality traits—all of which are in line with expectations and are reflected in the content of this book.[11] The propensity for having alpha *risks* relates to being male, to higher levels of stress and tension, and to a lack of self-reflection.[12] In other words, according to our data, the proto-typical alpha is a well-educated man with managerial experience and the hard-driving, urgent intensity of a type A. The more troublesome members of the alpha fraternity are men who are under a high degree of stress and are not inclined to introspection.

The scores for both men and women followed a normal distribution for all the factors analyzed, but the mean scores of men were markedly higher than those of women. Significantly, men scored higher on both alpha strengths and alpha risks (see table B-2 in appendix B). In practical terms, these findings mean that the overall patterns were the same for both sexes, but male scores were higher in general, reflecting overall differences in leadership style.[13] The results are consistent with our personal observations: more men than women are alphas, and male alphas are much more extreme in their expression of alpha qualities. These findings were instrumental in convincing us to focus the book on alpha *males*.

The data also revealed other intriguing patterns. While there were no significant differences between subjects born in America and those born elsewhere, minorities scored slightly higher in alpha strengths than did whites. However, no significant race or ethnic differences were found in alpha risk scores. Since "minority" encompassed a range of ethnicities, the findings might reflect what many minorities have reported: they have to perform better than whites to reach the same level of advancement. We also found that younger respondents scored somewhat higher than older ones on both alpha strengths and alpha risks; that level of education was not related to either strengths or risks (but did correlate with general alpha traits); and that holding a supervisory position correlated with alpha strengths but not with alpha risks. Taken together, these data suggest that as people mature and settle into leadership roles, they develop positive alpha traits and learn to modulate the extremes of alpha behavior.

One of the most significant findings corroborates a key principle in this book: alpha risks are closely related to alpha strengths. The data show a strong correlation between high scores in both categories. Although some subjects scored high on one scale and not on the other, in general, the greater the strengths, the greater the risks. (See table B-1 in appendix B.) This breakdown corroborates what we said earlier: your greatest assets can be your worst liabilities if you do not take control of them. Your goal should be to join the 3 percent at the top of the heap in alpha strengths and at the bottom in alpha risks. Those are the kind of leaders the world needs more of.

Dysfunctional Traits of the Alpha Male

In the animal kingdom, rivals compete for positions in the social hierarchy because ranking high assures access to necessities like food and to privileges such as mating opportunities. It's not much different in the human jungle, where alpha males strive to achieve positions of prominence. That drive can lead to healthy competition and achievements that benefit all of us. When it's excessive, however, it wreaks havoc, turning otherwise worthy alphas into bullies who intimidate, browbeat, and humiliate people to get what they want, often rationalizing their behavior as necessary to get others to shape up. Combative and pathologically competitive, unhealthy alpha males need to dominate; as a result, they are constantly on guard and always looking for an advantage.

Those statements are borne out in our study. When factor analyses were applied to the data on alpha risks, three distinct themes stood out: hard-driving competitiveness, interpersonal impatience, and difficulty controlling anger. (See table B-3 in appendix B.) The trio represents a compelling summary of alphas who create trouble: they see everyone as a rival and every situation as a contest for supremacy, they're demanding and impatient for results, and they're veritable powder kegs. Although people in supervisory positions have fewer alpha risks overall, they are somewhat more inclined to display anger, impatience, and competitiveness. It is unclear whether people with those traits are drawn to supervising others or if becoming a manager brings out these tendencies.

Alpha males want excellence, they want it now, and they're sure they know how to get it. When others fail to measure up, alphas let them know about it. Alpha males who operate with a sense of fairness, who give feedback appropriately and limit their outbursts to genuine crises and major screw-ups, become respected leaders. But those who can't control their anger can cripple a team or an entire organization.

One way alpha combativeness plays out is in a propensity for defensive behavior. Alpha males' intimidating style makes other people defensive, and alphas respond to that defensiveness with disdain. But, paradoxically, when someone disagrees with them, or gives them critical feedback, *they* get defensive—only to justify their behavior as honest truth-telling.[14] They think they're delivering a wake-up call when in fact they're hurling verbal grenades. In part, their defensiveness stems from thinking they have all the answers, and from having to prove it to others. They have a powerful need to explain, justify, and convince. If the other person doesn't get it, they say it again another way, louder and more forcefully. If that doesn't work, they pour on more data, more logic, and more evidence, pumping up the volume at every step. Discussion becomes debate, debate becomes argument, argument becomes war.

Put two dysfunctional alpha males together and, even if they start out with common objectives, they're likely to end up in a power struggle. When an alpha male pounces on someone who's *not* an alpha, the dynamic is different. As the other party tries to explain his or her thoughts, the impatient alpha either tunes out conspicuously or cuts in with a barrage of heavy artillery. The opponent slinks away in self-defense, pretending to get the alpha's point. Also disappearing are useful facts and important views, along with respect, trust, and support. People comply with alpha males and mindlessly implement their strategies, even if they don't agree with them. Effort diminishes, learning ceases, and collaborative dialogue is silenced.

As troublesome as it is, defensiveness pales in comparison to the most abusive alpha male trait: volatility. "We never know which Mike is going to show up in the morning, the effervescent guy with the big smile who can't wait to take on the world, or the maniac who's going to explode the first time someone rubs him the wrong way." That's from a series of 360° interviews we conducted at the request of the CEO of a major consumer products company. Like other volatile alpha males, Mike's sunny side was dazzling and infectious, but his dark side made Darth Vader look like Mr. Rogers. When "the happy warrior" showed up, everyone was ready to follow him to the barricades. When "the ogre" emerged from its cave, they wanted to hide under their desks.

In general, employees are willing to cope with an occasional outburst, especially if it's predictable. But arbitrary, frequent, and abusive tantrums cross the line into intimidation. And the flare-ups don't have to be volcanic to be debilitating.

This 360° excerpt about a senior executive named Candace captures a less explosive version: "She's like the big sister of your dreams: supportive, patient, understanding, and kind. She'll do anything to help you be the best you can be. An hour later, she's the wicked witch. She snipes at everything and everyone, cutting people down with nasty criticism."

In part, the difference between Mike's and Candace's anger is a matter of personality and style, but it also reflects a common gender distinction. In our study, male alphas scored markedly higher than female alphas on impatience and difficulty controlling anger (there was no significant difference in competitiveness). (See table B-4 in appendix B.) This jibes with our workplace observations. Male anger tends to be transparent, whether it's expressed in biting sarcasm or a blow-up. Angry women are usually less overt: their tone takes on a sharp edge, or they carp and criticize, pointing out what's wrong at every turn and ignoring what's working well. Women also *imply* you're in trouble and *hint* that there might be consequences, whereas a dysfunctional alpha male will get in your face and lay it on the line, paying no mind to packaging.

Whether it comes out in upheavals that shatter the Richter scale, or glares that melt icebergs, or callous slurs that cut to the bone, alpha volatility makes for an edgy, unpredictable workplace. Because of the sheer power of their inner furnaces, alpha males set the temperature of the group. Shift their thermostat from upbeat to surly, and watch the mood of the organization plummet. Raise it into the red zone, and you have a paranoid workforce. When an anger-prone alpha male leader is about to arrive on the scene, you'll see anxious people searching for clues about which personality will walk through the door. The price of that pervasive fear includes wasted energy, elevated stress levels, and employees who cover their behinds instead of getting their jobs done.

Many alpha males operate under the mistaken belief that fear moves people to productive action. They think the laws of the jungle apply to business, but it turns out that the chest-thumping leadership style not only doesn't cut it in today's office, it doesn't work all that well in the jungle either, as the research in the box "Lessons from the Jungle" indicates.

To be sure, the old-fashioned, hard-nosed alpha male style can be a legitimate management tool, not just in war or on a football field but in the corporate world as well. In turnaround situations, in severe crises, or at times of exceptional fear and uncertainty, tough command-and-control tactics can provide needed order and discipline. In ordinary circumstances, however, alpha male excesses are much riskier now than they used to be. More and more leaders realize that success in the corporate

Lessons from the Jungle

It used to be assumed that brute force determined which animals led the good life and passed along their genes. But new research on our close relatives, the baboons, paints a more complicated picture. In an interview with *Fortune* magazine, Stanford primatologist Robert Sapolsky notes that brutish baboons that fight for the top slots are the most stressed-out of the bunch.[a] Plus, they're not all that good at keeping the status they win through force.

Who gets to the top and stays there? Animals that are "great at forming coalitions." In the long run, cleverness, affiliations, and "suggestions of violence" work better than overt aggression. What's more, the tough guys don't do nearly as well in the sex wars as was previously assumed. Frequently, the kinder, gentler males quietly get it on with new mates while the macho dudes are beating each other up. In short, nice guys don't always finish last. In fact, they are quite well compensated, and their benefit packages are even better than the top alpha males'.

Sapolsky conjectures that primates with well-developed impulse control build strong coalitions, while those who lack impulse control and rely on force "can't prevent themselves from leaping out and doing some dumb-ass thing that blows their whole plan." For the human equivalent, compare a hot-tempered boss who intimidates people with a firm leader who treats people with respect. Bottom line: the animal drive to dominate will take you a long way, but you won't go *all* the way if you lack what it takes to inspire, affiliate, and truly lead.

a. David Grainger, "Alpha Romeos," *Fortune*, August 11, 2003, 48.

jungle requires keeping a lid on abusive tendencies, and alpha males who face up to their risks often learn with experience how to rise above them. Indeed, our study found that older alphas score much better on the controlling anger measure than their younger counterparts. It seems that maturity does lead to better command of one's frustrations.

Alpha Females

Our coaching experience, our own research data, and a large body of scientific research all suggest that women in general display their leadership traits somewhat differently than men.[15] Those stylistic differences are just as pronounced among male and female alphas. Like their male counterparts, female alphas are ambitious and drawn to positions of authority, but as a rule, they are less inclined to dominate. Better attuned to the emotional climate, they are more likely than alpha males to look for ways to collaborate and to find win-win solutions to conflicts. They can be just as opinionated and strong-minded, but they'll search for consensus and buy-in rather than impose their will.

In other words, alpha women want to lead, but they don't necessarily need to rule. A growing body of research supports those general observations. Studies indicate, for instance, that men are drawn to situations involving competition and risk taking, while women place higher value on cooperative relationships and working with people they like. In a study for the National Bureau of Economic Research, economists Muriel Niederle and Lise Vesterlund, of Stanford University and the University of Pittsburgh, respectively, decided to test the common observation that women are reluctant to compete, while men can be overly eager to compete. In groups of two women and two men, the subjects were given simple math problems to solve, under two different testing conditions. In the first, each participant received 50 cents for each correct answer, regardless of how the others did. The second round was done tournament style; the person with the best score won two dollars while the others received nothing. Each person was told how many questions he or she answered correctly, but not how the others compared. For the third round, they were allowed to choose between getting paid for each correct answer and competing in a winner-take-all scenario. Men were twice as likely to choose the tournament option, even though the maximum reward was the same and the potential for winning nothing was higher.

What explains this discrepancy? The researchers found that the men were far more confident in their ability to win. While none of the players actually knew whether they'd won the earlier tournament, 75 percent of the men thought they had, as compared with only 43 percent of the women. This bolsters our observation that alpha males are more likely than their female counterparts to see themselves as exceptionally competent—so much so, in fact, that they relish visible, high-risk competitions in which they expect to stand out. Depending on their *actual* competence, this drive either pays off big-time or leads to conspicuous disasters. Women, on the other hand, are more likely to shy away from competition even when they stand a good chance of winning.[16]

Other data suggest that female managers tend to be perceived as more consultative and inclusive, whereas men are more directive and task oriented.[17] There are also indications that men are biologically more dependent on the adrenalin of rapid-fire, high-risk situations, whereas women thrive on the calming influence of endorphin-producing activities, such as conversation and relationship building.[18]

In "The Art of the Decision," *Fortune* magazine reporter Janet Guyon wrote, "After 25 years of interviewing CEOs, I can say definitively: Men love to lecture, women like to listen."[19] It is a matter of ongoing debate whether such generalities reflect actual differences between men and women or whether people merely *perceive* those differences because of cultural stereotypes that no one can completely escape. According to Guyon, "a growing body of work" says there is an actual difference in male and female decision-making styles. "Women collaborate, listen, and try to build teams. Men are more apt to direct, blame others, and use the vertical pronoun." The article also reports that men are inclined to exercise decision-making power unilaterally while women with the same level of authority prefer to work through other people. Even at the higher rungs of the ladder, it seems, women get their self-improvement tips from Oprah and men get them from ESPN.

The jury is still out, but it's likely that scientists will eventually trace the differences between men and women to a complex mix of nature and nurture. Because these gender proclivities are accentuated when individuals are placed in strong leadership positions, it's safe to assume that alpha men and alpha women—on average—tend to evaluate novel situations in different ways. Because of her natural attraction to novelty, an alpha female might drive her organization toward something that hasn't been completely checked out, whereas an alpha male might cling too long to the known and be more conservative about exploring risks. Once on a novel path, women will likely fit the new situation into what's already established, whereas men might adapt by creating new systems.

It must be emphasized that neither style is better than the other. What's important is for individuals to become adept at using both under the appropriate circumstances, and to draw upon the natural strengths in the brains of the other sex.

Gender leadership differences show up fairly early in life. For example, in a study of teenagers at a summer camp, anthropologist Ritch Savin-Williams placed campers in cabins with strangers of the same age and sex.[20] The boys started competing for leadership privileges right off the bat; girls waited at least a week. Boys used ridicule and bullying to gain advantage; girls were conspicuously nice as they established strategic friendships. To assert their dominance, boys hurled insults, fists, or hard objects, and they didn't much care who got hurt. Girls employed subtle strategies such as gossip, backstabbing, or ignoring, and their empathy for losers was evident.

As described in the box "Systemizing and Empathizing," some scientists believe that such studies point to inherent differences: men tend to be systemizers while women excel at empathizing. Whatever its origin, the style we think of as "feminine" certainly seems to soften the edges of female alpha tendencies.

Meg Whitman, the CEO of eBay, is an excellent example of the differences between the alpha male and the alpha female. She has a robust drive to succeed, she likes being in command, and she's as metrics-oriented as most male executives we've worked with. Without those qualities, *Fortune* magazine would not have named her the most powerful woman in American business two years in a row, in 2004 and 2005.[21] But, like only the healthiest of alpha males, she balances her systemizing skills with solid empathizing skills. By all indications, her collaborative style has enabled her to assemble effective, highly motivated teams that serve as glue within a vast organization that has grown sevenfold since she took over in 1998.[22] "Her most striking attribute is to enable other people and other groups to get things done," says Tom Tierney, an eBay board member and the former CEO of Bain & Co.[23]

Systemizing and Empathizing

In his book *The Essential Difference,* Simon Baron-Cohen, a professor of psychology and psychiatry at Cambridge University, defines empathy as the ability to put yourself in the shoes of others and respond in a concerned way that resonates with their thoughts and feelings.[a] It's an essential skill for comprehending and communicating with human beings. Systemizing involves discerning the rules that govern how things work, a vital tool for predicting external events and manipulating objects. Because empathizers care about the feelings of others, they prefer to get what they want through collaboration and reciprocity rather than fighting. The systemizers' ability to manipulate systems is useful in combat, competitive strategizing, and political maneuvering. Quantitative analysis is systemizer territory; intimate communication is the terrain of empathizers.

Obviously, any population will have highly empathetic men who are lousy systemizers, and women who are outstanding systemizers with the empathy of a stone. *On average,* however, women score higher on measures of empathy and men do better at systemizing. These tendencies are evident early in life. Show infants *one day old* a mechanical mobile and a human face, and boys lock into the former while girls fixate on the latter. One-year-old boys are drawn to videos of cars; girls favor talking heads even with the sound turned off. Young boys push and shove to get what they want; girls bargain and persuade. On questionnaires, more girls check "I like to learn by working with other students" while most boys choose "I like to do better work than my friends." Girls make requests; boys issue commands. Girls allow for multiple viewpoints; boys draw hard lines of right versus wrong.[b]

By all indications, differences in the crib and on the playground get reinforced by society and later show up in the workplace. The ideal, displayed by healthy alphas of both sexes, is to be skilled at both empathizing and systemizing, and to use whichever is most appropriate to the situation.

a. Simon Baron-Cohen, *The Essential Difference* (New York: Basic Books, 2003), 2–6.

b. Ibid., 29–33, 47–56, 83.

Running a company with over 9,000 employees and more than 150 million customers, Whitman "leads by not leading, bosses by not bossing, and manages by not managing," writes William Meyers in USNews .com.[24] Elsewhere, venture capitalist Bob Kagle says that Whitman "represents both the emotional and rational side of the brand. She is an active and fair listener, and tough-minded and competitive."[25] That is not the combination of traits we associate with alpha males, except for outstanding leaders who are as venerated as they are valued. Many experts consider Whitman's balanced style the future of management, just as hybrid cars are the future of transportation.

Are female alphas the perfect antidote to the alpha male downside? In many ways they are. But they have challenges of their own. Emotional intelligence is a huge asset, but it can also create problems, and seeking consensus can either pay off big time or backfire in costly ways. If, for example, you're overly concerned about people's feelings, your communication might be so indirect that no one can figure out what you want and what you think. Politely worded instructions get construed as mere suggestions, and critical feedback is mistaken for gently offered advice. Plus, leaders with an aversion to conflict can stifle healthy competition and productive debate, depriving their organizations of a useful management tool.

Another reason sensitivity can turn from asset to liability is that women are often seen as *too* emotional. As many experts have observed, an enraged man is considered tough and strong, but an irate woman is hysterical and irrational. And if they lean in the opposite direction, female alphas run the risk of being considered too soft. Joyce Russell is the chief operating officer at Adecco USA, the world's largest staffing firm. Naturally warm and effusive, she is a talented and passionate executive who easily establishes rapport and builds good working relationships. Joyce feels that her "softer edges" are exactly what make her an effective leader. But many men perceive her as "fluffy."

Ray Roe, CEO of Adecco Group North America, fought hard to place Joyce in her current position, and wants to groom her as his successor. "She's as fine an executive as I've ever worked with," he told us. "But her warm, open approach fuels people's gender biases. She doesn't get the credit she deserves because her more feminine style makes it easy to discount her." In truth, there is nothing fluffy about Joyce. Underneath, she's as tough as nails and smart as a whip. But she has to work harder than men to prove it. "My challenge is to stay tough-minded about results and still keep my affinity for people," she says. She's learning to do things like begin presentations with hard facts rather than a more personal approach, and to confront issues directly while still showing concern for people's feelings.

Overall, the attributes we associate with masculinity, such as rationality, toughness, and physical strength, have historically made alpha males the natural leaders of human groups. But today's job description is different, and the slow emergence of women at higher levels of management is both a result of that change and a leading cause of it. It remains to be seen whether alpha women will transform the face of management entirely or become more like alpha males. What's required of both sexes is balance: balance within the organization as a whole; balance in individual departments; and above all, balance within each alpha leader. The tools you'll discover in this book will help you achieve that vital balance.

What's in It for You

We're often asked by CEOs to coach up-and-coming alpha males who have the talent, drive, and energy to run a company, but who are diamonds in the rough in dire need of polishing. In most cases, the clients themselves are surprised that anyone thinks they need help.

When told that their intimidating style can deplete morale and impair teamwork, these bright, savvy human beings are often dumbstruck. "I've been successful just the way I am," they say. "You're not going to neuter me now." No one wants to neuter them, of course; just fine-tune their strengths and scrape away their rough edges. They don't realize that the skills that got them to the playoffs are not enough to take them all the way to the championship. To truly realize their leadership potential, they need to build alliances and coalitions, earn the support of peers, demonstrate maturity and wisdom as well as talent, and show they can put the good of the organization ahead of personal glory. Unfortunately, many fail to realize the need for those skills until they're passed up for a major promotion.

If you're a typical alpha male, you might be thinking, "If it ain't broke, don't fix it." You may be tempted to give this book to someone who *really* needs it. Snap out of it! You may be hugely successful, but you're not yet where you want to be, and some of your traits may keep you from getting there. Even worse, some alpha male attributes can land you in a hospital.

We estimate that more than half of all middle managers are alphas. Thanks to their assertiveness, drive, and take-charge confidence, they rise to that level quickly, and they thrive there because they skillfully manage processes and day-to-day functions. Alphas also stand a better chance of rising higher than those who are *not* alphas. Indeed, middle managers who do not possess alpha traits—or don't make a concerted effort to add them to their functional competences—are likely to plateau at that level. But so are alpha males who don't overcome their inherent risk factors. Why? Because fewer and fewer companies are willing to tolerate alpha abuses, like denigrating people and driving one's agenda like a bulldozer. Bullies who lead through intimidation are likely to be kept under wraps by wise CEOs, self-destruct, or get brought down by insubordination, sabotage, and other forms of jungle retribution.

Like the hundreds of alpha males we've worked with, you can adopt new, more effective strategies. Doing so is a bottom-line issue: when you liberate your alpha gifts and reduce your alpha liabilities, you will stand a much better chance of rising to the heights your talent deserves—and everyone will be happy to have you there. Here are some of the benefits you can look forward to:

- Dramatic improvement in your leadership ability

- More productive and enjoyable working relationships

- Enhanced cooperation from peers and employees

- Increased respect and trust from colleagues

- Creative and harmonious teamwork

- Smoother flow of projects from conception to fruition

- More authentic self-expression and self-confidence

- Less stress, better health, and a happier home life

The Intention-Impact Gap

The starting point for obtaining these rewards is to expand your awareness. Only through honest self-reflection and self-monitoring can you effectively apply the tools you'll find in these pages.

In our coaching work with alpha males, we use the impact trajectory (figure 1-2) to demonstrate the central role of awareness in success. We begin by having clients enumerate their intentions in several categories, such as business outcomes, leadership results, and key relationships. We then compare their intentions to their actual impact, to make them more aware of the gap between their expectations and their results. We

FIGURE 1-2

The impact trajectory

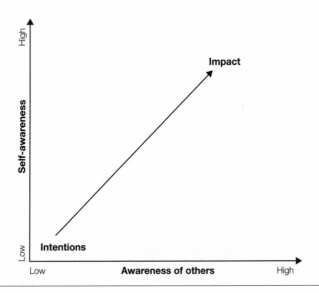

all know that factors such as knowledge, skill, and experience are vital for effective leadership, and high-ranking alpha males have all of those in spades. The wild card is their self-awareness (vertical axis) and their awareness of how they influence others, including peers, their teams, customers, and other key players (horizontal axis). As each type of awareness increases, so does the level of impact.

By becoming more aware of the impact of their behavior, alpha males can enhance their ability to communicate, collaborate, and create, leading directly to greater influence and sustainable business results. In turn, this improvement enables them to refine their intentions, bringing more authentic motivation to the surface. By asking questions such as, "What are my core beliefs?" and "What are my deepest values?" our alpha clients often realize the need to align their behavior with their truest intentions.

For example, in 2001, Kevin Rollins, then COO and president of Dell (now CEO), wanted to add explicit values of caring, integrity, and human connection to the performance-oriented corporate culture. From Kevin's examination of his own deepest intentions, and his commitment to move beyond his analytic alpha style to become a more inspiring leader, grew an initiative called the Soul of Dell, which greatly enriched the leadership training of executives and added new criteria to the metrics used to determine bonuses. Under this initiative, managers were evaluated not by the usual business performance standards alone but also by whether or not employees felt supported and coached.

Each increment of awareness narrows the gap between noble intentions and powerful impact—and, incidentally, brings welcome health benefits by reducing stress and strain. The more honestly you can reflect on the information in the book as it pertains to you, the more you stand to benefit.

How Alpha Are You?

If you have not already done so, we encourage you to begin the process of raising your self-awareness by taking the online Alpha Assessment (described earlier in this chapter in the box "The Alpha Assessment").

Meanwhile, the following checklist ("Are You an Alpha?") will give a quick sense of the extent to which you are an alpha, and the degree to which your alpha traits are assets or liabilities. Respond to each statement with "yes" or "no"; if neither choice fits perfectly, choose the one that seems most correct. Please reflect carefully and respond honestly; the awareness you gain will guide you to the most appropriate information and tools in the subsequent chapters.

Are You an Alpha?

Alpha Strengths

☐ No matter what, I don't give up until I reach my end goal.

☐ I always say exactly what I think.

☐ When I play a game, I always like to win.

☐ I have no problem challenging people.

☐ I expect the best from the people I supervise, and I help them deliver.

☐ I make the decision I believe is correct, even when I know other people don't agree.

☐ I have strong opinions on issues I know about.

☐ I seldom have any doubts about my ability to deliver.

☐ When leading others, I set high performance standards.

☐ Even when I am successful, I always think about things that could have been done better.

Alpha Risks

☐ I constantly compare myself to others.

☐ I don't care if my style hurts people's feelings, if that's what's required to produce results.

☐ When people disagree with me, I often treat it as a challenge or an affront.

☐ I tend to believe that others need to change more than I do.

☐ If I have a good idea and I'm asked to hold off and listen to inferior ideas, I can quickly become visibly annoyed.

☐ People say I become curt, brusque, or frustrated when I have to repeat myself.

☐ Sometimes I lose control of my temper and visibly express my anger.

☐ I have strong opinions about most things, even if I don't know much about them.

☐ Many of my work relationships have a competitive undertone.

☐ I don't invest much time in building collaborative relationships with peers.

☐ I've been told that I don't listen as well as I should.

While this is not a precise instrument like the online assessment, it does give you a rough idea of your alpha tendencies. If most of your responses to statements in the Strengths section were "yes," you are probably an alpha with many of the strengths that make alphas such dynamic and influential leaders.

If half or more of your responses to the items under Risks were "yes," you mostly likely have some alpha risks that deserve your attention. If you have seven or eight yeses in that group, it's very likely that your alpha liabilities are already limiting your success. With nine or ten yeses, you might well be on the brink of trouble.

Don't be confused if you scored high in both categories. Because alpha liabilities are mainly alpha assets taken too far or applied inappropriately, that is to be expected. (The exceptions to the rule are healthy alphas who have worked hard to reduce their negative tendencies.) Again, don't treat this as a definitive personality profile. As you proceed through the book, pay particular attention to information that resonates with your own self-perception and with the feedback you've received from others.

The Times They Are a-Changin'

As business has evolved, the alpha male drive for dominance that once assured the survival of the toughest has become increasingly maladaptive. In an environment where brains count a whole lot more than brawn, a physical pipsqueak can be a giant. In organizations that favor ensembles over solos, emotional intelligence does more to inspire loyalty than a loud roar or a puffed-up chest. Today's employees—well educated, increasingly female, and concerned about job satisfaction and work-life balance—would sooner quit than put up with abusive managers. In addition, the widely dispersed and culturally diverse teams created by globalization need managers who can communicate, teach, and consistently motivate. And, in the wake of Enron and other corporate scandals, unenlightened alpha males who scrap the rules or indulge in lavish displays of perks and privilege are no longer welcome.

Unfortunately, a great many upper-level executives still behave like classic enablers. By the time they wake up to the damage being caused by dysfunctional alpha males, it's too late for the leopards to change their spots. Like athletic coaches who coddle prickly all-stars without realizing how toxic they are for the team, some managers let abusive alpha males slide for years, even decades. "It comes with the territory," they say. They are seriously miscalculating the risks and rewards of unhealthy alpha behavior. For example, a study by business school professors Tiziana Casciaro and Miguel Sousa Lobo, of Harvard and Duke universities, respectively, found that personal feelings were more important than competence in forming effective work relationships. "We found that if someone is strongly disliked, it's almost irrelevant whether or not she is competent," said the researchers. On the other hand, if a person is liked, "colleagues will seek out every little bit of competence he has to offer."[26]

Creating an atmosphere in which trust, respect, and congenial relationships flourish is vital for success in today's environment. In a *Wall Street Journal* article titled "Malevolent Bosses Take a Huge Toll on Business," Kevin Voigt cited a Columbia University study of 1,000 workers in nine countries including the United States, Japan, Singapore, and Australia.[27] Ninety percent say they'd suffered abuse from bosses at some point in their careers, and on any given day, 20 percent have to put up with a bad boss. The cost in reduced productivity, low morale, and high turnover—not to mention health care expenditures due to stress disorders—is enormous. Plus, people who feel abused have no interest in being loyal. Many simply quit, contributing to what economists see as an alarming trend: worker shortages in key industries.

A study at San Francisco State University, for example, found that the main reasons people cite for leaving jobs is not money but the desire "to be respected, to be challenged, and to grow."[28] If companies want to retain their most valuable employees—which is, of course, more cost effective than hiring and training replacements—they have to realize that "no pain, no gain" is not a sound management style. It is, in fact, maladaptive: today's well-educated, highly skilled workers haven't got time for the pain.

Make no mistake, the magnificent strengths of alphas make them the most likely—and the most appropriate—people to assume positions of leadership. Yet, for many alpha males, the skills that today's leaders require—motivating, inspiring, teaching, communicating, modeling integrity and personal growth—do not come naturally, and those who fail to develop those skills will become increasingly out of place. In *Developing Global Executives: The Lessons of International Experience*, management professor Morgan W. McCall Jr. and organizational psychologist George P. Hollenbeck identified what they call "universal fatal flaws" of executives in the global environment.[29] They include bungled relationships with key people, lack of people skills, failure to ask for help, and failure to learn or to adapt to change. Those flaws are similar to the risk factors of alpha males. For all these reasons, the skillful management of alpha males is one of the most crucial tasks facing today's organizations. Our primary purpose in writing this book is to help alpha males leverage their strengths and subdue the flip-side weaknesses that stifle their effectiveness. Our other aim is to help the peers, teams, and managers of alphas work more effectively with them. By understanding alpha males, adjusting your attitude toward them, and taking command of how you behave toward them, you can make your workplace more productive, more agreeable, and more personally rewarding.

A Quick Look Ahead

In the next chapter you will learn about the four basic alpha types: the *commander*, the *visionary*, the *strategist*, and the *executor*. You will also discover the debilitating trap we call the "alpha triangle" and acquire a powerful tool for putting an end to it.

Chapters 3 through 6 describe each of the four alpha types in depth; you'll become familiar with the style each type brings to work every day and gain practical tools to maximize the strengths and subdue the risks.

Chapter 7 contains a crucial examination of the impact of alpha males on teams. It will give you powerful ways to deal with alpha-related problems and turn nightmare teams into dream teams.

In chapter 8 we address the care and feeding of alpha males. It will help you achieve a higher level of personal well-being. Don't think this is a throwaway topic: as you'll see, it's a vital bottom-line concern.

The final chapter contains a brief description of how to get the most follow-through from everything you've learned in the book. It focuses on the importance of coaching, something every alpha male—and everyone who works for or with alpha males—should take advantage of.

ACTION STEPS

- Become familiar with the full range of alpha male strengths and their flip-side weaknesses.

- Recognize that what separates healthy, well-functioning alpha males from dysfunctional alphas is primarily the area of interpersonal relations.

- Examine how alpha male strengths—yours and/or your colleagues'— contribute to the success of your organization, and how alpha male risks damage productivity, morale, and efficiency.

- Identify the leading alphas in your organization and observe the differences between the men and women.

- Take the online Alpha Assessment and contemplate the implications of your scores.

- Make a firm commitment to reflect honestly on the information in this book and to apply the tools that you find the most relevant.

CHAPTER

2

The Variety of Alpha Males

The Roles They Play and the Masks They Wear

One of the chief reasons for Dell's remarkable run from start-up to worldwide leader in market share, said *Fortune* magazine in 2005, is that "Michael Dell surrounded himself with mentors and consultants when he needed to."[1]

One of those consultants, Kevin Rollins, went on to become Dell's CEO, and he and Michael formed one of the most remarkable and productive working relationships we've ever seen between top leaders in a major company. They use their differences to full advantage, leveraging each one's strengths to complement the other's and canceling out their liabilities.

It wasn't always that way. In the early days of their relationship, those same differences created challenges and frustrations. Michael's nonstop creativity would continually run up against Kevin's rigorous, nuts-and-bolts analysis. He'd envision a bold possibility for the future and share it with Kevin, who would evaluate it rigorously and express his reservations. Frustrated by what felt like overly cautious naysaying, Michael started to bypass Kevin, diving deep into the organization to find engineers with whom he could work on his pet ideas. This, in turn, frustrated Kevin. His job was to drive each quarter's execution, which meant keeping everyone focused on tasks that had to be completed ASAP. The two men were in agreement on the company's long-term goals, but Michael's natural time horizon was much further into the future, and his imagination was so prolific that he could easily come up with more good ideas than the company could possibly implement.

Over time, both leaders came to realize that they were in sync in certain crucial ways: they were both passionately committed to winning, they were both analytical and data driven, and their underlying intentions were aligned. That's where the similarities ended. They then took the crucial step of learning from each other and candidly acknowledging their own limitations. Ultimately, they realized that their differences of perspective and style could make them far more effective together than either could be alone. Kevin learned to be more open to Michael's ideas, and to help him develop practical plans to fulfill them. Michael, meanwhile, saw that Kevin's concern about distracting people with a constant flow of hot ideas was not obstructionism but practical wisdom. In learning how to complement each other's strengths and manage their own respective risk factors, they enabled their giant company to soar from one innovation to another while continuing to run efficiently and meet its immediate goals without wasting resources chasing after unattainable dreams.

In working with powerful leaders like Michael and Kevin, we came to realize that not all alpha males are the same. Clearly, they all had certain characteristics in common—which we described in chapter 1—but many were markedly different from one another. In many instances, these variations caused explosive personal conflicts and corporate upheavals. But in other cases, the differences came together in a magnificent alchemy, leading to incredibly creative and productive alliances. Over time, we began to notice definite patterns in these stylistic differences. We identified four distinct types of alpha males, and the categories were validated by the data in our Alpha Assessment study. We named them the *commander*, the *visionary*, the *strategist*, and the *executor*.

The Four Types of Alphas

All alpha males are aggressive, competitive, and driven to achieve. They think big, aim high, and attack their goals with courage, confidence, and tenacity. But each of the four types expresses these common qualities in different ways. Think of them as spices that add flavor to the basic alpha male recipe. Understanding their nuances will give you deeper insight into yourself and the alpha males around you, enabling you to pinpoint strengths you can build upon and risks you need to address. With this more granular view, you can home in on a specific course of action, just as a doctor can devise a better treatment plan if she knows the exact type of infection a patient has rather than only the broad category.

Here is a brief summary of each type's primary behavior traits:[2]

- *Commanders:* Intense, magnetic leaders who set the tone, mobilize the troops, and energize action with authoritative strength and passionate motivation, without necessarily digging into the details.

- *Visionaries:* Curious, expansive, intuitive, proactive, and future-oriented, they see possibilities and opportunities that others sometimes dismiss as impractical or unlikely and inspire others with their vision.

- *Strategists:* Methodical, systematic, often brilliant thinkers who are oriented toward data and facts, they have excellent analytic judgment and a sharp eye for patterns and problems.

- *Executors:* Tireless, goal-oriented doers who push plans forward with an eye for detail, relentless discipline, and keen oversight, surmounting all obstacles and holding everyone accountable for their commitments.

You might say that *all* human beings can fit into those four categories, not just alpha males. To some extent that is true, but our concern is with alphas, and alphas bring to the four types an overlay of aggressive intensity, energetic persistence, and competitive drive that sets them apart from the rest of humanity. It is that distinctive collection of traits that led us to use the term alpha male *syndrome*.

It's important to note that the types are not mutually exclusive. While virtually every alpha has one dominant type, he or she will typically have one or two secondary patterns as well. So, for example, a visionary alpha might also have strong strategist tendencies, while another visionary might have commander traits as a secondary characteristic. The data from our Alpha Assessment study support the observation that alphas display the qualities of one primary type, but also possess traits of the other three in varying degrees. Although each type is statistically unique, there is an approximate 20 percent correlation between them.

To cite ourselves as examples, we are both visionary alphas, but Eddie has strong secondary arms as both a commander and a strategist, while Kate has a lot of executor traits. We both have big, expansive ideas, but Kate will offer practical comments about implementation challenges to justify her point of view, and she will persist until she can bring closure to the discussion. When Eddie wants to get his way, he first uses charm and humor to inspire support. Before bringing out the data, he appeals to the emotions by describing the impact his idea will have on other people.

In our experience, the most effective alpha leaders are those who blend the functional elements of more than one type—or are smart enough to surround themselves with associates who add the strengths of other types to the mix. For example, here's how the four types might look at a particular task:

- *Commander:* This job needs someone to take charge and lead the way.

- *Visionary:* I see a great possibility waiting to be unveiled and seized.

- *Strategist:* The potential opportunities and risks need to be analyzed and resolved.

- *Executor:* Getting this done requires structure and control.

You can see where all four styles have value, and that, depending on the circumstances, different combinations and proportions would be ideal. Michael Dell, for example, is a visionary alpha with a strong strategist arm, and Kevin Rollins is very strong in both strategist and executor alpha traits. The strengths of their dominant styles complement each other, and also neutralize their shortcomings.

Unfortunately, not all alpha males learn the priceless lesson of working with complementary types. As we write this, we are consulting for a company in which a pair of contentious alphas have created chaos and caused stockholders to lose sleep. One is a young, cocky commander with a short but impressive track record that propelled him to the senior VP level before he was 30. The other is the CEO, an alpha strategist who was one of the commander's principal champions on his way up.

Their relationship began to sour once the commander settled into his corner office. Charismatic, good-looking, and charming, he attracted a cadre of loyal followers who were also young, ambitious, and highly talented. His ability to motivate those energetic workers, stimulate their creativity, and bring them together in a strong team environment was so impressive that analysts thought the company was poised to soar ahead of its competitors and stay there for decades. But the commander began to believe in his own mythology. Whereas before he'd been smart enough to act humble when appropriate, he now dropped all such pretense. He was a star and he wanted to shine even brighter. The problem was, he still reported to the strategist, and the differences in their styles began to grate on each of them.

The strategist CEO not only had little charisma of his own, he had no use for it as a leadership tool. He was a nuts-and-bolts seer who could discern meaningful patterns in a pile of data that would make the commander's eyes glaze over. Where most people saw random pieces, he saw a finished puzzle. Methodical and systematic, he didn't trust emotion-based motivators, and he didn't like surprises, two good reasons why wild cards like the commander and his gang made him nervous. He had come to see his former protégé as clueless about the realities of life at the top. He also saw him as ungrateful. "He should thank me for helping him get where he is, but he dismisses me like yesterday's news," he complained.[3]

He wasn't wrong on that score. The commander saw the CEO as over the hill and out of touch. Less and less willing to be restrained by the strategist's insistence on methodical, tightly controlled procedures, he craved autonomy and he wasn't willing to wait for it. He'd grab an inch of freedom, and the strategist would counter with a new form of control, until finally he said he'd rather quit than continue reporting to his former mentor. The strategist, in turn, suggested that the company buy out the youngster's contract. Only the intervention of the chairman and founder has kept the dueling alphas in their positions. Not wanting to lose either of them, he soothed the strategist's ruffled feathers with some additional authority and the requisite perks, and told the commander to report directly to him. But the company was unsteady. Teams at every level were hampered by the tension, uncertainty, and communication breakdowns at the top. Like iron filings drawn to two different magnets, coworkers had taken sides, causing widespread polarization. Energy was being drained, and gossip lovers were having a field day.

It quickly became clear to us that the strategist and the commander could be an unbeatable combination if they learned to use their differences to create harmonious chords instead of dissonance. We used the awareness trajectory to show them how much greater their impact could be if they aligned around common intentions and stayed aware of the effects of their behavior. With the strategist's genius for creating infrastructure and processes, and the commander's brilliance for getting people to follow his lead and give their all, they could accomplish things together that neither could manage on his own, no matter how much autonomy he had.

By learning about their alpha types, they came to realize that the clashes between them stemmed from their different styles, not irreversible personality conflicts. They also saw that, as alpha males, they were naturally competitive, but they were fighting each other rather than teaming up to beat their competitors and achieve their common goals.

As of this writing, they are still wary of each other, but at least they're lining up on the same side of the ball. Now that they have the alpha typology as a framework, we will introduce them to the information and tools you're about to discover in these pages. We're confident that the chairman's faith in them will be vindicated.

Because you probably interact with a variety of alpha males in your work, it's important to learn about all four types, even the ones that don't seem to apply to you personally. Being aware of each type's assets and liabilities will help you form powerful alliances and avoid many of the problems to which packs of alpha males are prone. The categories are especially useful when working with alpha males in areas of recurrent tension, problems, and gridlock. When we explain to alphas that the colleagues they struggle with are not on totally different pages, but are, instead, coming at their common objectives from different perspectives, the tension tends to dissipate. Conflicts over style are easier to overcome than conflicts over substance, particularly when someone else's style can fill in the gaps in your own.

The Strengths and Risks of the Alpha Types

As with the general alpha male traits, each type has specific strengths that can turn into weaknesses. These are described in detail in chapters 3 through 6 and are summarized here. (For research supporting these points, see the data posted on our Web site at www.AlphaMaleSyndrome /assessment.)

Commanders. Commanders' noble intention is to make things happen, and they push people hard to accomplish their goals. Their primary risk is driving *so* hard they run over others like bulldozers. Their leadership challenge is to learn how to align people around a common direction and to inspire and orchestrate productive action rather than mandate it.

Visionaries. Visionaries' noble intention is to move an organization forward into an uncertain and unknown future. Fueled by a fertile imagination, they lead with passion and enthusiasm. Their primary risk is becoming so overzealous that they ignore reality, bite off more than they can chew, and lead their team over a cliff. Their leadership challenge is to become practical prophets by adding the skills of listening, planning, and executing to their intuitive gifts.

Strategists. Strategists' noble intention is to select the optimal direction and get the best result. They approach the task armed with data and exceptional powers of reason and analysis. Their primary risk is becoming overconfident know-it-alls in love with their own brilliance. Their leadership challenge is to invite others to contribute their unique intelligence and creativity.

Executors. Executors' noble intention is to get things done the right way. Masters of project management, they dig into the details with relentless determination. Their primary risk is becoming control freaks whose micromanaging creates roadblocks and paralysis. Their leadership challenge is to create ownership, commitment, and genuine accountability.

In our study, the scores for general alpha strengths and risks showed moderately high correlations with the strengths and risks of each of the types. Specifically:

- Most people who scored high in general alpha strengths also scored high in at least one of the strength subscales. The same applies to the risk subscales.

- About half of those who scored in the top 25 percent on the general alpha strengths scale also scored in the top 25 percent in strengths for one of the types. The same applies to the risk subscales.

The strength and risk scales for each alpha type were moderately correlated, meaning that people with one type of strength or risk tended to show other types of strengths and risks as well. The strongest correlations were between the risk scores for commanders, strategists, and executors, meaning that someone with the risks of one of those types probably has the risks of one or both of the others as well. Interestingly, we found no correlation between executor strengths and visionary strengths. This actually makes a great deal of sense; as we'll see in chapter 4, it's rare to find someone who sees the big picture and also excels at the details of implementation.

Table 2-1 summarizes the strengths and risks of each alpha type.

TABLE 2-1

Alpha types: When strengths become liabilities

Alpha type	Value to organization	Risk to organization
Commander	Decisive, strong, authoritative; exudes confidence; often charismatic; has a big appetite for achievement and thirst for victory; brings out the best in others	Solo player; domineering and intimidating; argues to win points; generates fear and self-protective culture; competes with peers; envious; loose with the rules
Visionary	High standards and expansive goals; inspires with view of future; makes creative leaps; strong convictions, unwavering faith, and tenacious will; trusts instincts	Overconfident about ideas; excessive bravado; defensive when challenged; closed to input; ignores reality, losing support of pragmatists; spins the truth
Strategist	Quick, probing mind; objective, analytic, data-driven, methodical; sees underlying patterns; leaps beyond the obvious and integrates disparate ideas	Opinionated know-it-all; smug, arrogant, pretentious; has to be right; can't admit mistakes; cold and unemotional; lacks team spirit; disconnects from others
Executor	Disciplined, tireless pursuit of results; uncanny eye for spotting problems; gives excellent feedback and wake-up calls; moves people to action; helps team grow	Sets unreasonable expectations; micromanages; prone to workaholism and burning out employees; impatient; overly critical; focuses on shortcomings; expresses displeasure, not appreciation

The Types of Alpha Male Anger

The three alpha risk themes we mentioned in chapter 1—hard-driving competitiveness, interpersonal impatience, and difficulty controlling anger—show up differently in the four alpha types. All alpha males tend to get irritated and frustrated by bad performance and the failure of people to meet their goals. But each type tends to express those tendencies in a different way and under different circumstances. Since dysfunctional anger is the most disturbing of all alpha male risk factors, let's look at how each of the four types tends to express it.[4]

Commanders are the most likely to raise their voices. They're yellers and shouters, and their primary trigger is the performance shortfall. They want everything that's supposed to get done to be done—now. Healthy commanders are masterful at building loyalty and creating accountability;

they use their intensity wisely to get people to take the hill. For a fair and reasonable commander, people will work extra hard and put up with the occasional temper tantrum because they don't want to let their leader down. But if they disappoint an *unhealthy* commander, they'd better bar the door. Earplugs might also be a good idea, although some commanders will raise their intensity level instead of their voice. Healthy commanders listen if someone they trust tells them they've gone too far. The dysfunctional ones feel entitled to their rage, regardless of the damage it does, because they feel that their poor-performing targets deserve it. They believe that fear motivates people to perform better, when in fact it merely coerces them into compliance.

Visionaries are the least prone of all the types to volatile outbursts, or to overt displays of any kind. Their anger is more likely to show up as annoyance when people think their grand ideas are far-fetched, not far-sighted. They don't like anyone to challenge their ideas, and they *really* hate it when someone says their vision is impossible and they ought to come back down to earth. Rather than confront the conflict head-on, they turn passive-aggressive. Seething inside, they'll use their anger as additional motivation, adding some "I'll show them" passion to their already fired-up drive. They'll keep the naysayers at a distance and try to accomplish the goal on the sly, looking forward to the day they can say, "I told you so! Who's the dreamer now?"

Strategists demean people with sarcasm or blunt comments about how stupid they are. They feel entitled to put people down, because no one is as smart as they are. Sometimes, their anger shows up as quiet irritation when others can't track fast enough to keep up with them as they glide through a huge amount of data, linking things together and drawing novel but logical conclusions. They believe it's the other person's responsibility to understand what they're trying to communicate. "You don't understand? That's not *my* problem. You're stupid!"

Executors chew people out, usually for not delivering on their promises. They can't stand excuses and "reasons why." They simply don't care. They just want the right job done the right way. They care a great deal about *how* people do things, and when someone takes a less efficient or more time-consuming path, they get frustrated. Unhealthy ex-

ecutors will micromanage and nitpick instead of coach, and they feel
entitled to criticize every little piece of every task that the person takes
on. Their criticism can be nasty, and it sometimes escalates to a major
scolding under the erroneous belief that a good dressing-down will help
the person perform better next time.

Figure 2-1 summarizes our research data linking each alpha type and
the three main risk themes: competitiveness, impatience, and anger.

FIGURE 2-1

Hard data on types

Our study found relationships between the four alpha types and several variables. *

1. The three major risk themes—competitiveness, impatience, and anger
   - Commanders scored high on the anger measure and moderately high in competitiveness and impatience.
   - Visionaries have a mild tendency to display anger, and a very slight tendency toward impatience and competitiveness.
   - Strategists are moderately inclined toward anger and have a slight tendency toward impatience.
   - Executors are quite likely to be impatient, and only moderately likely to display anger; they show a slight tendency toward competitiveness.

2. Gender differences
   - Men scored higher than women on commander risks and strategist strengths and risks, but not on the executor or visionary scales.
   - While not large, the differences as a whole tell a consistent story: men display more of the cold, domineering, calculating alpha behaviors.

3. Age, education, and status
   - Older people scored slightly higher than younger people on commander strengths and visionary strengths.
   - Younger people scored somewhat higher on commander risks, strategist strengths and risks, and executor strengths and risks.
   - The only subscale for which there was no age difference was visionary risks.
   - The higher the education level, the higher the scores on strategist strengths and visionary strengths.
   - Those who supervise others were especially strong in commander strengths and especially low in visionary risks.

*We did not look for statistical links with the Myers-Briggs Type Indicator, but we have noticed the following tendencies in our work: very strong visionaries score high on the MBTI intuitive scale; strong strategists score high on the thinking scale; strong executors score high on the judging scale. We have observed no association with commanders, although they seem to be slightly more extroverted than introverted.

What Type Are You?

Answering yes or no to the following questions will give you a general sense of which alpha type best describes you. Bear in mind, however, that the online Alpha Assessment is a far more accurate instrument. In about 15 minutes it will give you a description of your primary type and the relative strength of the other three, along with a personalized report that includes specific advice for your combination of types. If you haven't already taken it, we strongly encourage you to do so as soon as possible. (See the instructions in chapter 1 on how to take the assessment or go to www.AlphaMaleSyndrome/assessment.)

Commander Strengths

- ☐ People say they'll stand up for me and perform at their absolute best for me, and they do.
- ☐ I've always had an abundance of energy.
- ☐ I can be a very persuasive speaker.
- ☐ In new group situations, I almost always wind up in the leadership role.
- ☐ I'm exceptionally good at motivating others to take action.
- ☐ People have described me as charismatic.

Commander Risks

- ☐ I make it a point not to show my vulnerability.
- ☐ I can be highly argumentative at times.
- ☐ I can be harsh and overly direct when I'm stressed or worried about something.
- ☐ I occasionally bend the rules or spin the truth to accomplish what I want.
- ☐ I push myself hard to surpass the performance of my peers.

☐ I often feel jealous of peers who outperform me, or gain more recognition than I do, although I don't show it.

Visionary Strengths

☐ I prefer starting new projects and allowing others to finish them.

☐ I often come up with breakthrough ideas.

☐ When making important decisions, I have learned that I'm right to trust my gut.

☐ I like finding new ways to do things rather than take the accepted route.

☐ I'm more innovative than I am practical.

☐ I enjoy working in situations that demand improvisation.

Visionary Risks

☐ I get caught up in what's new and lose interest in routine work.

☐ When I feel excited about a new direction I tend not to see the risks.

☐ When starting a new project, people often tell me that my expectations are unrealistic.

☐ I often start new projects before finishing old ones.

☐ I get frustrated dealing with naysayers and worrywarts.

☐ Achieving my vision usually takes more time and resources than I initially thought.

Strategist Strengths

☐ I'm very analytic, logical, and data oriented in decision making.

☐ I operate from mental maps that allow me to pull important data together.

☐ I don't allow emotions to affect my decisions.

- ☐ I have laserlike focus once I lock onto something.

- ☐ People have praised my intellectual horsepower.

- ☐ If I have the data I'll come up with the right decision.

Strategist Risks

- ☐ I don't like selling my ideas; people should be able to recognize the superiority of my ideas.

- ☐ I generally don't need input from others to make good decisions.

- ☐ I have little respect for people who space out or get confused easily.

- ☐ I can almost always find a logical flaw with someone else's argument.

- ☐ I don't go out of my way to develop relationships at work; I focus on getting the job done.

- ☐ I focus more on getting good results and less on how people feel.

- ☐ I tend to make mental leaps and get annoyed when people can't follow me.

Executor Strengths

- ☐ When I begin a project, I immediately see the steps that must be taken to succeed.

- ☐ I always provide clear goals and expectations to those who work below me.

- ☐ Before starting a project, I make sure that a clear timeline and a detailed plan of action are in place.

- ☐ I like it when work projects follow a strict and reliable schedule.

- ☐ When I delegate, I follow up to make sure everything is on track.

- ☐ I like my team members to give me frequent updates.

Executor Risks

- ☐ Even when I'm in a leadership role I tend to get involved in the details.

- ☐ I've been accused of being a "control freak."

- ☐ I don't spend much time celebrating successes.

- ☐ I rarely find the work of others to be up to my standards.

- ☐ I can be very critical when I see problems in someone's work.

- ☐ I get irritated when people miss deadlines, don't keep agreements, or skip past significant details.

Did you answer yes more often on one of the strength scales than on the others? Chances are, that's your primary alpha type. If you answered yes to four or more statements in any of the other strength sections, you probably also have many of that type's traits. As with the questionnaire in chapter 1, don't be surprised if your risk scores are roughly parallel to your strength scores. In general, if you have the assets, you usually carry the liabilities as well. Again, we strongly encourage you to complete the full Alpha Assessment online, at www.AlphaMaleSyndrome/assessment.

The Alpha Triangle

Just as smoking constricts the arteries and erupts in any number of symptoms, the risk factors associated with all four alpha types constrict the flow of energy, information, and creativity in an organization, causing damage that can show up locally and systemwide. One common pattern is a deadly trap we call the *alpha triangle*. To paraphrase Shakespeare, all the workplace is a stage and all the alpha males are merely players.[5] Think of the alpha triangle as a dramatic theme that plays out in different variations, depending on which alpha types are acting in the three central roles. We're describing the triangle now because it is a very useful model for recognizing dysfunctional alpha behavior in any organization, and because we will be referencing it throughout the book.

The alpha triangle consists of three sides: villain, victim, and hero (see figure 2-2). Each character reinforces the other two: villains blame, victims whine, heroes fix. Each lays claim to a specific payoff: villains get power, victims get sympathy, and heroes get appreciation. As villains, dysfunctional alpha males are right out of central casting. Their noble intention is to get things done efficiently and well, but they pursue that goal with blunt instruments. They think they're helping people do their work better, but their victims don't feel helped; they feel misunderstood, mistreated, unappreciated, and maybe even abused. To complete the alpha triangle, someone has to take on the hero role by cleaning up the mess, perhaps by trying to get the irate villain to lighten

FIGURE 2-2

The alpha triangle

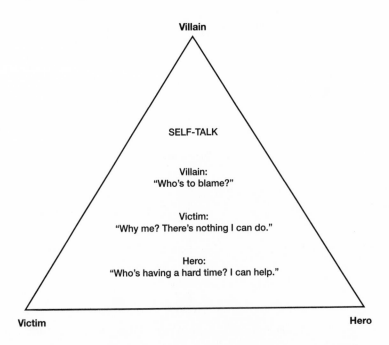

Source: Thanks to John Carpman for creating this model and to Kathlyn Hendricks for adding meaningful details.

up or by lending a sympathetic ear to the victims. In most organizations there is no shortage of actors auditioning for the part.

Here's a typical alpha triangle. A client of ours we'll call Glenn was a senior vice president at a multinational corporation. An alpha executor, his ability to dig deeply into problems, identify their causes, and quickly find the perfect solutions inspired awe. He was renowned for getting his staff to buy into impossible goals and achieve them. He was also known as a quiet assassin. When Glenn saw something he didn't like, which was often, he'd shoot daggers with his eyes and snap, "You're wildly off the mark" or "That's the dumbest thing I ever heard." To make up for Glenn and his morale-killing ways, one of the VPs under him would cheer up the casualties and restore their self-esteem. As is usually the case, however, the hero's damage control actually perpetuated the problem, because it gave Glenn less incentive to change his ways. The result was a tragic irony we call *alpha sludge*. Alpha males are hardwired for accomplishment, but when they turn into villains in the triangle they create so much inertia it's as if everyone's feet were mired in quicksand. As the sludge spreads, motivation is sapped, teamwork is destroyed, and performance plummets.

As in Hollywood movies, villains come in a variety of shapes and sizes. Each of the four alpha types has its own pattern of villainous behavior, each of which is rooted in the aggressiveness, competitiveness, and need to dominate found in all unhealthy alpha males.

- *Commander villains* demand extreme loyalty and subservience. They have to be number one, and everyone else has to be beneath them.

- *Visionary villains* believe in a bright shining future that no one else can even glimpse. They suck others into their jet stream, and before they know it they're on the brink of a precipice.

- *Strategist villains* are intellectual bullies who think they have all the answers. They think everyone else is an idiot, and they let them know it.

- *Executor villains* are irritating nags, constantly looking over everyone's shoulder, checking on them, telling them what to do and how to do it.

While everyone favors one side of the triangle over the others, most of us shift from one role to another, like Peter Sellers in *Dr. Strangelove*. A hero who always has to rescue someone might start to feel like a victim of that person's troubles, for instance, and a habitual victim might occasionally step into the hero role to help another victim. Alpha males typically vacillate between villain and victim: they bully people to the brink of tears and then feel sorry for themselves for having to deal with such incompetents. Sometimes they switch to the villain-hero two-step, so they get to put out the fires they start.

For example, an alpha male client of ours who runs a small company would assign more work than his staff could reasonably accomplish in the time allotted. Then, sensing they were overwhelmed, he'd charge in on his white horse and heroically complete the work himself. Naturally, to meet his ongoing need for victims, he unconsciously hired people with hard-luck stories and poor follow-through.

Breaking the Triangle

The alpha triangle is hard to break because each player has a stake in keeping it intact. Villains like to feel in control. Victims need to feel wounded. Heroes love to feel honorable. And all three get to feel justified. They might also enjoy the adrenalin rush: triangle dramas are exciting. But, as with other addictions, adrenalin jolts can be hazardous to your health, and they hijack your brain by shifting metabolism away from the higher centers of thought. Ultimately, everyone in the alpha triangle feels lousy, but their dependency keeps them stuck. And so the beat goes on. And on. And on.

Depending on the level of an alpha male's risk factors, the difficulties caused by his behavior can range from occasional minor annoyances to ongoing dysfunction to outright disaster. Alpha triangles can be as fragile as a paper hat or as sturdy as the Great Pyramid of Giza. The challenge for alpha males and those who work with them is fourfold: to recognize the need for change, to learn healthy habit patterns to replace dysfunctional behavior, to remain vigilant so they can spot the old pattern before it starts running on automatic pilot, and to make the necessary behavioral change. When they *do* shift to a healthier form of alpha male behavior, they find that everyone else in the triangle drama automatically adjusts.

Here is a bottom-line principle that runs through this entire book: *if you and you alone change, other people will also change.* Anyone, regardless of power or position, can dramatically transform a working environment by opting out of the alpha triangle. Think of it as simple geometry: if you remove any of its three sides, a triangle will collapse. In the absence of walls, the sludge that's gumming up the works can seep out.

Even triangles caused by alpha male volatility can be leveled once a key player sees the damage it causes. Take, for example, Walt, the chief technology officer at a prominent software company. Walt was a hard-driving alpha executor with a temper as hot as a power plant on red alert. What he thought was constructive feedback the people on the receiving end saw as a weapon of mass destruction. His staff cowered in fear, his peers tuned him out, and everyone in the company found ways to tiptoe around him. When the business team needed to make sure a shipment went out on time, for example, they would leave Walt out of the loop and work directly with his staff. Of course, when Walt got wind of this, *boom!*

Periodically, Walt would take his complaints to the CEO, an inspiring alpha visionary with the secondary traits of a take-charge commander. He loved the role of hero like actors relish Hamlet. He would soothe the wounded victims and sit them down to negotiate through their differences with Walt the villain. Soon, sanity and calmness were restored. On the surface, his approach might seem like a sensible solution. But the pattern kept on repeating. Imagine how much the CEO hero could have accomplished if he weren't smoothing ruffled feathers all the time. Think of what the victims could have produced if they weren't always trying to stay out of Walt's crosshairs. In the 360° interviews we conducted, Walt's colleagues clearly spelled out the syndrome. Here are some sample comments:

"Because he sees things others don't, he discounts what they have to offer. Instead of dominating every conversation, he needs to let it flow more before correcting people. When someone misses a detail, he should say, 'You might want to consider this,' instead of unloading on them."

"If Walt could communicate more tactfully instead of exploding, it would make a huge difference in how his message is received. He's incredibly insightful, but he can't get support or alignment with that temper."

"Walt wants to dig into the details right away. No 'How are you?' No pleasantries. He cuts people off abruptly. It makes you wonder, 'Am I wasting his time? Is he at all interested in communicating?'"

"His blunt style is off-putting. He challenges people in a demeaning tone that insinuates he doesn't trust them. I stopped engaging him directly; it isn't worth the risk."

"Walt comes across as knowing the right answers to everything, even in areas outside his expertise. There are people here with great ideas, but he doesn't listen to them."

When we started coaching him, Walt was not yet aware of how he was perceived and how he was affecting others. His self-assessment included these remarks: "People are intimidated by me. But I don't mind being abrasive, because I'm willing to clean up afterwards. It's a by-product of saying what I think. A lot of people don't have opinions, so I pick up the slack. But in this company, people are inclined to say, 'You've irritated me, so now I'll tune you out.'"

Using the awareness trajectory we introduced in chapter 1, we showed Walt how his style was impeding the flow from intention to impact. This information, plus his colleagues' 360° comments, which clearly portrayed him as the villain in the alpha triangle, killed his illusion that every problem in his organization was the fault of someone else.

We made similar progress with the other players as well. The victims began to see that by refusing to take corrective action they were perpetuating Walt's domineering villain behavior. The CEO admitted that he avoided confronting Walt because he liked being a hero and was afraid Walt would quit. He came to see that he was actually reinforcing Walt's dysfunctional behavior.

Breaking the alpha triangle requires behavioral change, not just a conceptual understanding. Ironically, it was Walt, the habitual blamer, who was first to take personal responsibility. The first thing he did was acknowledge that his volatility was a serious problem. For reasons we'll explore shortly, we encouraged him to give that explosive part of himself a name. He chose a good one: the Bomb. Realizing that he was letting negative feelings accumulate until the fuse ran out and the Bomb exploded, he did something most alpha males resist: he became familiar with a wider range of his own emotions—fear, sadness, and so on—than the narrow spectrum in his comfort zone. He also learned a new set of influence skills so he could impact people's performance without detonating.

The CEO also came around. Realizing that the cost of the Bomb's damage was unacceptable, he told Walt there would be consequences if he didn't change. They agreed that if Walt ever resorted to his explosive behavior in a meeting, the CEO would intervene and tell him to tone it down and listen to other people. They also agreed on an initial warning signal that would give Walt a chance to shift gears before the CEO said something publicly.

To his credit, Walt developed enough self-control that they never had to progress beyond the signal.

Once the two alpha men implemented these new response patterns, the triangle collapsed. The behavior of the victims naturally followed suit, and the performance of the entire group stepped up a notch.

The practical tools in this book will guide you safely beyond the alpha triangle, back to your authentic self and into effective teamwork. In the next four chapters you'll find advice aimed at each alpha type. You'll want to pay particular attention to those that apply most directly to you, but we strongly advise you to learn as much as you can from all four categories, since many of the tools have wide application.

First, we want to introduce a concept and a practice that we've found extremely effective in working with alpha males of all types.

The Masks We Wear

The Bomb was more than just a nickname Walt gave himself. It was his way of identifying what psychologists call a *persona*. Latin for *mask*, a persona represents the face we show the world at any given time. We can also compare a persona to a suit of clothing that can be put on or off, as needed. Having a varied wardrobe can be very useful, but problems arise when we unconsciously put on the wrong outfit for the occasion, like showing up at a country-and-western bar in a tuxedo, or, in reverse, attending a formal wedding in cowboy boots. Dressing inappropriately can cause enough problems, but imagine if you went a step further and *acted* in accord with your outfit, waltzing when everyone else was doing the Texas two-step, or vice versa. That's what happens when we slip into a persona that doesn't fit the circumstances: we present an inappropriate face to the world and act *as if* that mask were right for the circumstances. As other people respond to that ineffective persona, problems snowball.

Like everyone else, alpha males have various personas that they wear at different times, and each of the four alpha types favors certain styles. Understanding the personas you and your coworkers tend to adopt will help you understand how alpha dynamics play out in the workplace and, more important, how to break free of the alpha triangle and other dysfunctional patterns.

In childhood, we develop a collection of personas based on behaviors that help us cope with the world. Like directors assembling a cast of actors, we audition personas and "hire" those that bring us safety, love, recognition, and all the other things children crave. The adopted characters get embedded in the unconscious mind, and we carry them with us into the theater of adulthood, where they wait in the wings for their cue to come on stage. The more unconscious the persona is, the earlier it was probably formed, and the more likely it is that we'll think, "That's just the way I am." By the time we enter the workforce, we have developed layer upon layer of personas, and slip unconsciously from one role to another, until we recognize the pattern and consciously choose to make a change.

We started using the concept of personas with our clients about ten years ago, adding to our own previous experience the insights of Gay and Kathlyn Hendricks.[6] We found that understanding personas has a liberating effect on alpha males, because it helps them see their behavior as a collection of habits that were formed early in their lives rather than as an unchangeable genetic trait or a reflex hardwired into their brains. Once they see the potential benefit of replacing a dysfunctional habit with healthier behavior, they tackle the process of change with their typical discipline and learn how to shift out of autopilot when an inappropriate persona takes over.

That is what we help our clients do, and what you can do with the practice you're about to learn.

Getting Conscious About Personas

The first step toward gaining control of problematic personas is to identify them and name them. To help you in this process, take a look at figure 2-3, a list of the most common names that our clients have given

FIGURE 2-3

Alpha villain personas

Alpha commander	Alpha visionary	Alpha strategist	Alpha executor
Bulldozer	Dreamer	Biting Critic	Action Jackson
Chest Pounder	Eager Beaver	Chess Master	Bulldog
General	Far-Out Futurist	Contrarian	Broken Record
Head Honcho	Missionary Zealot	Cynic	Control Freak
My Way or the Highway	Pied Piper	Debater	Critic
Rant 'n' Rave	Pollyanna Good News	Hard-Head	Drill Down
Tyrant	Prophet	Mental Super Star	Hammer
Warrior	Rebel	Misunderstood Genius	Micro Manager
Wheeler Dealer	Super Salesman	Stealth Bomber	Shredder
			Timekeeper

to their personas, classified according to the alpha types associated with them. Bear in mind that these are simply nicknames that suggest a particular kind of behavior, not hard-and-fast categories. Feel free to use them, or to make up names that best capture the masks—or clothing— you put on at different times.

First, identify the three behavior patterns that are most troublesome at work. Once you've identified them, give each one a persona name. Then, answer the following questions about each one:

- What do you do when you're operating from this persona?

- How does this troublesome persona get activated?

- Describe the people or situations that get you hooked in the persona.

- Identify the positive underlying intention of the persona.

- Describe a better way to achieve that intention.

- Imagine a persona behaving in that better way and give it a name.

All of the personas listed in figure 2-3 have played the role of villain in the alpha triangle. The three personas you just named probably do the same. That's what dysfunctional personas typically do when alpha males wear them. But alpha males are sometimes victims of other villains, and sometimes they step into the breach as heroes. So, whether you're an alpha or someone who's not an alpha but is embroiled in alpha triangles at work, identify the personas you take on when you're a victim or a hero. Figure 2-4 shows some other persona names our clients have used. For each of your victim and hero personas, answer the same set of questions as before.

The Persona Interview

The following process is an effective way to free yourself of behavior patterns that lock you into the alpha triangle.[7] It practically guarantees a breakthrough into more authentic behavior and more effective decision

FIGURE 2-4

Other alpha triangle personas

Victims	Heroes
Accommodator	Cheerleader
Complainer	Energizer Bunny
Conflict Avoider	Flatterer
Overwhelmed	Harmonizer
Poor Me	Peacemaker
Procrastinator	Protector
Resigned to Whatever	Rescuer
Worrywart	Trooper

making. Keep in mind that the goal is not necessarily to get rid of personas. Your target is to escape their grip by hitting the "off" button when you catch yourself slipping into a troublemaking persona. Then you can be free to *choose* whether to wear the persona or shift to a more productive and successful one.

The process involves interviewing the *persona*. In other words, you step into that particular role and respond to a series of questions. You can have someone you trust serve as the questioner or do it on your own, essentially allowing one part of yourself to interview another.

First, select a situation or behavior that you want to change. Choose a real issue that's causing you problems at work. Next, name the persona you adopt in those circumstances. Choose a name that captures the unwanted behavior pattern; either make one up or select one from the lists.

When you're ready to begin the interview, enter fully into the persona. We find it extremely helpful to step into the role *physically* as well as mentally. Get out of your chair and embody the role as if you're a professional actor and your Oscar depends on it. Walk the walk and talk the talk. Ham it up. Assume the postures, gestures, and mannerisms of the persona. Use props if you wish.

Then, begin the interview, using the questions in figure 2-5. For the best results, go through them in the order listed, and answer *as the persona*, in his or her voice, from his or her perspective. And remember to have fun; just because the process is powerful doesn't mean you can't enjoy it.

Here is an example of how one of our clients used the persona interview to great advantage.

When Eddie conducted an offsite for Ken DiPietro, the senior VP we quoted in chapter 1, nearly everyone on his team gave him the same feedback: whenever anyone questioned his judgment, Ken would discount the feedback and push ahead strongly on his agenda. Recogniz-

---

FIGURE 2-5

Persona interview questions

1. *(Persona name)*, when did you make your first appearance in the life of *(your real name)*?

   If the answer is "at work," think of a related persona you used in childhood, one that this work persona might have grown from.

2. *(Persona name)*, from whom did you learn to play your persona?

   In particular, think about people who had a great influence in your early life.

3. *(Persona name)*, what are you most proud of?

4. *(Persona name)*, what are you most anxious about?

5. *(Persona name)*, what do you do in the present that feeds this fear? Which of your behaviors or choices trigger anxiety?

6. *(Persona name)*, how do you create difficulties at work?

7. *(Persona name)*, are you willing to find new ways to honor the value that you've brought to *(your real name)* in the past?

   If your answer is no, either you are not yet committed to change, or it's not really a problem. Reexamine your intention to change, or cycle back and summarize how the persona is creating a problem.

   If the answer is yes, create a new space to stand in by moving to another part of the room. Then name the new persona you want to develop.

8. *(New persona name)*, from this place of expanded awareness and confidence, what do you want to create?

9. *(New persona name)*, to accomplish those goals, what actions will you commit to taking in the next month?

ing this behavior as an automatic operating system he'd adopted early in his life, Ken explained that it had enabled him to fight for what he believed in, especially in the face of obstacles or confrontation. It was his way to drive results even though the side effects were often problematic. Ken named the persona Street Fighter.

Over the course of Ken's work life, Street Fighter emerged whenever he found himself in a tough, competitive environment. In his early jobs it seemed to work to his advantage. In his current position, however, Street Fighter was out of place.

The people around him became guarded and constantly vigilant, casting themselves as victims and heroes to Ken's villain in the alpha triangle. When, at the offsite, Eddie asked Ken's colleagues what personas of *theirs* showed up in response to Street Fighter, the victims' answers included Run for Cover and Go Silent, while the heroes chose names like Get Sneaky and Run Around because they got things done behind Ken's back.

Ken agreed to do the persona interview. To the question, "What do you most want?" Street Fighter replied, "To add value and get results." Could he think of replacement personas that would accomplish that intention with less carnage? Yes, he said, and he named the preferred persona Total Pro. Ken's colleagues lent support by brainstorming the different personas *they* might wear to help Ken adopt more positive behavior. Because his openness and vulnerability made them feel more comfortable with him, some of their supportive personas had coaching overtones, like Doctor Phil, Hand-Holder, and Cheerleader.

True to his nature, Street Fighter did not go away without a struggle. In the months following the persona interview, he showed up a few times, but Ken was usually able to recognize the takeover and even joke about it. Eventually, Street Fighter outlived his usefulness and appeared only rarely. Ken's team responded positively to his newfound consistency and equanimity, and as a result their teamwork, cohesion, and communications all improved markedly.

In the next four chapters, we'll delve more deeply into each of the four alpha types, beginning with a detailed look at the commander.

ACTION STEPS

- Determine which of the four alpha types—commander, visionary, strategist, or executor—best defines your behavioral style.

- Determine which types best describe the coworkers with whom you interact the most.

- Study the dynamics of the alpha triangle and ask yourself which roles you and your closest coworkers are most likely to play.

- Identify the reasons why you might be seen as a villain.

- Make a commitment to opt out of the triangle.

- Do the exercises in this chapter pertaining to personas.

- Commit to catching yourself when you take on nonproductive personas.

The Alpha Commander

The Top Dog Who Can Be a Pit Bull

In 2001, I became the director of the Defense Logistics Agency, a logistics organization the size of a *Fortune* 200 company, which supplies everything from uniforms to food to fuel for the armed services. At the time, complaints abounded from all levels of the military that DLA was expensive and nonresponsive. I received marching orders to orchestrate an immediate turnaround by slashing costs and improving our responsiveness to customers. To break through inertia without demoralizing the civilian workforce that accomplishes most of the work, I had to be forceful and direct. But if I came down too heavy with the hammer, I might cause so much fear that I'd stifle communication and destroy morale.

I struggled with this dilemma for two months. Then came 9/11. Suddenly, the challenge magnified a thousand times. Because of the massive increase in our workload, I had to create a sense of urgency and constantly drive for high performance, while at the same time not being overly impatient or intimidating.

—*Vice Admiral Keith Lippert, director, Defense Logistics Agency,*
    in interview with authors

Commander Strengths

"When the going gets tough, the tough get going" could be the motto of alpha commanders. Natural leaders who inspire trust, respect, and sometimes even awe, they are take-charge types who direct their abundant energy toward accomplishing their mission.

They think big, aim high, and run through brick walls to get what they want. And what do they want? To win! Whatever the game, commanders have a burning desire for victory. All alphas do, but commanders burn most intensely, and their internal scorecard constantly computes their standing. They want nothing less than a long, unblemished winning streak with records broken along the way. Exceeding each quarter's revenue goals is a must-do. Every potential customer is an absolute gotta-have.

As sports fans know, top athletes need more than superior talent; the legends stand out for their will to win. Michael Jordan, for example, was said to be just as intense at a charity golf tournament as in the NBA finals. Like Jordan, successful alpha commanders drive everyone around them to higher levels of excellence. Instinctively drawn to situations that cry out for strong leadership, they're the first to step up in a crisis, rousing others to tap into unexplored reservoirs of energy and follow them over every hurdle. To alpha commanders, demanding the best is a necessary leadership task and the only way to train winners. Coming from a healthy alpha in the right context, this challenge brings out excellence that people never knew they had. That's why rugged athletes and leather-skinned soldiers weep when they recall the tough coaches and officers who pushed them to their limits: "He was so demanding, I hated him at times, but he changed my life for the better."

When he was in the army, Ray Roe, now the CEO of Adecco Group North America, was that sort of officer. As a lieutenant colonel, he took command of a battalion that had failed the army's physical conditioning exam.

At age 40, the West Point grad was twice as old as most of his soldiers, but he modeled a dedication to fitness and put them on a physical training regimen that could literally kill. A marathoner, he ran long distances every morning with his two golden retrievers, and led his officers on a run once a week. One day, after a lengthy run, his favorite dog, Clyde, was found at the side of a road, dead of a heart attack. From that day forward, the incident was used to motivate new recruits who didn't think it would be very hard to keep up with a middle-aged officer. "The commander ran his dog to death," the sergeants would say. "He loved his dog, and he doesn't give a damn about you, so you better get in shape."

And they did. Years later, when he was a general in charge of a division, soldiers would ask, "Are you the General Roe who killed his dog running?" The reputation for toughness was coated with respect, as former soldiers spoke of Ray with gratitude. Since retiring as a brigadier general in 1993, he's successfully translated that leadership style to the business world.

Self-confident, courageous, and willing to take a stand for their beliefs, alpha commanders operate from a strong sense of mission, and they inspire their groups with the same dedication. Often that means getting people to see beyond their immediate concerns and serve the greater good. When Vice Admiral Keith Lippert took over as director, the Defense Logistics Agency (DLA) was a loose collection of fiefdoms with serious infighting between headquarters and the business units. The sense of mission Lippert infused into the agency after 9/11 remained intact long after the immediate urgency of moving supplies and cutting costs had diminished.

When Hurricane Katrina hit, DLA was poised to deliver $309 million in supplies, including 58 million meals, 4.5 million gallons of fuel, and $7.5 million in medical supplies. Today, the agency is viewed as so cost effective and customer oriented that the 2005 Base Realignment and Closure Commission significantly broadened the agency's scope.

Another commander motto is "The buck stops here." To commanders, personal responsibility is a supreme value, and they take it to the max. In today's intertwined, matrixed organizations, leaders must inspire accountability in everyone, including people who don't report to them. In the absence of 100 percent control, they can't just "order" ownership of results. While some leaders in those circumstances blame others for their problems, or play politics to protect their self-interest, alpha commanders fill the void and take charge. And because they exercise powerful influence skills, their actions generate endless ripple effects.

While some commanders have better interpersonal skills than others, they are all first-class motivators, using just the right combination of carrots and sticks. High-level commanders also combine firmness with warmth. They radiate "I've got your back covered" as well as "Don't cross me." For an example of a balanced commander, look at these admiring comments from some of Admiral Lippert's team:[1]

> "He always asks how I'm doing and seems genuinely concerned. He connects with people."

> "He cares about you even when he doesn't agree with you. He goes out of his way to be helpful in areas I wouldn't normally expect from my boss."

> "He's not 'buddy-buddy,' but he genuinely likes people, and they sense that. He's tough, but he cares."

For such leaders, people take orders, tackle risks, and stretch themselves for a higher calling. Those who add a healthy dose of charisma to the mix become commanders of commanders.

When commanders are in full command of their souls as well as their talents, their will to win is balanced by sterling integrity. Because they reward loyal, hardworking team members fairly and stand up for them when they're under attack, many commanders are revered even when they're not particularly well liked. They know it's important to be upright and ethical, and they attend to those virtues as much as their efficiency and productivity. "He has unbelievably high integrity," said one executive about his CEO, "and it makes me want to work harder, because I feel like my contribution will make a real difference." For many alpha commanders, integrity extends beyond their teams and their organizations, and maybe even their families. Whether their higher calling is to contribute to world peace, advance economic opportunity in their local community, or help individuals lose weight; whether the means to their larger purpose is waging a just war, providing job training for the unemployed, or marketing fitness equipment, they hope to leave a worthy legacy behind them. Many of history's greatest social leaders and philanthropists were alpha commanders who were as faithful to the moral bottom line as they were to their company's.

Taken together, this constellation of traits inspires the loyalty and trust of others. That's why commanders get to the top and stay there — unless their formidable strengths become their biggest weaknesses.

The Problem with Alpha Commanders

All alphas like to win, and all alphas demand a lot from others. Alpha commanders have those qualities in spades, but they can easily turn into twin Achilles' heels: the appetite for victory becomes ruthless competitiveness, and high expectations lead to frustration and explosive rage. *Star Trek* fans know the difference: Captain Kirk is a healthy commander; the Klingon warriors are dysfunctional commanders.

You can see how typical commander assets turn into liabilities in table 3-1. For the data our study revealed about commanders, see the box "The Data on Commanders."

TABLE 3-1

The commander syndrome: When strengths become liabilities

Alpha attribute	Value to organization	Risk to organization
Dominant, confident, take-charge personality	Acts decisively and courageously; brings out the best in others; makes quick decisions	Creates fear with intimidating, domineering style; suppresses disagreement
Aggressive	Focuses on winning; turns others into winners; commands respect	Creates anxiety; stifles open communication; forces employees to cover up mistakes and withhold ideas
High achiever	Drives others to productive action; motivates team to produce outstanding results	Takes high levels of performance for granted; doesn't create strong leaders under him
Competitive; demands the best from self and others	Brings out the excellence in everyone; motivates by encouraging healthy competition	Competes with peers; breeds resentment, contempt, retaliation; creates turf wars; reduces sharing of information
Takes on 110% responsibility for organization	Executes dependably; follows through personally to ensure goals are met	Tries to do too much; fails to delegate; wastes talent of others; prone to premature burnout

The Data on Commanders

In our study, commanders who scored high in strengths also tended to score high in risks, but the correlation was not as strong as it was for the other alpha types, and there were more exceptions. With the other types, for instance, someone in the top 25 percent on the strength scale was very likely to be in the top 25 percent of risks as well. Not so with commanders (see table B-1, appendix B). The data suggest that commanders are more prone to extremes: excellent strengths with few risks, which makes for outstanding leaders, or perilous risks with few strengths, which makes for disasters. When they're good, they're very good, and when they're bad, they're awful.

Men scored significantly higher than women in the overall commander traits and also in commander risks, although the difference in commander strengths was not statistically significant. In other words, men are more likely than women to display the risks associated with being a commander (see table B-2, appendix B).

Fully half of the commanders in the upper 25 percent of risk scores were also in the top 25 percent in anger. That same group also scored high in the other two risk themes, impatience and competitiveness, but the proportions fell to about a third. Notably, these patterns are almost exactly the same for male commanders and female commanders. This finding is consonant with our experience in organizations: while anger is a problem for most alphas, commanders of both sexes are especially vulnerable (see table B-3, appendix B).

How Excessive Competition Leads to Defeat

When their healthy appetite for victory crosses the line of good sense and civility, alpha commanders epitomize Vince Lombardi's famous maxim: "Winning isn't everything, it's the *only* thing." They see *everyone* as competition—not just real opponents such as rival companies, but also their colleagues, other departments within their organizations, and even their teammates. Friends become foes; teammates become rivals. They have to win the Super Bowl *and* be MVP. They have to win the war *and* fill their chests with more medals than anyone else. They have to exceed their business objectives *and* get the biggest bonus.

At their worst, alpha commanders not only have to win, they have to dominate. They not only fight to the death, they eat the opposition for lunch. While leaders like Ray Roe can be tough and *gain* respect, a take-no-prisoners style in the hands of a bully breeds mistrust, resentment, contempt, and even retaliation. To alpha commanders who see the world as a zero-sum jungle where everyone is as ruthless as they are, anything goes, including cheating, lying, and chopping off the heads of others to make themselves look tall. When they direct that cutthroat attitude toward those who ought to be their allies, they wreak havoc within organizations.

Making matters worse, many alpha commanders are allergic to asking for help. If, in your mind, you are always in a boxing ring and everyone else is Mike Tyson, you're not about to turn your ear toward them. And if you think it's dangerous to show any sign of weakness, you miss out on one of the best influence skills of leadership: the capacity for self-disclosure. As a consequence, difficulties drag on and eventually impact other groups. The result is a CYA culture marked by a compliance that often degenerates into defiance; people who are abused by bellicose commanders find subtle ways to undermine them.

Some commanders seem to go through life whistling the tune from *Annie Get Your Gun*: "Anything you can do, I can do better." Obsessed by trivial rivalries, they jeopardize their worthy goals with envy-driven schemes. As bosses, they often create contests among employees, because they love the spectacle of gladiators in suits fighting to the finish.

Like former Notre Dame football coach Dan Devine, who provoked brawls among players to test their mettle, some commanders incite conflict among employees as a way to assess their prowess, with the winner gaining admittance to the inner circle. Certainly, healthy competition can bring out the best in people, but unnecessary and demeaning warfare can bring out their worst. Dysfunctional commanders can create work environments that mix *Dynasty* with *Sports Center*, fostering rampant paranoia, backbiting, and gossip, along with constant chatter about who stands where on the scoreboard. The emotional brutality saps office morale, encourages self-preservation over teamwork, and sometimes ends in mutiny.

The tendency of unhealthy alpha commanders to pit their team against other teams, and themselves against everyone else, makes it hard for them to work directly with peers to solve mutual problems. They see teamwork, collaboration, and consensus as wimpy, unexciting, and slow. They demean their rivals in public. They even cripple their own teams by making it treasonous to share information with other groups. In self-defense, peers who want to collaborate with them pull back and circle the wagons. The result is a key commander dilemma: they want desperately to rise above their peers, but if they get overly competitive they fail to advance. Why? Because they can't move up if their strongest peers don't want to work for them. Those who have been stabbed in the back or manipulated by a ruthless commander fear that he'll always look out for number one and won't do right by those who contributed to his success. They think, "If he's promoted, I'm outta here."

The relentless competition of alpha commanders creates one of the great drains of corporate energy: the turf war. Manager A scuffles with manager B over who would do the best job on a project. Meanwhile, manager X refuses to share his data with manager Y. The message is, "You're in my territory. Stay away." In the worst cases, the result mirrors nature: while members of the same pack slug it out for dominance, another pack swoops in and takes over the territory.

In our experience, it is imperative to redirect this competitive energy into genuine teamwork and synergistic cooperation, bearing in mind that collaboration can be a major challenge for alpha commanders. Reflecting on his highly successful experience running Dell Americas with Ro Parra, Joe Marengi told us, "I spent my whole life throwing sand in the eyes of anybody who jumped in my sandbox. Now I'm co-managing a business with someone else. I found co-anything *very* tough at first, but I came to realize how valuable it is to have someone to share responsibilities with."

Alpha commanders who don't believe they can win unless everyone else loses are capable of stopping an entire company in its tracks. At a huge global corporation where we consult, two young men who arrived within a couple of years of each other were singled out as rising stars. Each now runs a business unit with 8,000 to 10,000 employees who interact constantly. Both of them are alpha commanders, equally committed to results, equally intense, and equally stubborn about being right. But they're hardheaded in different ways. The one we'll call Harry is creative, passionate, and farsighted, but he lacks the influence skills and patience to garner broad-based support for his ideas. He gets his way only when he's in charge; at other times, the company misses out on his innovative thinking. Tom is just as driven, but his interpersonal skills are as well honed as his ability to run a tight ship. Whereas Harry is a long-term thinker, Tom has a more incremental and shorter-term perspective. People outside of his business unit, most notably those in Harry's group, consider him manipulative and underhanded. In an ideal world, these two gifted commanders would make their differences work to their mutual benefit, and the company would thrive. But their reciprocal mistrust spread to their business units, crippling effective interaction, and eventually caused a serious fracture in the company.

It has also caused a rift in the upper echelon. The CEO and the chairman want to keep both men happy, but they disagree on how to accomplish that. We advised them to *require* Tom and Harry to resolve their differences directly. So far, they've rejected that idea. The chairman is afraid to provoke one or both of them to leave the company. The CEO is reluctant to confront *anyone* directly, not just Tom and Harry. Like many alpha commanders with a hair-trigger temper, he would rather create a major scene in public than deal with difficult issues one-on-one. In terms of the alpha triangle, both Tom and Harry see the other as the villain and themselves as victim, while the chairman and CEO are classic heroes. As of this writing, the battle continues to rage and the sludge gets thicker by the day.

How Explosive Anger Demolishes Productivity

The pioneering humanistic psychologist Abraham Maslow once observed that if the only tool we possess is a hammer, we'll treat everything like a nail. Dysfunctional alpha commanders often look like hammers on the lookout for a good nail.

While anger management is a central challenge for all four alpha types, enraged commanders tend to be the scariest. They're blunt, loud, in-your-face screamers who strike fear in the hearts of others. As a leadership tactic in times of crisis, aggression can have value. No one would criticize an officer who berates a slacker soldier in wartime, or even a football coach who screams at players on the sidelines. But when General George Patton, a celebrated World War II hero, laced into a wounded soldier in a hospital bed, and Ohio State's legendary coach, Woody Hayes, socked an opposing team's player, they were seen as abusive, out-of-control Neanderthals, and their fall from grace was swift.

If there is a time and place for hotheaded alpha eruptions, it is rarely in a modern business setting. Yet the abuse of alpha commanders is often seen as a cost of doing business with powerhouse leaders who get results. The side effects can be devastating, however, particularly when two volatile alphas lock horns. Internecine wars break out, hostile takeovers occur, and the goal becomes not only to defeat one's rivals but to annihilate and disgrace them as well.

Kate recalls the time she was brought into a major corporation to coach the CEO and COO. Working individually for several sessions, she established pleasant relationships with both men. Then she attended a meeting of 16 senior executives and about 25 vice presidents and directors. The senior vice president of operations began his presentation, standing right next to the COO. Within minutes, the COO stood up, pointed his finger at the senior VP, and began to drill into him with withering, demeaning remarks. Kate was shocked: this man who had been warm and charming in private was so brutal in front of an audience that the VP kept backing away until he was literally pressed against a wall. Instinctively, Kate sprang from her seat and marched toward the raging COO.

She had no idea what she was going to do; she only knew she had to stop the abuse. Fortunately, the COO spotted her and immediately called for a break. Kate took him aside and told him, clearly and frankly, that such behavior had to stop. To drive the point home, she informed him that she would not work in a company where such behavior was condoned, much less modeled by the COO. Fortunately, like most mature alphas, he did not mind being called on his excesses when it was done in the right way by the right person. Rather than costing Kate the job, standing up to the COO earned her added respect and set the tone for a productive coaching relationship that grew into a warm friendship.

In their meetings, Kate pointed out that he was confusing people by terrorizing them in public and acting like a lamb in small groups and one-on-ones. Such blow-up-and-make-up behavior is the exact opposite of the principle everyone learns in Management 101: praise in public, criticize in private. At first, the COO rationalized his behavior: "I don't want to waste thirty people's time because someone is off track. I pick up ideas fast, and I want to make the decision and move on. When I feel frustrated I get very brusque. In a small team I can talk to the person the next day, but in a large team of middle managers, I may not see them for six months, so I need to make my point then and there." Like other dysfunctional commanders, he knew he upset people, but he viewed it as a necessary aspect of productive leadership. Then Kate showed him the practical consequences of his Jekyll-and-Hyde behavior spelled out in the compelling remarks of his colleagues during 360° interviews. For example:

> "He's so belligerent in meetings that people edit themselves and filter out any information that might trigger his rage."

> "Privately, he's very approachable. But in large groups his bluntness is so offensive that people miss the essence of what he's communicating."

> "I learned not to argue with him in public, and to talk to him later. But this keeps us from having honest, open discussions, and bringing issues to resolution as a group."

> "We actually leave a ten-minute slot in the agenda to accommodate his flameouts. Once he leaves, the real work starts; we go through the facts and figure out what to do."

Once he saw that he was the villain in dozens of alpha triangles, the COO was willing to buckle down and get to work on reconciling his private Teddy Bear persona with the Thumper persona that surfaced in meetings.

The Power of the Commander's Presence

Alpha commanders are not always aware of how much power their mere presence carries. Admiral Lippert, for example, has all the commander strengths and very few of the flip-side weaknesses. The epitome of a team player, he is a firm, directive leader who never raises his voice or loses his temper. Yet his 360° interviews, conducted six months after he filled the top spot at DLA, showed that some of his team experienced him as intimidating, threatening, aloof, hard to read, and unconcerned about people's feelings. We told him that by establishing a tough, results-oriented atmosphere he had delivered a necessary wake-up call, but he had not yet established trust. In the long run, the organization would surely suffer, because fearful workers don't communicate honestly or take the required risks to solve complex problems. In fact, intimidated and apprehensive civilian employees were already holding back, unwilling to own up to the problems in their departments until they felt they were fully on top of the issues.

If a humane, well-balanced leader like Admiral Lippert can inadvertently strike fear in the hearts of workers, imagine what a raging bully can do.

After hearing our report, the admiral hit the ground running. He quickly called for open communication and honest feedback, and he allowed his authentic self to show. A turning point came at an offsite we facilitated in June 2002. In one exercise, we had top agency leaders list on a flip chart both their strengths and the areas they needed to improve—and then walk around the room adding comments to each person's chart. To the group's astonishment, Admiral Lippert participated as a peer, openly responding to developmental feedback and committing to make the recommended changes. That single bold stroke overturned the inaccurate perception created by his earlier style. Later, he put the intimidation factor to rest for good by admitting to his senior management team that his effort to shake things up had inadvertently created problems.

In our next round of 360s, we received comments like these:

"Admiral Lippert has opened up and let us in, which reflects his trust in us. We're all growing as a result, and we knock ourselves out to perform at our best for him."

"Admiral Lippert has modified how he approaches people. He was always effective, but now he's moved into an entirely new zone of broad leadership impact."

As a direct result of Admiral Lippert's change in style, DLA responded remarkably well to the demands of the Iraq war. Improvements in teamwork and communication enabled the agency to significantly increase productivity while markedly reducing the size of its staff. As a result, DLA earned greater respect from their military customers and picked up significantly more responsibility as military bases were scheduled for closure.

Unlike Admiral Lippert, many intimidating commanders refuse to acknowledge their negative impact on others. They insist their behavior is necessary for success, and no one dares to contradict them. Rather than tell the truth, people stay out of their crosshairs, a conspiracy of silence that often extends to senior management. When, finally, someone in authority tells them that belligerence and intimidation are not acceptable, commanders respond in terms that management likes to hear: "I get that way sometimes because I want so badly for us to succeed." They promise to curb their tempers and work better with others. But only the exceptional ones pursue self-improvement with the zeal they apply to competitive goals. Why should they, when shortly after the wrist-slap they're handed another plum assignment?

As we've mentioned, all of that is changing rapidly. As organizations become less and less tolerant of abusive executives, bellicose alpha commanders who rant and rave their way to middle management are likely to stay there unless they change their ways.

Female Alpha Commanders

Female alpha commanders not only are fewer in number than their male counterparts; they are also less inclined to exercise their authority through intimidation and domination. Just as results-oriented as men, they are driven to win and they like being the "go to" person, but they pursue their objectives while also paying attention to how they treat people. Not surprisingly, men scored significantly higher than women on the commander risks scale in our study (see table B-2 in appendix B).[2]

Both male and female commanders can be driven by a sense of mission, but the women are more likely to motivate their troops by calling them to a purpose higher than the bottom line. Especially when they sense a loss of focus, they'll invoke concepts such as destiny and legacy.

Both male and female commanders also inspire the loyalty of those around them, but they go about it in different ways. Women tend to create a sense of community on their teams by showing genuine caring, paying more attention than men to people's interests outside of work and giving people small but clever gifts and cards. In short, women tend to soften their aggressive commander traits with maternal nurturance.

For example, an alpha client named Kathy Mankin was a middle manager at Heller Financial, a large financial services company. Strong, assertive, and highly competent, her managerial style was so motherly that she was known around the office as Mom. She made sure her team got the recognition they deserved and lobbied for promotions on their behalf. When she asked them to work weekends, she rolled up her sleeves and worked alongside them. All of which made her a highly respected leader.

At the same time, people questioned whether she had the authoritative presence required of a high-level executive. When employees didn't get their work done, for example, she chided them with guilt-inducing remarks that lacked the punch of real consequences. She was also as controlling as she was protective. Conservative by nature, she doggedly pushed her views and used her influence to defeat out-of-the-box ideas. Her staff felt grateful to be taken care of, but they resented her overcontrol and resistance to new approaches.

To her credit, when Kathy's career stalled, she took corrective action. She learned to be more of a director and an orchestrator, and less of a rescuer and nurturer. She developed the skill of building on other people's ideas instead of just pushing her own. She even made her appearance less maternal, updating her rather frumpy wardrobe and old-fashioned hairdo and trimming down with regular workouts. Within four years, she jumped three levels to become president of the firm's largest income-producing division.

Not every female alpha commander learns those lessons, however, and perceived softness can render them less effective and stall their careers. This is especially true of women who take it personally when colleagues push back. Getting emotional or judgmental when someone disagrees with you plays right into the stereotype that women aren't tough enough to lead at the highest levels. Similarly, expecting your instincts to be followed without backing them up with facts and data—something intuitive male commanders are less likely to do—can also work against you.

Commander Tools

If you're an alpha commander, your central challenge is to enlarge your area of concern. You have to shine while allowing others to shine; compete by collaborating effectively; blow minds with your competence and strength while also winning hearts with fairness and empathy. You need to stand tall without making others seem small; take charge and also share control; earn acclaim and also give credit. In addition, you have to model those vital qualities for those you lead, encouraging your team to build cooperative relationships with other work groups based on common goals and shared resources. You're used to meeting big challenges. If you can meet this one with the same competence and tenacity you bring to the others, it will pay off big time.

Is your hand poised, ready to turn the pages and skip to another chapter? Are you already thinking, "I don't need any advice; I'm at the top of my game"? That's exactly what many alpha commanders do when they start hearing feedback that hits close to home. They crank up their personal charisma and can-do energy and shift into high-gear productivity, sidestepping the crucial task of modifying their behavioral style. Don't make the classic commander mistake of confusing kick-butt action with results.

Expose Your Vulnerabilities

As superheroes in their own minds, alphas want to appear confident and strong, even invincible. They fear that if they don't come across that way, their credibility will be undermined and opponents will pounce

like sharks that smell blood. Because they tend to use intimidation as a
management tool, commanders are especially loath to expose their un-
derbelly. They express this tendency in various ways, ranging from outright bullying to leaping to conclusions. Because they need to appear
decisive, they'll act on their assumptions without gathering needed facts
or attending to important details. That tendency can destroy trust: in a
survey of 700 people, conducted by Development Dimensions International, 30 percent said that jumping to conclusions before checking
facts was the most unforgivable thing a boss could do.[3]

But, as paradoxical as it may seem, when strong, successful leaders
own up to their shortcomings, they're actually seen as *more* self-confident
and courageous. Leaders who openly reveal their human frailties, while
still projecting strength and dependability, command more respect than
those who strut around with their chests puffed up, afraid to show a
chink in their armor.

Let's face it: everyone already knows you're human. Trying to maintain an image of perfection just keeps people at a distance. Exposing
your foibles and quirks shows them what they might *not* know: that
you're self-aware, humble, and eager to improve. The respect and trust
you stand to earn by being candid will enable you to build loyal, productive relationships and raise your leadership to a new level.

Are you willing to be vulnerable for the sake of building stronger
working relationships? Honestly owning to the following behaviors will
give you a sense of how open or self-protective you are:

When people ask me something, I have trouble saying, "I don't know."

I find ways to let people know I'm smarter than they are.

I often exaggerate the extent of my experience.

I try to cover up my problems until I find a way to solve them.

I deflect attention from anything that makes me look bad.

I sometimes pretend to understand things when I'm actually confused.

I try to project an image of decisiveness even when I'm not sure what
to do.

If you responded "yes" to most of those, you can use an infusion of self-disclosing candor. This is not psychobabble; it's a nuts-and-bolts, bottom-line concern. In our experience, companies that place a premium on openness and self-awareness are more creative, more energetic, and more profitable.

If you doubt that, try this mental experiment. Suppose your alpha boss has problems with how you've executed his directives, which you consider vague. Imagine that he storms into your office, slams the door, and lets loose a barrage of demeaning remarks. Now imagine the same scenario, except your boss sits down and calmly says, "I'm aware that I'm not doing a very good job communicating what I'm looking for. I have a sense of how it should be done, and I really want you to execute it, but you obviously can't read my mind. So let's try to tease it out together." Which approach would make you bust your butt to get the job done? Which manager would earn your loyalty and trust?

In 2002, Eddie was asked by Vice Admiral Dan McCarthy, at that time the head of the Naval Supply Systems Command (NAVSUP), to help his senior staff deal with the competing demands of supporting the global war on terrorism while contributing to the navy's need for significant reductions in its overall cost of operations. McCarthy himself was highly coachable and eager to learn. He could also be quite intimidating. His rank, his imposing physical stature, and his booming, emphatic voice added up to the forceful presence of a classic alpha commander. When Eddie invited members of the group to describe their experiences working with the admiral, a long-time civilian executive named Jane said she once invested a tremendous amount of time and energy accumulating information for McCarthy only to be treated curtly when she reported it to him. In response to this mildly critical feedback, the admiral pounced like a defense attorney, launching into a long, factual explanation that was as defensive as it was rational. Jane visibly backed away and clammed up.

McCarthy's reaction effectively undermined his own stated purpose for the meeting, which was to engage in a genuine dialogue about the organization's problems. To his great credit, he quickly realized what he'd done. After the lunch break, he shocked everyone by taking the floor and admitting that he'd been highly defensive at the morning meeting. He hadn't been aware of it at the time, he said, but upon re-flection he saw it clearly and he wanted to take full responsibility for his behavior. McCarthy's courage changed the atmosphere radically. Almost immediately, other members of the staff followed his example, engaging in honest self-reflection. Difficult issues that had been suppressed were readily brought up, making them infinitely easier to resolve. From that day forward, the entire NAVSUP executive team interacted more openly and more effectively.

At that pivotal event, Admiral McCarthy demonstrated several skills that every alpha commander should learn: (1) he took a good, honest look at himself rather than blaming others or discounting their contri-butions, (2) he dropped his defensiveness and opened up to genuine learning, (3) he candidly admitted his mistake, and (4) he exposed the flaw in his behavior. In short, he made himself vulnerable. A gesture like that by an alpha commander is rare, but when it occurs it invariably has a powerful impact.

Here's a potent example of self-disclosure that also shows the power of working with personas. A *Fortune* 500 company's top executive team was engaged in a heated debate about a possible new acquisition. As the in-tensity escalated, the group became polarized. The CEO, who had a persona he called Wheeler Dealer, pushed hard for the acquisition, backed by about half of the team. The more conservative members, led by the CFO, were reluctant to go along with what they considered a risky move. The room crackled with tension. Suddenly the CFO sat up straighter and taller in his chair. A very large man, known for his gruff, tough manner, he instantly commanded the room. Waving his arms, he bellowed, "Mr. Rant and Rave is about to show up and I can't stop him!"

Bursts of belly laughter cascaded through the room like water from a se-ries of faucets. Mr. Rant and Rave was the name the CFO had given to the persona that showed up when he got mad. He had come to dread that per-sona as much as everyone who got caught in its fire-breathing path, be-cause it had caused a great deal of damage over the years. Had Mr. Rant and Rave taken over, the CFO would have tried to bully his way to victory, and the opposition would surely have stiffened. Instead, his lighthearted self-revelation allowed the tension to dissipate. Now the group could review the facts with cooler heads. Even Wheeler Dealer could now see the wisdom in the CFO's argument, which swiftly carried the day.

The lesson in these stories is that by revealing your vulnerability you send this meta-message: it's OK to be less than perfect. Your candor models the values of self-awareness and continual improvement. When offered appropriately, self-disclosure also draws people closer to you, making them much more willing to give you their trust and respect.

Here's the bottom line: if you want to establish a learning organization in which people are committed to exploring new and better ways of doing things, the first and most important step is to model those priorities yourself.

Put an End to Needless Bickering

You and the colleagues with whom you argue need to recognize that while a good debate can be healthy, continuous bickering is not. You're passengers on the same ship, and power struggles can sink all of you. Preventing this from happening requires honest, heartfelt communication, especially where there's been a history of intense competition. Since commanders are even more reluctant than other alpha types to display vulnerability, breakthroughs usually occur only when one of the rivals finds the courage to get the ball rolling. Sometimes, however, it requires direct intervention. Here's how we got two alpha commanders onto the same page for the good of their organization, a pharmaceutical company.

Ben was a senior research executive, known for his technical expertise and his ability to line up others in pursuit of results. Standing six feet six and moving with great self-assurance, his authoritative presence was reinforced by a deep voice that reverberated through the building. His big challenge was one shared by millions of alpha commanders: he wasn't commander in chief.

Like countless other leaders, Ben was also being led. He reported to Gil, the head of research and development, a leader of high intensity and powerful demeanor. The relationship was productive, but contentious.

At meetings, Ben and Gil would challenge each other with such intensity that they eventually lost the trust of their employees. Here's some of what we heard in Ben's 360° interviews:

"They're like the Battling Bickersons. Gil yells at Ben in a way that makes the hair on my neck stand up. Ben doesn't seem to take it personally, but he lashes back."

"Ben and Gil have an odd-couple type of relationship that gets very volatile at times. When they go at each other in meetings, it wastes a lot of time, and it's really unhealthy for the organization."

"They seem to make a sport of sparring in public and creating dramas in staff meetings. But I hear that Ben avoids conflict when they're one-on-one."

We advised Ben and Gil to learn how to resolve their differences promptly and privately. The changes we recommended required more of Ben than of Gil because Ben not only reported to Gil, but he was also much more volatile. Indeed, that was one of their major issues: Gil knew that Ben's belligerent, autocratic style was alienating his peers in other business units. Ben realized that he absolutely had to change. Naming his contentious persona Bad Ben, he made a public commitment to behave differently, and asked his colleagues to give him feedback if he ever resorted to his default position.

Both men agreed to work on catching themselves before becoming combative. To keep from storing up bad feelings, they learned to stay on top of their issues. Once he saw that Ben had modulated his commander excesses, Gil was able to relax his vigilance, becoming far less intrusive and critical. Predictably, they not only worked better together, but everyone around them grew more confident and productive.

Anger Management for Commanders

People can put up with a lot from alphas, but their nervous systems can stand just so many angry outbursts before the stress shows up in water cooler venting, absenteeism, turnover, and markedly reduced productivity. We have found the following two strategies especially helpful for alpha anger control. While all alphas will benefit from them, we placed them in this chapter because commanders tend to express their anger more overtly and more explosively than other types.

Take a Breather. It takes willpower and presence of mind to stop yourself when your temper is building. But stepping back instead of letting loose gives you a chance to cool off before you do something regrettable. It also gives you time to reflect. What do you really want to accomplish? What is your noblest intention? What's really best for the team? The company? Your future as a leader? Taking a break will help ensure that the impact of your actions is aligned with your best intentions.

Of course, circumstances don't always allow for lengthy reflection. But a great deal can be accomplished in even a brief recess, especially if you introduce calming elements. We have found that breathing practices and some form of movement, whether vigorous exercise or a simple walk or stretch, are extremely effective in defusing angry reactions and helping people "reset" before taking action. It doesn't take much. A few deep breaths, with the emphasis on holding the exhalation, can quickly trigger a calming reaction. It also diverts energy from the animal portion of the brain, which might be urging you to punish or pummel someone, to the higher centers where rational thought and creativity reside. Similarly, getting out of your chair and moving your body—a quick walk, some floor exercises, running in place, stretching—can quickly discharge the volatile energy that leads to emotional upheavals. (See chapter 8 for detailed instructions.)

A Little Help from Your Friends. Do you have a trusted colleague with whom you can be candid, and from whom you're willing to hear the truth? Why not ask for help in managing your anger? Allies can often spot the warning signs of a shortening fuse and help you avert an explosion. They might let you know that you're getting testy, that you sniped at someone inappropriately, or that you've scared the heck out of someone. They might help you understand the situations that trigger your rage and help you formulate more appropriate responses. The ideal ally is someone who's been around you enough to know your nuances and quirks. Make sure to give the person explicit permission to give you feedback. Tell him or her exactly how you'd like to receive that feedback, and pledge not to kill the messenger.

A client we'll call Mario had the full arsenal of commander strengths, but his volcanic eruptions made him an arch villain in one alpha triangle after another. A senior VP in charge of an entire continent for a global corporation, Mario rose through the ranks with lightning speed. But the price of his heavy-handed style—in lost energy, alienated personnel, and a soiled reputation—kept mounting. In 2002, we received these 360° assessments:

"Mario's hands-on, roll-up-your-sleeves approach makes work exciting, and it stretches me to improve. But when he gets riled up, you better get out of his way."

"Every time I think I can't reach any further, he pushes me through another ring. But he's so impatient, and he's so quick to the jugular, that it gets awfully bloody around here."

"He's extremely persistent and tenacious. But he's like a dentist who won't come off the nerve. He makes his point, he makes it again, and he persists until you cave in."

"Mario has strong opinions, but he's not always clear and people are afraid to ask. They say, 'Yes sir,' and pray nothing goes wrong because his reaction can be truly painful."

"In a sense his style is motivating because you'll do anything to avoid getting hammered. But it's ultimately *demotivating* because it creates tremendous anxiety. He needs to balance 'Sergeant Mario' with 'Partner Mario.'"

That's exactly what we set out to help Mario do when we began coaching him. We knew he was capable of changing when he told us, "I'm brutally honest with people, because I want to bring out the best in them. But sometimes I go too far. How can I modify my style to be more effective?" He named his troublemaking persona the Bulldozer, and created a replacement called the Samurai, a warrior with the presence of mind to restrain from violence unless absolutely necessary. Then we focused on three areas of improvement.

One was his communication skills. We helped Mario listen more patiently and deeply, so he could create a more genuine connection with people. We also helped him use appreciation as a motivator instead of only fear and intimidation. The second front was learning to pause before pulling the trigger. He developed a repertoire of exercises, from taking deep breaths when anger welled up to shadow boxing when he was really enraged and could spend a few minutes alone. Finally, we encouraged him to open up about his problems. In addition to speaking to us, he formed a confidential buddy system with a trusted colleague who also had a temper issue. They turned to each other whenever they needed to be defused, and met once a week to discuss their progress.

Two years later, we received comments like these in his follow-up 360:

"Everyone jokes about the 'kinder, gentler Mario,' but it's true. In the past he'd say, 'If you don't make this number this quarter we're going to make some changes.' Today, he'll say, 'You've made a lot of improvements, but I'm counting on you to step up even more.' He focuses on the requirement rather than threatening the consequences."

"He used to bottom-line his comments in one negative sound bite. Now you get more detail and less emotion, which makes it easier to grasp what he's communicating."

"He's not exactly a diplomat, but he's developed some tact to go with his tenacity."

"He still loses his cool occasionally, but he doesn't use profanity anymore, and he doesn't raise his voice."

"If something went wrong in the past, Mario would leave dead bodies in his wake. Now, he lets you know he's upset and moves on without letting it cloud the issue."

"In a recent meeting, a director two levels down was recommending a particular direction with no facts or data to back it up. In the past, Mario would have totally lost it. Instead, he made a few pointed remarks and let it go, and when the presenter left, he said, 'That guy needs our help.'"

The result of learning to manage his anger was predictable: far better follow-through from people who had resisted Mario's leadership in the past, and a great deal more enthusiasm and creativity from those who had subdued their talents and kept a lid on their ideas rather than risk Mario's rage.

How to Work with Alpha Commanders

The more belligerent, demeaning, and unreasonable an alpha commander is, the more likely you are to convince yourself that you're a true victim. But no matter how justified you are, casting him as pure villain locks you into the sinkhole of the alpha triangle with no escape hatch. Instead, make the powerful move of claiming responsibility for the one thing you *can* control: your own reactions.

It's especially important to avoid complaining. Alpha male commanders have an unusually low tolerance for grumbling. Witness this comment we received when we interviewed an alpha commander's direct report: "Jack once barked, 'Shut up and quit whining,' when I was sharing the problems I was having while working with peers on a cross-functional project. He fails to take into consideration other people's hard work, commitment, and challenges." No matter what's going on outside you, therefore, when the "poor me" voice in your head starts to moan, find another attitude, another way to view the situation, or another approach to solving the problem. Embrace the learning challenge: ponder how you might work more effectively with the commander, so that your ideas and insights become useful resources.

If, for example, you feel that a commander boss expects too much of you, instead of searching for a way to say no, ask yourself what changes you can make to deliver the same results more efficiently. How can you satisfy his objectives in a way that works for you too? Taking this path can lead to a big three-way win—for you, the commander, and your company.

Also, watch out for the tendency to call forth personas that actually reinforce the alpha commander's worst tendencies. Chief among these are three cousins—the Accommodator, the Pleaser, and the Complainer.

Accommodators and pleasers dislike conflict so much they pretend to be in agreement when they don't mean it. They need to learn that it's usually more important to make things happen than to make things nice. Outside of meetings, accommodators and pleasers often become complainers, venting about the alpha commander behind his back. If you see these tendencies in yourself, instead of complaining, summon up the courage to take action. Learn how to gather the details, expertise, and support to solve the problems you so perceptively notice. Take the necessary action, even at the risk of being wrong or getting criticized.

Here's how one highly competent executive who is *not* an alpha brought honor to himself and his company by dealing masterfully with an intense and powerful alpha commander. Hector de J. Ruiz, chairman and CEO of Advanced Micro Devices (AMD), made the cover of *BusinessWeek* in 2005 as one of the ten best business leaders in the country.[4] Back in 1999, when he was offered the position of president and COO of AMD, his friends tried to talk him out of it. They couldn't see how Hector, a strong leader with a humble, collaborative style, could work with W. J. (Jerry) Sanders III, the flamboyant alpha commander who founded the company and still served as chairman and CEO. But, intrigued by the opportunity to turn around a struggling organization, and having been told by board members that he'd be first in line to succeed Sanders, Hector accepted.

Life with a volatile CEO who's famous for his tirades can easily turn into a cutthroat reality show. Hector chose not to get dragged into the alpha vortex. "I reached out to make the transition as smooth as I could," he said. "I didn't think it would be productive to take Jerry on, even if I won." While Jerry ranted and raved in meetings, Hector stayed calm. Following Kate's guidance from coaching sessions at Motorola, his previous company, he waited out the tirades and refused to take Jerry's eruptions personally. Rather than get defensive, he found ways to disagree that led to reasonable discussions.

At the same time, Hector saw the need to adopt some positive alpha traits himself. Otherwise, he could not have moved AMD in the right direction. "I made sure everyone knew I wasn't making changes casually. I asked for their support and listened to their concerns, but I made it crystal clear, without being harsh, that it's my decision and they needed to sign up or leave. Ultimately, about two-thirds supported the changes, and I dealt with the other third firmly but constructively." By remaining true to his principles and his personal style, Hector was able to steer AMD on a steady path of recovery. He replaced Sanders as CEO in 2002, and in 2005 he became chairman of the board.

Dealing with Alpha Anger

Whether or not you're an alpha yourself, dealing with a volatile alpha can be one of the great workplace challenges. Here are some vital tips:

- *Don't get defensive.* No explanations. No excuses. Take 100 percent responsibility for whatever happened. It might not have been your fault, but you can still take ownership of your share of it and, more important, do what you can to find a remedy.

- *Avoid feeling victimized.* Of course, your alpha boss is a bully. Yes, you might be a scapegoat. Sure, no one should be treated that way. Don't get even, get curious. Delve into why you're the one getting yelled at. If you focus on learning instead of sulking or venting, you'll stay out of the alpha triangle. Just because he's in the villain role doesn't mean you have to play the victim.

- *Look in the mirror.* Just because you don't deserve the abuse doesn't mean you didn't put the bull's eye on your back. Is being a target for someone else's anger a pattern from your long-ago past? Does it serve a purpose? If the drama offers you some secondary gain, you're likely to keep it going. Before you can truly protect yourself and set appropriate boundaries, you need to learn how and why you trigger those alpha explosions.

- *Get curious.* Adopt the attitude that you can always learn from the alpha, no matter how explosive he gets. Calmly restate his message. Ask clarifying questions to let him know you want to understand him. Look for the pearls of wisdom concealed in the angry packaging. Affirm what you've learned and summarize the action you intend to take.

- *Clarify your standards.* We train people how to treat us. If you're being yelled at or humiliated consistently, you've somehow made that OK. Look at the alpha's anger as a sign that you're not yet firm in your commitment to being treated better. Get clear with yourself that abusive behavior is not OK and the abuser will start to change.

- *Stand your ground.* Get clear on what behavior is unacceptable. Then make your boundaries known. Let the alpha know that if he crosses the line in the future you'll walk away. If you have to follow through on that threat, don't storm off in a huff or strike a judgmental pose. Simply remind him of your commitment and walk away knowing that you've sent the message that you're not willing to be abused. Alphas might not like it, but they'll really respect it.

How Women Can Hold Their Own with Alpha Commanders

For women, surviving in a commander culture can be a major challenge. Linda Furiga, the chief financial officer for the Defense Logistics Agency, found that the key was making wise use of coaching. Linda had worked her way up through the ranks, seizing every opportunity to display her competence, and was finally handed the purse strings of an enormous organization at the heart of U.S. military operations.

Because of her quiet demeanor, Linda's insights often got lost in the shuffle despite her obvious qualifications. In a room filled with male alpha commanders, her soft voice would literally go unheard. Sometimes, colleagues would recall the substance of what she'd said but assign credit to someone who spoke with greater force and volume. Painfully aware of the situation, Linda was not surprised to see 360° comments such as these:

"She needs to assert herself in meetings and to stand up for what she believes is right."

"She's very articulate, but she's not convincing because she's too soft in style. She needs to be far more forceful in her public demeanor."

"Her tone of voice conveys a sense of timidity when she should be exuding confidence."

Linda knew her soft-spoken style was a significant risk. As the executive in charge of over $30 billion in revenue and budget, she had to make sure everyone got the information they needed, and also keep self-serving department heads from manipulating the system. Plus, she had to persuade the Department of Defense and the U.S. Congress to make available the funds DLA needed to carry out its mission. She knew she had to be seen as a strong leader, but she had no idea how to change the situation. When Admiral Lippert asked us to help her, we started by asking her to identify the personas that diminished her authority. One she called Truth Broker; the other was Peacemaker.

As the first persona, she facilitated truth-telling by others but was not forthcoming herself. As Peacemaker she was so focused on keeping the peace that she did not stand her ground or deliver needed feedback.

To help her see how those two personas appeared to others, we videotaped her giving a presentation in each of the roles. We then worked on the intensity, rhythm, and timing of her communication so she came across with greater strength and conviction. We showed her how to speak forcefully and to assert herself into the circle of conversation. Before long, she had a crucial test of her new skills. Delivering a presentation to a roomful of alpha commanders—high-ranking government and military officials—she conveyed a powerful, convincing, and inspiring presence. As the change carried over into everyday interactions, Linda started to receive the recognition she'd always deserved. She was awarded the prestigious Presidential Achievement Award in 2005. Nothing had changed except that she had learned to hold her own with dominating alpha commanders, and she took a page from their book by tapping into her own dormant leadership traits. In short order, she spearheaded a successful campaign to obtain the resources the agency needed to meet post-9/11 demands. Based on her briefs with the Office of the Secretary of Defense (OSD), she got DLA an additional $6 billion in vital funding.

In the next chapter, we'll explore the creative world of alpha visionaries; they are quite different from alpha commanders, but their challenges are no less critical.

ACTION STEPS

If you're an alpha commander:

- Heighten your awareness of how you impact the attitudes and productivity of your coworkers.

- Get familiar with the habitual lenses through which you see the world, as well as their attendant blinders.

- Enlarge your sense of ownership beyond your immediate area to include the entire organization.

- Become familiar with your dysfunctional personas, such as Bulldozer, Tyrant, and Hammer.

- Get control of your personas early in discussions, and replace them with more effective leadership approaches.

- Learn to lead without intimidation, and to teach without coercion.

- Find ways to stand out without diminishing others.

- Learn to manage your anger.

- Don't be afraid to expose your shortcomings and vulnerabilities.

- Learn the fine art of partnering to compete against your real opponents instead of your peers.

If you work with or for an alpha commander:

- Consciously adopt useful alpha traits so you can achieve better results and be recognized for your contributions.

- Do everything you can to help commanders achieve their goals.

- Become aware of any hint of dysfunctional personas such as Accommodator, Pleaser, and Complainer. Replace them with behavior that empowers you.

- Keep your defensiveness in check; don't take the commander's style or eruptions personally.

- Find ways to be direct without triggering the commander's ire.

- Avoid the temptation of playing good cop to his bad cop, or victim to his villain.

- Confront commanders one-on-one or in small groups rather than large groups.

- Don't compete with commanders; make the good of the team or organization your top priority.

CHAPTER

The Alpha Visionary

The Dreamer Whose Dreams
Can Be Impossible

I'm the proverbial fool who rushes in where angels fear to tread. I've been fearless all my life, and I've always had an overbearing optimism. I sometimes pound straight into the wall for a long time before I stop and wonder if there's a way around it. In the early seventies, my colleagues and I discovered the first angiotensin receptor blocker, which led to a huge advance in hypertension treatment. We were making $11,000 a year and, as academics, if we wanted a patent we had to pay for it ourselves. So we just published our findings. What drove me was the joy of the hunt and the pleasure of the kill—the hunt for a scientific breakthrough and the "kill" of bringing it to fruition so people receive real benefits. The difference between having a vision and being a dreamer is that a dreamer just has ideas. For me, drugs don't count unless they get to people who need them.

When I discovered the existence of COX-2, I realized it could lead to a whole string of therapeutic drugs, so I left academia for Monsanto, which had the resources to do the sophisticated analysis we needed. All of a sudden I had a team of five hundred people, whereas in academia I worked alone with my students. I had to learn how to partner with others, and infuse them with passion through the ups and downs of multiyear projects. Within two years we had a big COX-2 breakthrough, which led to Celebrex, the only COX-2 drug still on the market.

My biggest leadership challenge came when Monsanto's CEO sent me to co-run Searle, their Pharma division, over the objections of the Searle CEO.

In coming aboard, I singed a lot of eyelashes, but I worked hard to engage with people at all levels, so everyone understood the vision and where they fit. I learned to put aside my own opinions at times and embrace ideas that welled up from the bottom. The result was a dedicated team that kept on learning and growing.

I know that I come across as intimidating. I still have trouble listening to the end of a sentence without interrupting. I hear a problem, and I immediately jump in with questions. No time wasted on diplomacy. But I work at letting people know I'm attacking the science, not them, so they know I'm approachable and they can disagree with me.

—*Phil Needleman, former chief scientist and head of R&D for Searle and Pharmacia*

Visionary Strengths

The immortal Renaissance artist Michelangelo once said, "The greater danger for most of us lies not in setting our aim too high and falling short, but in setting our aim too low, and achieving our mark." That could be the motto of the alpha visionary.

Visionaries think big. Then they think bigger. Imagining possibilities that would never occur to most people, they ask, "Why not?" when others say, "No way." They think expansively, adding and multiplying where others might subtract and divide. To dream the impossible dream is not extraordinary to alpha visionaries, it's just how their minds work. And reaching for the unreachable star is not some crazy gesture; it's what makes their lives worth living. They don't like limits or naysayers or words like *can't* and *unfeasible*.

Some alphas get what they want through pushing hard and standing firm. Visionaries use their infectious enthusiasm to convince, influence, and inspire. They like facts, but their main tool of persuasion is pure, contagious passion. And, when necessary, they'll spin the truth a bit to pull others across the threshold. Combine their charisma with the rich imagery and evocative metaphors that pour from their mouths, and the effect is intoxicating. Despite your reluctance, you find yourself tagging along on their adventure, muttering, "I can't believe I'm doing this." Regardless of the outcome, you're in for the time of your life.

Naturally curious, alpha visionaries are wide open to other people's ideas—as long as they're *big* ideas. Preposterous? Not to them. Too daring? Au contraire. The pantheon of innovators, artists, and courageous entrepreneurs consists largely of alpha visionaries. They're not always a good fit in large corporations that stick to the tried and true or in organizations that embrace innovation slowly and only when the risks are minimal. Their natural homes are start-ups and established companies on a fast growth trajectory.

Curiosity may kill ordinary cats, but it brings visionary cats to life. With minds as open as the Grand Canyon, they see the potential for a payoff where others see fuzziness, chaos, or danger. As natural optimists and risk takers, they seize the moment, keeping their long-range destination clearly in mind while navigating every hazardous intersection on the way. Once they begin their journey, they remain proactive and flexible, always adapting, always pushing the edges of the envelope, always pouncing on opportunities. Even animal alphas benefit from this visionary trait. In *The Human Zoo*, Desmond Morris makes this observation about the head baboon: "Even if a group is cruising happily along on a set and satisfactory course, it is vital for him to change that course in certain ways in order to make his impact felt. It is not enough simply to alter it as a reaction to something that is going wrong. He must spontaneously, of his own volition, insist on new lines of development, or he will be considered weak."[1]

Skillful alpha visionaries combine cloud-covered dreams with an ability to make things happen on the ground. As Phil Needleman, former head of R&D at Pharmacia, told us, "To make a difference in life, you have to see the curves in the road and also see the stars."[2] They know how to dig deep into an organization's guts to marshal the support and skills to realize their vision, and they bridle when the system pulls the reins on them. "Not so fast," cautious colleagues tell them. "Look, I gathered some data that show . . ." Too late! The crafty visionary is already off and running, with an eager posse behind him. If he's a visionary whose grip on reality is as firm as his imagination is bold, you'd be wise to drop your graphs and catch up to the pack.

Often accused of being grandiose and imprudent, alpha visionaries are not constrained by lack of evidence. They don't need to know *how* something will happen to feel in their bones that it *can* happen and *will* happen. They're the kind of dreamer of whom others say, "He may sound crazy, but he sure has the courage of his convictions." Their unflappable faith in their own instincts keeps them moving forward in the face of resistance and organizational inertia, and their tenacity inspires everyone around them to reach higher and take on bigger goals. "Show me someone who can throw a ball a hundred miles per hour and I'll show them where the plate is," said Needleman.

Well-rounded alpha visionaries are as inventive about management as they are about their schemes. They find the right methods to realize their audacious goals, often challenging conventional wisdom in the process. Those who don't have that gift—and only a few do—had better be smart enough to surround themselves with competent, bold-thinking pragmatists who can help them evaluate their ideas and realize their visions. At their best, alpha visionaries have a sixth sense for choosing partners who match up with them; they're smart enough to pay attention to people whose expertise is different from their own, and to coach raw talent in the service of their goals. A great example was the late Bill Kimpton, an alpha visionary who founded the Kimpton Group, a multibillion-dollar restaurant and hotel company. Once, during a stagnant period, Bill realized that his dislike for dealing with everyday minutiae was damaging the company. He hired Tom LaTour, an alpha executor with a genius for managing details. As president, and later CEO, Tom freed up Bill's energy for the creative visioning at which he excelled, and in which he found delight. The company, which at the time consisted of two hotels and one restaurant, today has grown to 43 hotels and 41 restaurants that have won countless industry awards.

Healthy alpha visionaries attract the right people to their teams because they are inspiring, larger-than-life personalities who make you want to say "How high?" when they ask you to jump through hoops. Being close to them is energizing. Just don't rain on their parade. Try to restrain them and you can quickly go from hero to zero. They won't yell or scream; they'll just ignore you, write you off, and cut you out of their loop. It's not that they're cruel or cold; they're usually likable, and they can be quite emotional—so emotional, in fact, that they get passionately attached to their dreams, and they don't want anyone bringing them down. They're as wary of stagnation as most people are of change.

When things don't go well, their sunny dispositions can darken radically. But they know how to rebound. Before you know it, they're back on their feet, reenergized, having thought things through in a new light and ready to chase a fresh new vision, and their energy and creative pizzazz is so infectious that people want to go along for the ride. Those who hop aboard often talk about the visionary leader the way one person spoke of Phil Needleman: "He's passionate about his work and devoted to making a difference in the world. I feel honored to work with him, and privileged to be his colleague."

The Problem with Alpha Visionaries

"If you have built castles in the air, your work need not be lost," said Henry David Thoreau. "That is where they should be. Now put the foundations under them." It's that last step that alpha visionaries often forget. As a result, the same Peter Pan qualities that make people want to follow them straight to never-never land can also turn them into Pied Pipers who lead the charge right off a cliff. And visionary zealots who also have some charismatic commander traits seldom have a shortage of eager followers.

Table 4-1 shows how the same alpha visionary qualities can lead to an exhilarating run to glory or a wild ride to ruin. The box "The Data on Alpha Visionaries" outlines the data from our study.

TABLE 4-1

The visionary syndrome: When strengths become liabilities

Alpha attribute	Value to organization	Risk to organization
Bold, creative, innovative thinker	Dreams up ingenious ideas; sees far into the future; turns ideas into opportunities; moves organization in new and profound directions	Comes across as arrogant, stubborn, overly opinionated; generates more ideas than company can implement; wastes time chasing unattainable goals
Farsighted; sees what's possible	Recognizes gap between today's reality and tomorrow's potential; stays one step ahead of competition	Focuses on the future and neglects the near term; loses sight of business viability; ignores planning and the nuts and bolts
Resilient, indefatigable, strong sense of mission and commitment to vision	Energizes teams to reach impossible goals; bolsters the confidence of those who falter; willing to make personal sacrifices to achieve vision	Overreaches and overstretches the organization; doesn't consider resources needed to make dreams a reality; unable to finish every project
Passionate, enthusiastic, and energizing	Sells ideas and creates buy-in for new directions; attracts creative employees to the organization; unites people around vision	Spins truth to get people on board; gets attached to dreams; ignores pragmatists; avoids dissenters; thinks rules don't apply to him; circumvents chain of command
Strong appetite for newness and change; naturally curious, open to the ideas of others	Drives needed change and rapid growth; adds tremendous value to start-up businesses	Undervalues organizational alignment; launches into action before gathering support from others; changes for change's sake; wastes resources on ill-conceived quests
Optimistic and confident about the future	Keeps others motivated and willing to take risks; not disheartened by criticism; willing to keep trying after setback	Conceals doubts from others; overlooks obstacles and contrary information; cuts self off from feedback; may not be grounded in reality; retaliates against those who doubt his vision

A Matter of Confidence

Reality, as a comedian once said, is a matter of opinion. In the opinion of alpha visionaries, if they have a big idea and they want badly enough to realize it, it can happen. In their universe, time is ever-expanding, resources are infinite, and downside risks are mere supersti-

The Data on Alpha Visionaries

I n our study, those who scored high in visionary strengths were also likely to score high in visionary risks; about half the subjects in the top 25 percent on the strength scale were also in the top 25 percent in risks. Only a very few (2.4 percent) were in both the highest strength group and the lowest risk group; even fewer (1.9 percent) were in the highest risk group and the lowest strength group. In other words, if you're gifted with the imagination and passion of an alpha visionary, you're probably prone to reality-bending, Don Quixote–like quests.

We found no significant relationship between visionary risks and the trio of anger, impatience, and competitiveness; this is the opposite of high-risk groups in the other alpha types (table B-3, appendix B). We also found no significant differences between men and women in either the strength or the risk category (table B-2, appendix B).

tions. That indomitable faith is a magnificent asset in the service of a workable plan. Wrongly applied, it's a recipe for disaster.

Fortunes have been made by healthy alpha visionaries who refused to back down when bean counters said their ideas couldn't possibly pan out. In the 1990s Michael Moritz and his partners saw possibilities in start-ups like Yahoo! and PayPal that no one else did. Their vision propelled their partnership, Sequoia Capital, to the top rung of venture capital firms.

In the summer of 1999, Michael met a couple of visionary geeks named Larry Page and Sergey Brin who were looking for funding for their new search engine. Because he saw something special in them and their product, Moritz stayed in the game while other VCs shied away or passed because of the inordinately high valuation at the peak of the dotcom craze. "They thought we had lost touch with our senses," he recalled. When Page and Brin insisted that Sequoia Capital coventure with Kleiner Perkins, a rival firm led by John Doerr that had initially funded Amazon.com and other blockbuster start-ups, Moritz renewed a long-standing investment alliance between the two firms. The rest, of course, is history. Six years after investing $12.5 million in Google, Sequoia's stake was worth $4.3 billion.[3]

Michael told us he doesn't consider himself a visionary. "Whatever contribution I make comes from recognizing people who have really interesting ideas," he said. "I'm constantly alert to possibilities and don't get too wound up in needing the future to be similar to the past. We have come up with things that have worked very well and also things that have turned into nightmares. There has to be someone who tugs the train forward, otherwise it's all too easy to say no to new ventures or fresh ideas." In fact, those self-described qualities mark him as a visionary. As you can see from these 360 comments, his colleagues agree:

> "He's a bold, visionary thinker. He's also a very sharp, straight-line thinker. Creating truly great companies requires vision plus conviction, and Mike has both."

> "Mike has good over-the-horizon radar. Even though his ideas are often shot down, he brings us huge value from this level of creative thinking."

> "He can distill what a new company is all about down to a clear and simple phrase, even if it's a complicated business."

During the dot-com bust, Michael took Sequoia Capital's losses personally. That too is a mark of alpha visionaries; they stand behind their ideas and take full responsibility for them. The mark of a *healthy* alpha visionary is to learn from the setbacks. "Mike's recent losses have helped to further shape and refine his creativity," said one of Sequoia's senior partners. "His creativity and boldness are still there, but now he's gotten much more frugal and clever about the investments." Those attributes are among the reasons why Sequoia Capital is one of only two early-stage venture funds from the Silicon Valley halcyon days in the 1970s that are still at the top of their game.

But not all alpha visionaries are that balanced. Fortunes have been lost and businesses have gone belly-up because of reality-challenged visionaries who were great at the *what* but not the *how.* Those who also have a strong strategist streak are especially likely to be stubborn dreamers who can't stand challenges to their thinking. Nuts and bolts bore them. Caution makes them antsy. Worrywarts drive them crazy. Ironically, they actually *create* worrywarts, turning realistic people who want them to succeed into handwringers who fret about their reckless optimism. In the natural push and pull of organizational life, the more a visionary expands, the more the pragmatists contract; the more manic the visionary, the more anxious the pragmatists. Naturally, the friction hardens the cement in the alpha triangle, with the visionaries being seen as villains by their careful colleagues, who feel like victims whose future is in the hands of high-flying daredevils. Completing the picture, various heroes try to calm everyone down and work both ends against the middle.

Having self-assurance as a default mode can be a magnificent virtue, but dysfunctional alpha visionaries abuse that trait by suppressing every doubt that sneaks through their filters. Afraid that if they reveal any sign of hesitation the troops won't follow their lead, they steadfastly conceal their qualms, often overcompensating with extravagant cheerleading. To a certain extent, they're right; people *do* rally behind confident leaders, and the visionary's confidence can be as magnetic as the North Pole. But the refusal to acknowledge doubt cuts them off from needed feedback, from both experts and their own intuition. Lacking the opportunity to scrutinize their ideas and turn them into strong, pragmatic strategies, they fall prey to impaired thinking and foolhardy behavior.

Eddie admits to doing exactly that, as only an alpha visionary with strategist traits can do. Inspired by Frank Shorter, an underdog whose disciplined training regimen enabled him to win the Olympic marathon in 1972, Eddie became enamored of endurance sports such as cross-country ski racing and 100-mile runs. Up to a point, his body tolerated those activities very well. Then he succumbed to the visionary's magical thinking. He'd sign up for events he didn't have time to train for. To compensate, he devised the concept of "in-event training," where he'd use the first half of the event to train for the second half. As a physician he knew it didn't allow for any recovery time and that once fatigue set in, his muscles were unlikely to do more work. But he convinced himself that his mental power could make the difference. Full of blind optimism, he entered a 50-kilometer ski-skating race that involved techniques he'd never learned. Everything was fine for the first 3 kilometers. Then the technical aspects that he was beginning to grasp faded into clumsy and exhausting efforts. He managed to finish, and spent the next few days licking his wounds. He repeated this process several more times, then signed up for a 100-kilometer run. He completed the race, but sustained nine stress fractures!

Worse than his own visionary self-deception was the impact he had on others. By convincing friends that they too could do in-event training, he often did more harm than good. For instance, he got a couple who had never ridden more than 20 miles on a bike to do a 200-mile ride. Their pelvises went so numb they couldn't have sex for weeks, and they haven't been on a bike since.

Only later did Eddie realize how deluded he was, saying, "In my arrogance, I invented a strategy to rationalize my impatience, and I gave it a cool name—in-event training—when I should have called it the dumbest thing I ever did." That's what visionaries do when their assets morph into liabilities: they have the fatal flaw of hubris.

Checks and Balances

Many alpha visionaries find details boring and planning tedious. They respond to events brilliantly, but they don't always have the patience to undertake the necessary preparation. In itself, winging it is not necessarily bad. But problems arise when alphas fail to listen to people who can ground their vision in the reality of time, resources, and risk. To visionaries, "Be careful" sounds like "Don't do it," and "Wait until the funding is in place" translates as "Drop this dumb idea." Raise questions about feasibility and you're a gloom-and-doomer. Challenge their optimism and you're chicken or paranoid.

Many visionaries view dissent as a nuisance rather than as raw material that can fine-tune their dreams into workable plans. While they're generally the most likable of all the alpha types, they can get nasty when they feel the need to put a challenger in his place, often eliminating from their inner circle anyone who disagrees with them. It's not that they need sycophants and yes-men; it's that they like to be around people who stoke their fire and fuel their ideas. As a result, they become insulated. They don't realize until it's too late that the counsel they tuned out was not saying "Drop it," but "Let's look at how we can realize your vision."

Healthy alphas are sharp enough to notice this Achilles' heel and wise enough to do something about it. "My biggest risk is that I have trouble listening all the way through to the end of a sentence without interrupting," said Phil Needleman. "I hear disagreement, and I immediately have a solution under way. This doesn't create a positive spiral. You need people who will tell you they disagree and why."

Then there's David Neeleman. The visionary CEO and founder of JetBlue Airways has more in common with Phil Needleman than a nearly identical last name. He openly acknowledges having attention deficit disorder, a diagnosis that might have stigmatized many successful alpha leaders—visionaries in particular—had it been prevalent when they were in grade school. Their voracious, rapid-fire imaginations propel them from idea to idea like bees sipping nectar in a flower garden. Having a perpetual motion machine for a mind can be a challenge. "I never stop thinking," says David. "I can't turn it off. I'm always fidgety, always looking for what's next." His mind is so restless that he can't even stop to celebrate his achievements: "When I sold my software company, $20 million got wired into my account, and I didn't even take my wife to dinner. I couldn't even relish it for a minute."

But the same propensity can be a blessing if it's properly harnessed. Because he fully understands both the strengths and risks of his visionary attributes, Neeleman surrounds himself with people who complement the assets and compensate for the liabilities. "Sometimes I feel like there are too many people around me with attention *surplus* disorder,'" he told us. Although having such people at his side can sometimes be a nuisance, he knows that they're indispensable. "I always think, 'Don't worry about it, just do it,' and they want to test the idea. But the company needs both. My strength is not in carrying ideas through to execution, it's in coming up with the ideas and inspiring others to get on board."

Joking that "It takes three to balance me out," Neeleman says that four people run JetBlue: him, the president and COO, the executive vice president of Legal and Treasury, and the CFO. "It forces me to be disciplined instead of shooting from the hip. I know I have to go over my ideas and present them in a way that's so compelling that they'll go for it."

How Alpha Visionaries Create Triangles

Unlike David Neeleman, dysfunctional alpha visionaries resist the pragmatists, preferring to surround themselves with people who feed their addiction to hot new ideas. As a result, they create alpha triangles in which they're either the villain, victim, or hero, depending on one's point of view. Realists cast them as villains for overloading the system with too many half-baked ideas and incomplete projects. At the same time, the visionaries themselves feel victimized by unimaginative colleagues who want to limit them to predictable, easy-to-implement projects, or by rivals with ideas of their own. They will often shift from victim to hero, riding the white steed of a bold idea to free the organization from its chains. Will he save the day or lead them to ruin? That depends largely on whether the visionary is open to reality checks. It also depends on the leadership of other executives. All too often, overzealous visionaries polarize management, with believers rallying behind the grand idea and opponents lining up against it. The result is sludge.

An alpha visionary we'll call Charles was hired by his former mentor, the CEO of a major consumer products company, to head up R&D. Charles hit the ground running, jazzed by the thought of steering the organization in a bold new direction. Before long he announced an ambitious plan to re-envision the company's future in the light of new technologies. The CEO was as pleased as he was proud, and Charles's staff awakened from a long slumber to hop aboard the vision.

But not everyone was happy. The senior vice president of marketing, an alpha commander named Marv, had worked at the company since college. A brilliant motivator with a glistening track record, Marv thought he was in line to become the next CEO when the current officeholder retired in a few years. Now those expectations were shattered; he assumed the CEO would groom Charles for the job. He also did not agree with Charles's vision for curing the company's slump. To him, scientific research into new products was a waste of resources. Improving a best-selling line of household cleansers should not require rocket-science expenditures. He wanted to invest that money in a fresh, creative marketing campaign.

Fearing that his rival would have undue influence on the CEO, Marv started living up to the persona name he gave himself: Machiavelli. He launched a two-pronged campaign: positioning himself politically as the right successor to the CEO and undermining Charles's plan. He cut R&D out of strategic planning sessions and kept them in the dark about anything that might give Charles a power edge.

Charles quickly got the message. While alpha visionaries are often oblivious to corporate intrigue, they can become veritable Caesars when their dreams are under siege. Determined to protect his vision, which he equated with the good of the company, he was prepared to do whatever it took to make sure R&D did not take a back seat to marketing. He took on the persona of the General.

For the next two years, these two alpha males, each running an integral part of the same company, acted like warring chieftains. At staff meetings, they avoided each other. When they absolutely had to communicate, they kept the dialogue brief and functional. Every punch and counterpunch further eroded the synergy between their two departments.

Naturally, each one saw himself as a victim to the other's villain. And there was no shortage of heroes. Both Marv and Charles took on that role within their divisions, plus various colleagues tried to foster peace and get the rivals to work together. Neither one would yield an inch.

Kate was called in to facilitate a resolution. She got Charles and Marv to commit to staying in a room until they resolved their issues, even if it took all night. Gradually, their misperceptions and self-delusions were peeled away. Among other things, Marv learned that Charles had no desire to be CEO; he liked R&D too much, and he knew he wasn't cut out for general management. Even more important, both men realized that neither one could fulfill his ambitions if they didn't learn to work together. They started having joint strategic planning sessions, and agreed to spread the available funds between their two groups. Gradually, they learned to trust each other.

Spearheaded by Charles's R&D team, the company introduced a line of new products, which sold extremely well, thanks to a spectacular marketing campaign by Marv's group. Ironically, neither one became CEO. Charles went on to head up R&D at corporate headquarters; Marv left the company when he realized that his ruthless competition with Charles had cost him the trust of upper management.

The Secrets of Secrecy

Many alpha visionaries learn early on that it's hard for people to appreciate their visions in seed form. So, rather than deal with the inevitable resistance, they take their ideas underground, carrying out experiments and trial runs with selected colleagues. The clandestine operations have three purposes: to avoid getting shot down before they get to the starting gate; to work out the kinks behind closed doors; and to build momentum out of sight of anyone who has the power to slow them down. The strategy can certainly enhance creativity, but it can also disperse energy and resources and create a climate of suspicion.

Alpha visionaries work around organizational obstacles in other ways as well. They'll go behind people's backs, ignore procedures, and circumvent the chain of command to get their ideas to whatever managerial level they think will serve them best. Kate's first corporate management job was at Shaklee, a major manufacturer of nutritional supplements. Passionate about the company's mission, she had the idea to create a series of consumer videos. The VCR was a brand-new technology in 1979, and Kate got so excited that she spent every free weekend for three months designing materials, using available research to project sales, and devising a sophisticated business plan. Her manager's response was lukewarm: good idea, but not something he'd go to the mat for.

That should have been that. But Kate, being an alpha with a vision, went over her boss's head, and over *his* boss's head, and pitched her idea to senior VPs. Understandably, her manager was furious that his authority had been undermined. That she'd damaged her relationship with someone she respected caused Kate a great deal of anguish.

Also distressing was the decision of the senior VPs to reconsider her proposal in 18 months. To an impatient alpha, that seemed like an eternity. Three months later, she left to pursue an opportunity in another company. Eventually, Shaklee launched a line of videos that followed Kate's model right down to the packaging. It was the best new product launch the company ever had, but it was not as big as it could have been: WeightWatchers, which was an unknown company when Kate first had her idea, had meanwhile emerged as a strong player and had introduced a similar product six months earlier. The episode taught Kate vital lessons that every alpha visionary should learn. First, don't get so attached to your view of reality that you forget the rules. Second, breakthrough ideas are nothing without buy-in. Had she aligned with the sales training department, the project might have been green-lighted sooner. Instead, she succumbed to the alpha visionary's fatal flaw: she was so in love with her dream that she wouldn't risk diluting it with the ideas of others.

Shading the Truth

Even alpha visionaries with high ethical standards will occasionally shade the truth as they maneuver through the land mines of resistance. In their minds, they are simply protecting young ideas that are now as fragile as sprouts, but will, when they mature, be good for the organization, if not the world. Among other problems, their duplicity gives rise to a misuse of time and energy. Instead of making careful assessments and soliciting feedback, visionaries put all their efforts into selling their schemes. Sometimes they spin the truth so much, they spin into orbit, fooling *themselves* along with everyone else. Eventually, either the full truth is exposed, leading to the visionary's embarrassment or downfall, or so much suspicion is aroused that his influence plummets.

Lance Glasser, chief technology officer and executive vice president at KLA-Tencor, was a classic example. A true visionary whose extraordinary scientific ideas led to breakthroughs in semiconductor technology, his PhD from MIT did not teach him how to gain organizational support for his ideas. In his eagerness to win people over, he responded to resistance by telling everyone what he thought they wanted to hear. Over time, his colleagues grew suspicious: Why would someone bend his story to suit his audience except out of personal ambition? In fact, advancing his career was the furthest thing from Lance's mind. What drove him was a powerful desire to get the right thing done. He simply did not know a better way to garner support. Because he wasn't as direct as he should have been, he lost the trust of the very people he needed most.

Lance tackled the problem head-on. At an offsite, he asked his peers for direct feedback. Afterward, he shared what he learned with his own team and declared his intention to acquire more straightforward influence skills, so he could not only get his points across but solicit helpful input and earn people's trust.

Half Begun Is Not Well Done

Alpha visionaries walk through the cafeteria of life like hungry tourists whose eyes are bigger than their stomachs. Easily seduced by the Next Big Thing, their operations take on a "flavor of the month" quality, as they launch one new program after another in a frenzy of beginnings. As a result, they're often left with a collection of dangling incompletions that create sludge and distrust.

Dashing wherever the adrenalin takes them while the other balls they've been juggling crash to the ground behind them, overextended visionaries blur their organization's focus. People run around in too many directions at once, and resources get stretched to the breaking point. Not that chaos is always bad; it can be a cauldron for magnificent creativity. But taken too far and dragged on too long, it can turn an organization into a wheel spinning wildly in the mud, going nowhere.

One of the most frustrating things about dealing with alpha visionaries is that they're smart enough to know better. When they put their brilliant minds to it, they can be excellent tacticians. They just don't want to be bothered. Planning and execution don't turn them on. They assume that if they come up with an elegant scheme everyone else will figure out how to get it done, and if they come up with *ten* glorious schemes, or a hundred, those will get done too. The August 2004 issue of *CFO* magazine raised the question: Why do bad things happen to good plans?[4] The article concluded: "The problem is that most planners don't think hard enough about what might go wrong before putting an idea in motion." This remark from Rick Funston, national practice leader for the governance and oversight group at Deloitte, captures the alpha visionary dilemma perfectly: "There's a natural tendency for executives to focus on the positives of a plan and deemphasize the risks. It's like saying, 'Let's climb Mt. Everest this weekend because it will be great fun,' without stopping to think that the risks of the climb will probably get you killed."[5]

Female Alpha Visionaries

Our research found no significant differences between male and female visionaries. In our personal observations over the years, we have likewise noticed very few clear-cut gender distinctions. It seems that women who are alpha visionaries are just as likely as the men to grab hold of a far-reaching idea and push it forward as if it were the greatest discovery since the silicon chip. They can be just as inspirational, just as reality challenged, just as prone to leading people over a cliff, and just as impatient when others fail to appreciate their vision and raise the banner high.

We have, however, noticed one significant difference, one that is consistent with the gender differences we've recounted elsewhere: women visionaries tend to handle opposition differently than men. As we've seen, male alphas in general are much more prone to frustration, direct confrontation, and angry outbursts than women (needless to say, this is a generalization; individual women can be as volatile and impatient as any man). Visionary women tend to respond to disagreement in a more collaborative way, sharing ideas with others and incorporating everyone's most valuable contributions into their developing vision.

If Meg Whitman had thought that her ideas were the only ones with value—the default position of many high-ranking alpha male visionaries—eBay could not have built the sense of community and democratic input that has played such a large role in the company's success. "She knew she had to build the eBay brand," wrote Loren Fox in a *Salon.com* story about Meg's early days with the company. "But she also listened to the auction site's founders and conferred closely with them. Her style—collaborative yet decisive, serious but loose—set the tone for the company."[6]

As we've seen, healthy *male* visionaries have the same qualities. They're just somewhat more likely to be found in women.

Visionary Tools

If you're an alpha visionary, your primary challenge is to reach for the stars while keeping your feet on the ground. For help getting anchored, you'd be wise to turn to those around you as well as within.

Surround·Yourself with the Right People

The gap between intentions and impact can reach Grand Canyon distances with dysfunctional alpha visionaries. They have a heightened awareness of what is possible but a dim awareness of what's needed to realize their dream—and they don't like hearing about it. The first step to overcoming that risk, therefore, is to recognize it; the second is to align yourself with colleagues who can pick up the slack. Roderick M. Kramer, a professor of organizational behavior at Stanford, put it this way in an article for the *Harvard Business Review*: "It's great to have a chorus of loyal aides and advisers who march to your orders. But you also need someone to let you know when the team is marching toward an abyss." Leaders who are "most prone to recklessness and folly," he adds, "are often too adept at creating an organizational world that reflects their own optimistic values and forward-charging inclinations. It's critical for such leaders to have someone who can speak up and give them an honest assessment of the situation."[7]

We've already mentioned some crackerjack teams in which other alpha types complement a visionary leader. Perhaps the best-known example is the dynamic combo of Bill Gates and Steve Ballmer. Although we've never coached the Microsoft duo, we've worked in depth with executives on their team and have spent enough time with them to be confident that Gates is an alpha visionary (who else would say, "Intellectual property has the shelf life of a banana"?[8]) and Ballmer is an alpha commander. The natural checks and balances of their respective styles have been a key factor in the Microsoft success story.

They're likely to be key to the company's future as well. When Gates named Ballmer CEO, he said the move would free him to invent new software. His latest vision just might revolutionize electronics. As described by *Fortune*'s Brent Schlender, Microsoft's Longhorn project imagines linking every conceivable electronic device, from cell phones to PCs to home entertainment centers, "in a mesh of software that will make the entire Internet and everything on it a single, programmable entity."[9] While Gates dreams magnificent dreams, Ballmer combines his commander leadership with the secondary skills of an alpha executor. "To put it simply," says Schlender, "his job is to refashion Microsoft into a rocket that can reach that moon," by combining his "rabid team spirit" and his "fixation on imposing order."

If you're an alpha visionary, your best asset outside of your own mind might be the people you gather around you. Find trustworthy allies who are expansive enough to respond favorably to your big ideas, but also objective enough to spot potential problems, confident enough to express their concerns, and expert enough to formulate plans to help you actualize your vision. Look for people with diverse styles, backgrounds, and expertise. One major reason that some alpha visionaries succeed while others falter is that they work effectively with advisers who think in different ways. Which of the visionary's ideas should be acted upon? Which should be discarded? Which can be combined, modified, or refined into workable schemes? Which warrant an experiment or a pilot program? Such decisions are best made collaboratively, in an open exchange of ideas among people with different outlooks. That kind of team play requires patience and listening skills that don't come easily to visionary alphas, who would rather deliver an inspiring speech and march into the sunset with a thundering herd behind them. But if you want people to get behind your visions, adjust your frustration thermostat and work patiently to garner support.

Gaining alignment might also require learning new influence skills. Instead of trying to win people over with sheer exuberance and optimism, learn how others think and offer them facts, figures, logic, and anything else that will break through their opposition. In general, you'll find that being direct, straightforward, and fully transparent works better than spinning the truth.

And stop resisting resistance. Visionaries love data that *support* their ideas, but they treat contrary facts like creationists treat Darwin. There is much to gain from examining the opposition's rationale and data. Ask not "How can I get rid of them?" but "What can I learn from them?" and "How can I integrate this new information into my vision?" If you look only for information that supports your thinking, you're more likely to dupe yourself than others. Try to see unpleasant facts as data to build upon. Ironically, this is the best way to get worrywarts off your back: once they're listened to, naysayers relax. Next thing you know, they're open to your most audacious ideas.

Fine-Tune Your Intuition

Like artists, visionaries tend to have easy access to their intuition. This gift enables them to see the future with an accuracy that facts and reason alone cannot achieve. The problem is, insights and imaginings pour into their minds like waves onto a beach, making it hard to sort out the useful from the junk. The exercise in the box "Stepping into the Future," is a powerful way to combine intuition and reason, so you can select the alternative that's most likely to yield results.

Stepping into the Future

Step 1. Choose a point in time, possibly a date in the near future or maybe many years out. Identify the date by month and year.

Step 2. Assign a place in the room to this date.

Step 3. Walk purposefully to the spot for this future date, feeling yourself moving forward in time as well as in space.

Step 4. Station yourself in that location, and fully imagine what the period between now and this date has been like.

Step 5. Respond to the following questions one at a time. Speaking into a recording device or writing out your answers, describe any and all impressions that arise, whether visual, sensory, or auditory. Do not censor yourself or edit your thoughts; there are no right or wrong answers. If you feel stuck, just use your imagination to intuitively make up an answer.

- Where are you?

- What are you doing?

- What are you feeling?

- What did you do to make this period successful?

- What contribution or impact do you feel best about?

- What has been more difficult than you expected?

- What problems could you have anticipated and planned for?

- What has been easier than expected?

- What changes surprised you?

- Where did you really make a difference?

Step 6. Return to your original location—the one that represents present time. Reflect on the intuitive information that surfaced. How would you interpret it?

Step 7. Which idea that emerged in the future do you want to explore further? Select one that could make a big difference in your success. In the best possible future, what do you want to have happen?

Step 8. Identify the actions you plan to take. Write them down or speak them into the recording device, specifying dates by which you will take these actions.

Step 9. Do you notice any resistance arising inside you? Explore that question by asking yourself:

- Which concerns feel familiar to you?

- How do these concerns reflect your previous behavior patterns?

- How do the concerns relate to the roles you typically take on in the alpha triangle?

Step 10. Take a moment to acknowledge and accept that your resistance represents an outdated behavior pattern. Then, move back into your expanded space and reaffirm your noble intention as it relates to this specific goal or action.

How to Work with Alpha Visionaries

People react to alpha visionaries in different ways. Some get inspired by their vision and eagerly follow without stopping to evaluate the plan. Others immediately look for limitations and obstacles. In the second group are two types: those who eagerly point out the yawning gap between the vision and reality as they see it, and those who either keep their concerns to themselves or start a whispering campaign because they're afraid to speak up. The fearful response is especially likely when the visionary displays the usual alpha risks, such as arrogance, belligerence, and competitiveness. Whichever camp you belong to, the following tips will help you respond more productively to alpha visionaries.

Stretch Yourself

Try to see what the alpha visionary sees. What's good about his idea? Why might it work? What would things be like if it *did* work? If you realize that details are missing, fill them in yourself. Allowing your own imagination to expand can liberate the dormant visionary in you. If you've been setting your sights too low, raising them might ignite your passion and purpose. Don't be afraid of getting lost in the clouds; once you've seen the view from the visionary's vantage point, you'll be in a better position to assess the potential impediments.

Speak in Visionary Language

Let him know you understand his vision and are intrigued by it. Don't fake enthusiasm; he'll see right through you. Simply reiterate the message in different words: "It sounds like you're thinking . . ." "If I understand you correctly, your goal would be . . ." Once you establish that you've heard him correctly, ask clarifying questions to flesh out his thoughts. But be careful, or he'll suspect you're looking for ways to punch holes in his thinking.

If you find weaknesses and limitations in the vision, try to be solution driven rather than problem driven. Speak in terms of what it will take to realize his dreams. You don't have to squelch your concerns; just let him know you're on his side. In other words, don't say, "It sounds way too expensive" but rather, "We'll have to find ways to keep the costs down." Not "Our customers won't go for it" but "We can run some focus groups to find ways to win over our customer base." What if the idea is totally off the wall? Continue to speak about what it would take for the plan to succeed, and back up your reasoning with facts, figures, expert opinions, and impeccable logic, always focusing on potential solutions.

Harness the Visionary Energy

Add value to the visionary's inspirations by grounding them in the reality of time, money, implementation strategies, and other facts of life. Brainstorm with him to formulate workable plans for bringing the visions to reality. Modify his ideas, reconfigure them, and build upon them. Find ways to control the speed with which his visions are rolled out. Make him feel that you're a partner, not an opponent—a fellow dream maker, not a dream slayer. If he sees you as an ally, he'll welcome the practical support.

Working effectively with visionaries is a balancing act: you have to be sensible without being cynical and open without being gullible. If you can hang on to the visionary's magic carpet and also keep your bearings, you're in for a thrilling ride.

In the next chapter, we'll examine a very different type of alpha: the methodical, systematic, data-driven strategist.

ACTION STEPS

If you're an alpha visionary:

- Surround yourself with people who have a talent for execution.

- Pay attention to pragmatists who can spot potential problems and formulate plans to actualize your vision.

- Engage people with different styles and outlooks in creative exchange rather than power struggles.

- Work patiently to garner support; use facts and logic, not just charisma.

- Learn from the resistance you encounter.

- To gain alignment, be direct, straightforward, and transparent.

- Accept the limits of time and resources, and don't overcommit.

- Scrap the nonessentials and delegate what you can't complete yourself.

If you work with or for an alpha visionary:

- Let visionaries know you understand their vision and are intrigued by it.

- Stretch yourself; show curiosity rather than cynicism.

- Look at the possibilities, not just the flaws and risks.

- Summarize what they've said and ask clarifying questions.

- Tell them what it will take to make their vision a reality.

- Let them know you want to help them actualize their dreams.

- Use facts and data to show them what it will take for them to succeed.

- If you can't partner with them, make sure they team with colleagues who can help them actualize their visions.

- Let some of their exuberance, optimism, and imagination rub off.

CHAPTER 5

The Alpha Strategist

The Analytic Genius Who Can Be a Stubborn Know-It-All

I learned early in life that if I wanted to improve something I had to gather facts and be clear about the data. Even as a kid, I tried to pull things together. In the fifth grade, I organized the neighborhood football team—everything from coaching to fundraising to equipment to scheduling—and I've worked this way ever since, through school, my law practice, and my twenty-seven years as an executive in major league baseball.

People need to understand the basics, the underlying facts, in order to make sound agreements, and language is often too imprecise to be dependable. So I often go back to the data to be sure we're on the right track. The downside, of course, is that people can get tired of revisiting the original facts, but memories can get blurred and we need to know we're operating from the same basic data.

In the past, when people got the facts wrong or said something I disagreed with, I sometimes responded too strongly. Some people thought I didn't want to hear from them. But it's important to really know what colleagues are thinking. I thrive on getting input from disparate sources and making the necessary links. So I learned to tone down my initial reactions. I still get frustrated, but I'm learning to make sure people know it's not about them personally. Still I'm often frustrated with myself for not being able to get the factual clarity I need to make sound decisions.

—*Larry Lucchino, president and CEO of the Boston Red Sox*

Strategist Strengths

You know those kids in school who are called "brainy"? The ones who always have their hands in the air and tear up opponents on the debating team? Some of them grow up to be alpha strategists. Alphas tend to be smart, but each type is smart in a different way. Commanders know how to get people to do things. Visionaries see possibilities others can't imagine. Executors are brilliant at implementation. Strategists come up with remarkable plans that lead to breakthroughs, innovative procedures, and margins that warm the hearts of shareholders. If you need a shrewd plan to actualize a business model, make sure an alpha strategist is on board.

Strategists excel at evaluating complex conditions with clear-headed reason and astute judgment. Quickly assessing how varied information fits together, they ground their goals in facts and prescribe actions that are likely to bring about the desired results. Objective, analytical, and methodical, their intellects glide from premise to conclusion like a prima ballerina stepping lightly across a stage, making leaps that leave people gasping. They think hard and reason proactively, playing out permutations and connections that reach beyond immediate problems and extend into a future that others can glimpse only dimly. At their best, they are as inventive as they are precise, often solving a number of problems at once, including some that don't yet exist. They can look at a broad plan, detect where things might go awry, and fill in the blanks.

Healthy, well-balanced alpha strategists have interpersonal skills that match their analytic genius. Skilled at winning alignment, they catalyze discussions, ask probing questions, and orchestrate the group's resources to reach the best decisions. "He's a great facilitator," said a colleague about one such strategist, George Nguyen, the president of Eaton Heavy

Duty Light Trucking and China Truck. "George may have strong opinions, but he listens carefully and shows genuine interest in everyone's perspective. He challenges their thinking without discouraging them, fleshes out their best ideas and integrates them to create the best approach."[1]

The nickname that another of our alpha clients was given by his colleagues captures the strategist mind-set: the King of Data. Like alchemists who can pick out the right ingredients to create gold, strategists synthesize disparate facts, opinions, and impressions to chart a decisive direction. They draw upon anything and everything. These qualities make them excellent teammates for alpha visionaries. That combination can turn into the odd couple when the strategist constrains the visionary's expansive nature. But when the strategist gets as excited by a fresh vision as he does by a spreadsheet, you have an unbeatable combination—especially when they're contained within one person, as they are in Larry Lucchino, the president and CEO of the Boston Red Sox. "Larry has broad vision and keen strategic insight," said one of his fellow baseball executives. "He has the rare ability to see the big picture as well as the important details."

Of course, any realm governed by a King of Data is bound to contain risks. In this case, the risks revolve around this fact: alpha male strategists tend to be a lot more skilled with data than they are with people.

The Problem with Alpha Strategists

When George Nguyen was named president of Heavy Duty Light Trucking and China Truck at Eaton Corporation, a diversified equipment and technology company, his mandate was to drive change and growth. The technology for building truck transmissions was in a state of flux; the supply chain needed revamping; and it appeared vital to develop global markets, particularly in Asia. In many ways, the assignment was made to order for George. He had worked with similar challenges in his previous company; as a Vietnamese American he brought unique cultural insight to the Asian expansion; and as an alpha strategist, he was adept at understanding what needed to be done and how to implement it. These comments from his 360° interviews attest to his strategist strengths:

"Before George came, we had talked of growth, but George spotted opportunities we hadn't tapped and quickly came up with effective strategies. He took on big business challenges and succeeded far beyond expectations."

"George grasps concepts and information quickly and takes people to the next level in solving strategic problems. His sense of urgency drives us to succeed."

"George stands out in developing strategy. He takes risks, pushes growth, and locates resources to support his initiative."

But there was a downside to George's style, and it was exacerbated by Eaton's corporate culture. A Midwestern company with an America-centric orientation, Eaton's workforce consisted largely of longtime employees who felt they would always be part of the "Eaton family." New directions made them nervous; their way of growing was to do what they'd always done, only better. George's plan did not take into account the need to bring on board people with entrenched positions and long-standing alliances—an oversight that was compounded by his alpha strategist risk factors. Witness these critical remarks in the same 360:

"When I talk to him, I get the impression he thinks he's smarter than everyone else."

"George is so mentally quick that it's hard to keep up with him. He gets ahead of people and becomes so frustrated and impatient he jumps to a unilateral decision without our input."

"He goes a hundred miles per minute; he's urgent and intense and won't stop to receive information. If you don't cut to the chase quickly, you lose his attention and he'll interrupt you."

"George displays extraordinary business acumen and technical knowledge, but he lacks people skills. He focuses on driving his strategies, but he pays no attention to *how* he does it or whether he's offending someone."

"Even asking him questions can generate a deprecating response. People end up feeling stupid, so they learn to just comply."

George was damaging morale by being the villain to a lot of victims who worked under him. To make matters worse, many of his peers felt he was self-aggrandizing; they accused him of inflating his own strategic input while failing to acknowledge *their* contributions or owning up to his share of the problems. A performance review said that his style was "not conducive to motivating his team," and that he "needs to develop humility," "solicit input," and "trust the competence of others."

George had the typical liabilities of an alpha male strategist. As you can see in table 5-1, when the King of Data turns into Prince Know-It-All, his analytical genius can become a weapon of destruction instead of an instrument of instruction.

Although George had worked with several coaches, his team had not seen him make observable, sustained changes, so the company called

TABLE 5-1

The strategist syndrome: When strengths become liabilities

Alpha attribute	Value to organization	Risk to organization
Fact-based, rational, logical, analytic decision maker	Finds solutions to intractable problems; reasons purely, uncontaminated by emotion	Discounts intuition and ideas that are unsupported by data; weak at reading self and others; unlikely to share feelings or connect emotionally with others
Finds nuggets of opportunity in piles of data	Able to discern trends and strategic implications; recognizes gap between today's reality and tomorrow's potential	Prone to narrow thinking and hasty closure
Highly intelligent; committed to accurate thinking	Identifies flaws in others' arguments and ideas; generates the right solutions	Perceived as a demeaning know-it-all; makes people defensive; pushes own ideas on others; gets frustrated with slower thinkers
Curious about ideas; eager to find the best approach to solve problems	Brainstorms well; works effectively with others to generate fresh ideas	Overly attached to own perspective; gets defensive and justifies his opinions; doesn't build on others' ideas; unable to build alignment and work with team
Intellectually confident; holds strong opinions	Takes decisive action; solves problems quickly and efficiently	Fails to consider alternatives; doesn't question assumptions; arrogance and stubbornness inhibit creativity; forces ideas on others

us. Eddie decided to see if he could break through George's defenses or join the used coaches club. He quickly found that George had certain healthy qualities that many alpha strategists lack. He might come across as a know-it-all, but he had enough humility and awareness to see his liabilities clearly. "I was brought into this company to create change," he stated in his self-assessment, "but as I've pushed for change, I've seen people resist. They see me as arrogant and impatient. They feel that I'm not open to their feedback. I've got to fix that. My parents and the Boy Scouts taught me to be helpful, and that's what I want to be, but I'm so opinionated that people think I don't want to hear their ideas. I need to pay more attention to the messages I send, and to accept that people have different styles and different ways of getting things done."

George entered the coaching relationship with a firm commitment to do whatever was necessary to improve his leadership. The turning point came when he summarized his 360 for his whole team in July 2005, and then met one-on-one with his peers and his manager. With Eddie's participation, he described what he had learned about himself and invited his colleagues into a candid dialogue about the changes he needed to make.

Once George became fully aware of his impact on other people, he instituted a process of checking in with himself after every interaction to see if he'd been fully effective on an interpersonal level. Shifting his priorities from proving he's right to realizing his most noble intentions had a powerful impact on George. It motivated him to solicit honest feedback and to implement some of the tools you will discover later in this chapter. His 360 six months later documented his growth:

> "George is far more patient and tolerant. People feel less intimidated and seem to enjoy working with him more."

> "He's engaging at a more personal level, and his level of patience has increased dramatically. You can see in his body language that he's less combative and more receptive. He listens to people and gives them time to present their point of view."

> "He's become more tolerant, more open, less locked into his opinions."

"Honesty and integrity were always immensely important to George. Now the values he talks about seem more genuine and heartfelt, because he's treating people so much better."

His next performance review included four-star praise in areas that had previously been singled out as shortcomings: "solicits input from peers and directs; effectively contracted to receive timely feedback; less autocratic; provides public recognition to others." George still had work to do, but his turnaround was dramatic. In the quarter following George's leadership transformation, Eaton Trucking showed a 24 percent increase over the same period the previous year, and trucking became the company's leading profit contributor despite being one of the smaller segments. More important, George's colleagues were fully aligned with the direction he set, making it very likely that the business would continue to exceed its goals.[2]

Like George, every alpha strategist can gain control of his potential liabilities. The process begins when the strategist becomes more aware of how those risk factors play out in interactions with coworkers. The next section spells out those risks in more detail. (Also see the box "The Data on Alpha Strategists" for a summary of our study's findings.)

The Data on Alpha Strategists

Our study found a moderately strong strengths-risks relationship for strategists (table B-1, appendix B). If you're a strong, confident, analytical thinker, with a gift for discernment and rational decision making, the chances are good that you're liable to use your intellect as a sledgehammer, forcing your views on others and closing yourself off to valuable perspectives.

As to gender, men scored significantly higher in both strategist strengths and strategist risks. In other words, male alphas are more likely than female alphas to be strategists, and male alpha strategists are more likely than females to exhibit the downside of defensiveness, know-it-all

---

pushiness, and other forms of intellectual bullying. (See table B-2 in appendix B.)

As a group, the three risk subthemes—competitiveness, impatience, and difficulty controlling anger—correlated with high strategist risk scores. (See table B-3 in appendix B.) Of the three, the anger correlation was especially strong, for both men and women.

How the Brilliant Thinker Can Become a Know-It-All

Think again of those brainy kids in school. You probably knew one who was kind enough to help others with their homework, and who patiently tried different tutoring methods to get them to understand. Then there were the obnoxious brainiacs who showed off their IQs and spat out snide remarks that made ordinary kids feel like idiots. That's the difference between healthy, balanced alpha strategists and dysfunctional alpha male strategists with zero people skills. No one likes a know-it-all. Just as the other students can't wait for a conceited classmate to fail a test, coworkers root for the arrogant alpha strategist to get something wrong, the more humiliating the better. And just as the pretentious student does not get invited to the big parties, the self-important strategist eventually fails to get the promotion he craves. The more obnoxious he is about being right, the more others will want him to be wrong. They might not even admit he's right when he is.

With their quick, precise minds, alpha strategists are often the first to spot the flaws in others' thinking and surface the right answers. But, as George Nguyen's 360s indicate, those assets turn into liabilities when their insights are expressed with impatience or arrogance. Strategists who get a kick out of proving other people wrong invite resistance and resentment. Other alphas will argue toe-to-toe with a pompous strategist, to the point where each cares more about winning than what's best for the organization. Those who are not alphas will do anything to avoid the strategist's condescending superiority, even shut down their brains and comply half-heartedly with a flawed plan.

Alpha strategist show-offs have strong opinions about nearly everything. The more dysfunctional ones ask for input when they know they're expected to, but merely pretend to listen. They have monologues, not conversations. Notorious interrupters, they'll jump in the instant they see where you're headed, and the discussion quickly becomes a lecture. And woe to those who disagree; alpha male strategists take it as a personal affront. They'll counterattack, bludgeoning you with facts. Only those with healthy self-esteem can survive without feeling like their IQ is lower than their age.

The strategists' dilemma is compounded by their uncanny ability to unearth the roots of a problem. That capacity puts them a step ahead of everyone else, and they don't always have the patience or skill to pull others along. "My lifelong challenge is that I have the right idea but I can't get other people on board without pushing my views on them," said Ken Schroeder, the former CEO of KLA-Tencor. "In meetings, I'm crystal clear on what we need to do, but my team members don't see what I do. I can't let us march off and do the wrong thing, but if I'm not careful I come across as too sharp. I had to find a way to communicate so others find my style palatable, even when they don't agree with me."

As they dig into the heart of things, unhealthy alpha strategists mine for flaws in others' thinking. Their intention is honorable: to get to the truth. But their low tolerance for slower minds turns a mutual exploration into an interrogation. People cower like kids in a classroom praying not to be called on. Of course, alpha strategists don't see themselves as intellectual bullies. They're just committed to accurate thinking. "I process data and arrive at answers so quickly that many people are left in the dust," said one self-aware strategist. "I get intense, and they complain that I'm playing 'stump the dummy.' I don't intend to be patronizing, I just get frustrated and I want to move on."

Strategist dysfunction begins with the strategists' firm belief that they have the right answers and it's their duty to convince others to go along with them. When persuasion doesn't work, the most impatient alpha strategists simply declare the game over and order their strategy put into action. One of Larry Lucchino's Red Sox colleagues described him as "an effective collaborator and a great facilitator and integrator of many interest groups—partners, fans, politicians, media, and management. But," he added, "under pressure he defaults to command-and-control tactics."

When persuasion fails, alpha male strategists often move on to manipulation, perhaps by asking clever questions designed to maneuver people into their line of thinking. If the person still fails to come up with the right conclusion, the strategist tells him exactly why he's wrong, often implying that he's not only misinformed but dumb. The most dysfunctional alpha strategists are intellectual bullies who *enjoy* demolishing the self-esteem of others. "I like to see them sweat," one manager admitted. "I give them wood shampoos"—his colorful way of saying he hits them over the head verbally with intellectual bats. He said he did it to get people to think more rigorously, but by turning it into a blood sport he actually caused brain freeze. Once he realized that his contempt had a devastating impact on his team's intellectual firepower, he learned to ask questions that led to discovery rather than intimidation.

The net result of these risks is a tragic irony: the alpha strategists' success is built on clear, objective thinking, but their need to be right can cloud that very clarity and destroy their vaunted objectivity. Even worse, their attachment to being right closes alpha strategists off to people who have information they need. It also alienates those who try to help by pointing out flaws in their thinking. Once burned, potential allies stay out of the know-it-all's line of fire, often going over his head or working in clandestine groups to do things their own way.

How Objective Thinking Can Negate the Human Factor

Like Mr. Spock in *Star Trek*, alpha strategists can be so rational that they appear to have the soul of a calculator. As we saw with George Nguyen, their cool objectivity is a definite asset, but the absence of the personal touch makes it difficult for them to build loyalty or get buy-in for their initiatives. Alpha visionaries who turn a blind eye to practicality also have trouble getting buy-in, but their passion and inspiration make it easier for them to overcome that problem. Alpha strategists try to get people on board by proving how right they are, and in the process they end up turning everyone off because they make others feel intellectually inferior. Some are so focused on numbers and points of logic that people call them robots behind their backs.

The strategist version of "Build it and they will come" is "Create a brilliant plan and they will get it done." But enrolling others takes more than a convincing strategy. You also have to engage their hearts and stir their souls. "The central challenge of change is not strategy, not systems, not culture, but changing people's behavior," writes the well-known expert on culture change, John P. Kotter.[3] And changing behavior, he notes, "is less a matter of giving people analysis to influence their thoughts than helping them see a truth that influences their feelings."

We recently worked with a senior vice president in a major consumer products company. Having taken charge of a 2,000-employee engineering department a year earlier, he'd made significant headway in fixing major problems with product quality. But customers still did not fully accept the products. After interviewing the top 75 people in the organization to figure out what was keeping them from achieving their goals, we discovered that the senior VP's intimidating, short-tempered style had created a lack of trust. At first, he was remarkably receptive to this feedback. Then we shared the comments we received about his lack of a coherent strategy. He hit the roof. Leaning forward menacingly in his chair, he pounded his desk so hard the crashing sound alarmed people in nearby offices. Like a lawyer displaying evidence, he showed us a document that detailed his strategic plan. In a loud, sharp voice, he said he'd referenced the plan countless times in meetings and memos. How dare those idiots accuse him of not having a comprehensive strategy!

People knew perfectly well about the strategic plan. But they did not understand how it would translate into action or produce the needed results. The senior VP had fallen prey to a common problem with alpha male strategists: magnificent conception, poor explanation, no enrollment. He was like a football coach with an ingenious game plan, who can't get his players to understand it or execute it. Once he calmed down, he was able to see that brilliance is worthless if you can't rally others behind your ideas. Eventually, the company set aside one afternoon a month to deepen its strategic plan and communicate the results throughout the organization. As a result, the firm has made significant headway in penetrating the market.

Like that senior VP, unhealthy alpha strategists turn the asset of intellectual confidence into the liabilities of arrogance and stubbornness. If they have power, they impose their schemes by fiat, even in the face of reasonable disagreement, and they cling desperately to their strategies even when all the evidence indicates they're failing because they can't admit they were wrong. Even when their minority-of-one viewpoint turns out to be *correct*, the long-term impact can be devastating: with their pride reinforced by victory, alpha male strategists are less likely to listen to dissenting opinions in the future.

Female Alpha Strategists

Our research indicates that men are significantly more likely than women to exhibit strategist traits. (See table B-2 in appendix B.) The finding is consistent with scientific studies showing that men tend to be linear, sequential thinkers who easily separate emotion from thought, while women think in a more integrated fashion, perhaps because different thought processes are more dispersed in the female brain and more localized in the male brain.[4] As society continues to change, and more and more women learn thinking skills that their grandmothers didn't dare aspire to, we're likely to see a shift in the ratio of male to female strategists.

In our experience, female strategists in general match the analytic skills of their male counterparts but don't carry the same interpersonal risks. They're less likely to be seen as arrogant know-it-alls, because they tend to welcome different perspectives and to validate the ideas of others. This is not always the case, of course. Ellen McMahon, a senior research scientist at the Pfizer pharmaceutical company, used her alpha strategist skills to become a standout figure in the male-dominated field of cardiovascular physiology. She saw herself as smarter, quicker, and more tenacious than most researchers of either sex, and worked extra hard if someone said she couldn't do something because she was a woman. Her competitive drive and her analytic sense about the direction research should take led to major advances in drug development.

But Ellen also exhibited the alpha strategist downside. Seen as overly opinionated, excessively critical, and too attached to her own ideas, she earned the nickname Iron Maiden. Instead of bringing out the best in others, she scared them away. "She's so authoritarian and inflexible that people stop presenting her with creative ideas," said one colleague. "She's usually right, but she'll say, 'You're wrong' before anyone has a chance to think, and people get tentative and defensive." As with the alpha male strategists we work with, Eddie helped Ellen develop influence tools to complement her intellectual horsepower, and she went on to become a persuasive spokesperson for women in science and for the process of drug development.

Louise O'Brien, Dell's former vice president of strategy and formerly an editor at the *Harvard Business Review*, is more typical of female alpha strategists. A clear, analytic thinker whose outstanding ability to articulate her ideas always earns the respect of alpha male peers, she not only stands strong in toe-to-toe debates, she also knows how to listen to her colleagues' ideas and build upon them. Before moving to Dell, Louise was a partner at Bain & Company, where, she says, "I always migrated toward the more quantitative cases and the more masculine industries. I did that deliberately, because as a woman I knew I could easily get labeled as a powder puff. I tried to hit home runs with dazzling analysis that no one else had thought of." Those home runs earned her a partnership at Bain, a rarity for women even now.

As a leader, Louise lacked the go-for-the-jugular quality that many alpha male strategists bring to the job—either to their advantage or to their detriment. At one point in her career, when she was a vice president for sales, she came into conflict with a brutish peer who treated her like an opponent in a fight to the death. In one meeting, he looked at her with smug self-confidence and asserted that he would end up with all her accounts and she'd either report to him or quit. "I reminded him that we were on the same team, but he didn't see it that way," said Louise. "To him it was a zero-sum game, and that's not how women approach things." In that particular case, her approach won out over her confrontational colleague's. He got neither her job nor her accounts, and he ended up leaving the company long before Louise did.

As Dell's VP of strategy, says Louise, "I was powerful because my bosses, Michael Dell and Kevin Rollins, were powerful. To be honest, I liked having the benefits of referred power without having to fight the battles." Alpha male strategists who need to sit atop the pyramid would have trouble working in the shadow of two such influential figures. But it worked beautifully for Louise, who says, "I'm motivated by personal achievement and a desire to have an impact, not by organizational power or dominating and controlling people."

For gifted strategists like Louise, the qualities that characterize female alphas can be an asset. Indeed, to a certain extent they're shared by healthy alpha *male* strategists as well. When taken too far, however, they can easily become liabilities. If you're overly concerned about hurting people's feelings, for example, you won't stand up for your views or oppose a wrongheaded idea. You might also let your heart overrule the tough conclusions of your analytic mind. At times, for instance, the best course of action for a business carries unfortunate side effects for individuals; women may find it more wrenching to make those difficult choices, while men run the opposite risk, of being too cut off from the human consequences. Healthy alpha strategists—male and female alike—balance the traits of heart and head, acting with concern for individual interests while courageously making the right decision for the organization as a whole.

Strategist Tools

Alpha strategists face three basic dilemmas: (1) how to communicate what they know without making others feel stupid, (2) how to point out errors in others' thinking without alienating them or making them defensive, and (3) how to balance their exceptional minds with the ability to team productively with others. If they don't learn to do those things, they discourage fresh thinking, dampen energy, and extinguish team spirit. Frustrated by the lack of results, alpha strategists become even more convinced that they're the only ones who can get things right. The result? An alpha triangle and a deluge of sludge. Feeling like victims of slow minds, strategists turn themselves into heroes and take over, which of course makes them even bigger villains to everyone around them.

A consumer products company in New England was going through an unprecedented growth spurt brought on by sudden changes in the market. With the company's resources outstripped by the soaring demand, the CEO, whom we'll call Chris, was forced to deal with a new set of challenges. He had to continue meeting the needs of his loyal customer base while at the same time recruiting and orienting additional staff and asking more of his longtime employees. The stress brought on by this balancing act put Chris's alpha strategist style at odds with the alpha commander traits of the company's COO, Steve.

Chris and Steve had worked together in varying capacities for more than 20 years, and they had been a productive team in their current roles for the previous five years. Throughout that time, their styles complemented one another. But, as is often the case under extreme stress and strain, their alpha qualities now intensified and they found themselves clashing for the first time. A brilliant analytic thinker, Chris made decisions in the classic strategist manner, through step-by-step information processing based on solid metrics. Gripped by a sense of urgency, he would seize the data on hand and quickly process it to closure so he could make a rational decision. Once he came to a conclusion, he solidified his position and presented it to others as if it had been engraved by a burning bush. Under some conditions this alpha strategist mentality can be just what the doctor ordered. But it carries the risk of reaching premature closure, depriving executives of potentially valuable input and shutting out the opportunity to align the team. This cocky stubbornness can also frustrate colleagues who think differently and are also confident that they're right.

Steve was one of them. A true commander, he led by instilling energy and motivation in the workforce with his gung-ho charisma, and he sized up situations quickly, making on-the-spot decisions with his gut. Unfailingly confident in his own perspective, Steve's way of reassuring Chris when the CEO got anxious, was to say, essentially, "Trust me, I have it under control." But reassurance in the absence of facts doesn't work with strategists; on the contrary, it compounds their anxiety and makes them even more vigilant. Several times during the crunch of the growth spurt, key decisions came down to Chris's way versus Steve's way, and Steve had to bite the bullet because, after all, Chris was the head of the company. Steve not only felt shut out and discounted, he also felt that his authority with the people under him was being under-mined—and nothing is harder for an alpha commander than the thought of being seen as not in command.

As Steve grew more frustrated, so did Chris. He felt unsupported by the COO with whom he'd worked successfully for so many years. He became suspicious, thinking Steve was working around him, using his charismatic personality to line up support for his own agenda. He didn't know what Steve's agenda might be, but he suspected it was different from his own. In fact, Steve was using his influence skills to line up the workforce behind Chris's decisions. As an alpha strategist, Chris be-lieved that data rules: show people the facts, announce the conclusion to which they logically lead, and that should be enough to get them to go the extra mile. Steve knew that most people don't read numbers like a strategist. He tried to drive them by instilling a sense of mission and by dangling the carrot of future rewards in front of them.

These leadership differences, which balanced each other nicely under ordinary conditions, were beginning to have serious consequences. Em-ployees were complaining about both the CEO and the COO. They felt that Steve was driving them too hard without providing an adequate road map. "Saying 'Just win, baby' isn't enough," said one senior executive. At the same time, they complained that Chris demanded so much analysis that they had no time to get their jobs done. Strong performers had left the company, and the rumor mill swirled with other pending departures.

Eddie brought the two old colleagues together to clear the air. The first thing he did was ask them each to describe what they really wanted for the company. They quickly saw that they were in perfect alignment on the level of intention, but they had let their methods and styles become discordant. To their credit, both men dropped the tendency to blame the other, and in-stead examined their own behavior. Steve saw that it was not enough to tell Chris what he'd decided. As a strategist, Chris needed facts, not just faith. Steve agreed in the future to share the data and the analytic processes that led to his conclusions. On his end, Chris saw that he had to accept that most people don't have his knack for gathering and reading data, and that they need other, more human forms of motivation. He also realized that he had to be more tolerant of uncertainty in times of change, to keep from closing off creative options. And both men agreed to guard against locking themselves into either/or situations, where they felt forced to choose between their two positions. Instead, they agreed to generate several possibilities, work together to select the best alternative, and communicate to key leaders that they, the two men at the top, are aligned with one another.

The Chris and Steve story illustrates some of the challenges faced by alpha male strategists in an organizational context. It also demonstrates the importance of expanding awareness, openness to feedback, and the willingness to be vulnerable. Here are some more specific tools for overcoming strategist risks.

Stop Defending and Start Learning

Unhealthy alpha males defend their positions so aggressively they could win the Butkus Award for outstanding linebacker, and strategists are particularly adept at intellectual goal-line stands. The wise ones learn that the penalties for unnecessary roughness are costly.

Defensiveness *always* creates the alpha triangle. Here's how it typically works with alpha strategists. Whether in a managerial role or in a peer-to-peer context, their coercive manner of offering feedback puts the other person into the victim role. The victim's defensiveness might be passive—nervous explanations, timid justifications—or aggressive—a counterattack or an attempt to shift the blame. Naturally, alpha male victims are aggressive defenders, who often leap quickly into the villain role. At that point, the alpha strategist who provided the initial feedback does one of two things: (1) mentally throws up his hands and shuts up because the other alpha isn't listening (a subtle form of hero behavior designed to keep the peace and protect the relationship), or (2) intensifies his aggressiveness, in which case he reinforces his villain status by escalating the conflict. Either approach will perpetuate the alpha triangle.

As you can see in table 5-2, healthy leaders profit from feedback and make needed changes, while unhealthy leaders fend it off in different ways.

When the competitive nature of alpha male strategists gets the better of them, they barricade the gates of their minds to keep out intruding ideas, opinions, and facts. No learning or collaborative dialogue can take place. Stepping out of this morass requires a willingness to shift out

TABLE 5-2

Responses to feedback

Dysfunctional alpha leadership	Healthy, self-aware alpha leadership
Pretend the problem doesn't exist or deny that it's yours.	Acknowledge the problem and take responsibility for solving it.
Assign blame, showing how the problem is someone else's fault.	Look for ways you contributed to others' errors.
Get defensive; act huffy about how hard you work and how much you do; counter-attack.	Acknowledge your lapses and mistakes. Accept all feedback as an opportunity to learn.
Create a smokescreen by firing a barrage of unrelated complaints or criticizing the presentation or the decision.	Proactively solve the problem, considering what information needs to be communicated and who should complete which tasks.
Spin the truth to make yourself look better, or conveniently forget what you were told or what you agreed to do.	Focus on getting the job done and addressing the challenges.

of that know-it-all posture and into a more open stance. In our earlier example, Chris and Steve did exactly that, demonstrating skills that every alpha male should learn: (1) they took a good, honest look at themselves rather than discounting their own contributions to the problem or blaming the other person completely, (2) they were willing to drop their defensiveness and invite genuine learning, and (3) they openly admitted their mistakes.

Figure 5-1 is a powerful tool for monitoring defensiveness. The higher the score on the (+) scale, the lower the defensiveness and the greater the openness to learning. A high score on the (−) scale indicates the opposite: a lot of defensiveness and a mind closed to learning.

You can use the scale to understand your own pattern of escalation. If, for instance, you find that you're frequently operating at levels −1 and −2, you're stuck in a habit of defensiveness and not very open to learning. You can also use the scale to track others and adjust your own behavior accordingly. If someone is very high on the defensiveness chart, for instance, save your breath; he's not capable of listening. Better to pause and listen to *him*. If he sees you're genuinely trying to understand his perspective, he's likely to shift out of defensiveness and listen to *you*.

FIGURE 5-1

Turning defensiveness into learning

High openness to learning	+10	Plan the change, engage others, set milestones, and implement.
	+9	Communicate genuine enthusiasm about making a change.
	+8	Think out loud, making new associations about the issue.
	+7	Take full responsibility for the issue and the results that have occurred.
	+6	Request information and examples about the issue.
	+5	Openly wonder about your role in creating the issue.
	+4	Communicate genuine curiosity about the issue and how to resolve it.
	+3	Express appreciation to the messenger, regardless of the delivery style.
	+2	Summarize key points without interjecting your own ideas.
	+1	Look interested; breathe; demonstrate an open posture.

BREAKTHROUGH: CHOOSE CURIOSITY OVER BEING RIGHT

High defensiveness	−1	Show polite interest, while inwardly preparing your rebuttal.
	−2	Overexplain details and provide more information, assuming issue will then disappear.
	−3	Justify actions with forceful and compelling logic, plus an interpretation of key events.
	−4	Interrupt to give your perspective, while feeling misunderstood.
	−5	Interpret what the person is saying as an undeserved attack; feel unappreciated.
	−6	Blame someone or something else; disclaim any responsibility yourself.
	−7	Make snippy replies and show your irritation nonverbally.
	−8	Intimidate or attack the messenger; get sharp, brusque, and harsh.
	−9	Pretend to agree, then complain about decisions and criticize people who aren't present.
	−10	Comply by implementing the person's idea, while hoping it will fail.

Note: This is a modification of a chart developed by Gay and Kathlyn Hendricks, www.hendricks.com.

You can also use the chart to track an interactive sequence between you and someone else. Suppose you need to offer critical feedback to a staff member. Your purpose is to help the person change, but you're frustrated by his previous performance failures, so the content and tone of your comments are flavored by blame (−6). The employee becomes defensive and launches into an explanation (−1 to −3). You intensify your commentary, coming across as sharp, harsh, and intimidating (−7 or −8).

Sensing that if he keeps on explaining he'll be humiliated, the employee shuts up and acquiesces (–10). Later, he complains to coworkers about you (–9). What happens as a result of this dysfunctional interaction? Mistaking the employee's compliance for agreement, you leave, thinking you've taught him a valuable lesson and the problem will be fixed. In reality, he hasn't learned a thing, and neither have you.

Such an analysis can help you formulate a better way of doing things in the future. Simply shift your own behavior from the high scores on the minus side to the high scores on the positive side. You'll quickly see the other person's scores move in the same direction.

Learn to Use Strategic Pedagogy

Because they believe they're smarter than everyone else, alpha male strategists are prone to taking more than 100 percent responsibility for thinking up effective lines of attack. The problem is, once they come up with a brilliant plan, they now have additional responsibility: winning others over. Although well-rounded strategists rise to the occasion, others take *less* than 100 percent responsibility for garnering support. When people don't understand their reasoning, instead of finding a better way to influence them, they respond with shouts or put-downs, or just throw up their hands and give up: "If they don't get it, it's their problem. I can't be responsible for their stupidity." A key challenge for alpha male strategists, therefore, is to take responsibility for communicating effectively.

Do you get frustrated because people can't follow your thinking? Don't just write them off as dumb. Their minds simply may not be as quick or as agile as yours. Maybe you can leap gracefully over steps of logic like a deer, but if others are plodding behind you like bears, don't just leave it to them to catch up. Try slowing down to match their pace. Find out what they know and how their minds work. Bring them along with language and teaching tools they can relate to.

One of our clients whom we'll call Pete, a senior VP at a major high-tech firm, is an excellent example of a brilliant alpha strategist who became even more effective when he sharpened his influence skills. "I see the holes in people's logic," he told us early on in our relationship. "When it's clear that the path they're on isn't going to get us where we need to go, I drill in, hoping they'll see the problem. If they don't get it, I show them *my* way, which invariably turns out to be correct. But in the process I alienate people. They feel demeaned." His team would become so fearful that they'd stop asking questions. They'd leave meetings confused, then get together on their own to figure out what the client wanted. All too often, their results were far removed from his expectations.

In his 360° assessment, Pete's colleagues stated his dilemma clearly. "He convinces people they're not smart, so they quit contributing," one commented. "If he engaged people instead of pushing them away, he'd be phenomenal." Another person remarked: "Pete devalues people who are not as smart, and his rudeness causes a terrible loss of energy, creativity, and trust." All strategists would benefit from our recommendations to Pete:

- Use your genius to help others become smarter, instead of making them feel dumb.

- If you think someone doesn't "get it," own it as *your* communication problem.

- Take full responsibility for explaining your ideas clearly enough for people to follow.

Pete learned to convey his ideas slowly and sequentially, and to check with people frequently to see if they understood. When we followed up a year later, his 360 featured comments like this: "He's still very passionate in his desire to get us to the right point, but he's much more measured. He still gets annoyed sometimes, but now he expresses his concerns constructively so people are more willing to contribute."

Ray Roe, the CEO of Adecco Group North America, is an excellent example of an alpha strategist who learned the value of linking accurate data to high-level communication. When the Enron scandal erupted, Roe (whom we met in chapter 3 because he also has strong commander qualities) was the COO of Lee Hecht Harrison, an executive search company owned by Adecco. Six months later, at a time of heightened scrutiny on corporate finances, Adecco found itself in a massive accounting crisis, and Ray was brought in as the new CEO for the U.S. business.

Faced with cleaning up the crisis at Adecco, he addressed the most essential need: to standardize operating procedures so every branch of the company could be audited according to the same rules. "We're a huge, decentralized organization with a lot of turnover, and the problem was extremely complicated," he recalled. "The biggest challenge was getting thousands of people at all levels of the organization aligned, and to follow through on all the day-to-day habits that were required to sustain the changes." Remembering a lesson he learned as a lieutenant colonel in the Army, commanding a battalion of 800 soldiers, Ray created a clear, consistent strategy and then focused as much on *communicating* it through the ranks as he did on the strategy itself. An integrated set of processes quickly took hold throughout the company, leading to the most significant turnaround the company's auditors had ever seen. In one year, the number of recorded items with serious weaknesses plummeted from 192 to zero, and the company improved its margin by 1 percent, which translated to $34 million on the bottom line.

Like Ray Roe and the client we called Pete, you too can become far more effective if you raise your coaching and communications skills closer to the level of your analytic brilliance.

Use Engaged Listening

Alpha male strategists would rather dictate than dialogue. They think that command-and-control tactics in conversation allow them to use their verbal proficiency as a tool to achieve influence. But research suggests that they're mistaken: people are more likely to change their views when they're given a chance to speak as opposed to being lectured to.

Don't underestimate the power of listening. Those who listen carefully and ask incisive questions based on what's said—and what *isn't* said—gain tremendous power to influence others. But don't underestimate the *challenge* of listening either. Good listening calls for openness, respect, and genuine interest. Skilled listeners follow the speaker's lead wherever it takes them. They remain fully present with the speaker, without multitasking in their minds or rehearsing what they're going to say next. Most important, they're willing to change their minds based on what they hear.

There are three levels of engaged listening skills: accuracy, empathy, and intention. The combination can enhance your influence enormously.

Listen for accuracy. Briefly summarize what you heard. You might think that taking the time to summarize will slow the conversation, but in fact it often saves time by preventing misunderstandings. It also says, loud and clear, "I heard you," and such validation can defuse tension when feelings run high.

Listen with empathy. Tune in to what the speaker is feeling and name it matter-of-factly: "I can see why you'd be upset by this" or "It sounds like you have some doubt, and I can understand why you would." Don't try to talk him out of his feelings or make him wrong for having them. Empathy does not mean you have to agree; you can be empathetic and still hold a different opinion.

Listen for intention. What is the true intention behind what is being said? Discerning what's implied but not clearly stated is an incredibly powerful tool. If you begin by reflecting on the intentions with which you agree (a major challenge for alpha strategists, who like to pounce on areas of disagreement), you'll find that it's easier to create alignment.

The three levels of engaged listening can be conveyed separately during the course of a conversation or all at once in a single response. Table 5-3 depicts what happened when we coached a CEO who was trapped in an argument with an opinionated executive we'll call Norm about how to portray the company's values.

If he hadn't learned the art of engaged listening, the CEO would have resolved the debate like a typical alpha male strategist, by stepping into the persona he called Bulldog and forcing everyone else to shut up and comply with his plan. The result would have been a classic alpha triangle, with the Bulldog as villain and Norm and other executives as assorted victims and heroes. Instead, the CEO made Norm feel heard and valued. He then shifted from his rigid, defensive stance to one of relaxed openness. A healthy dialogue followed, in which Norm and the

TABLE 5-3

Engaged listening

Listen for:	Action	Example
Accuracy	Summarize the key points of the message.	"Norm, you've presented a diagram showing the four key values, along with a detailed ten-page document that describes the day-to-day behaviors that the values represent."
Empathy	Highlight the mood and feelings of the speaker.	"You seem to feel passionate about continuing with the values statement in its current form. I wonder if you feel concerned, perhaps even afraid, that changing the statement might create a distraction and derail the progress we've made."
Intention	Point out the speaker's unstated noble intentions.	"It sounds like you want to ensure that our values govern everyone's behavior and create positive, sustainable habits."

CEO built on each other's ideas to modify the values statement in a way neither could have anticipated.

Get in Touch

The alpha strategists' genius in reading data is matched by a weakness in reading emotions—their own and others'. They see feelings as illogical viruses that can infect decision making. Chief among these contaminants is fear. They see fear as a major weakness that has to be concealed from everyone, including themselves.

Alpha strategists, who love facts, need to learn these facts: fear afflicts even the most self-assured people; it can serve a useful purpose by prodding us to question our assumptions; and it can be a stepping-stone to higher insight and creative breakthroughs—if we face it squarely.

You're right to think that people want fearless, self-assured leaders with strong convictions. But that's not all they want. They also want leaders who are honest and human. Alpha strategists who are willing to let their guard down enough to share their fears with others dramatically change the way they're perceived: less arrogant, less self-important, less threatening—and that shift in perception alters the behavior of the people around them. We're not advocating ostentatious displays of anxiety, just a subtle shift from "I know what has to be done and anyone who doesn't see it is a moron" to "I believe I know the right way to go, and I'd like your input to confirm or change my thinking." If you can make that shift, you'll find that people will be far more likely to respect you and to follow you, not less so.

Understand Thinking Flaws

Alpha strategists excel at what Harvard education professor David Perkins calls "reflective intelligence": the ability to reason to a correct answer. With lightning speed, they analyze complex situations, discern critical variables, and work out the steps that follow logically from each possible occurrence: If we do X and they do Y, then Z will follow, but if they do A and we do B, then C will probably happen; so to make sure they *don't* do A, let's do M—and M is often something no one else would have dreamed of. Much of the frustration strategists experience—and the grief they cause others—stems from their inability to cope with people they consider less smart than they are. Some of those people might actually be *smarter* in some ways, but alpha strategists assume that everyone's mind works in the same basic way, only theirs is a whole lot better at it. In fact, there are many forms of intelligence, and wise alpha strategists—as opposed to those who are merely smart—cultivate all their mental skills and also help others to improve their reflective thinking.

The first step is to understand how other minds work. In his book *Outsmarting IQ*, Perkins describes four "intelligence traps" to which everyone is prone:[5]

Hasty thinking. We react impulsively, mindlessly, without thinking about what we're doing. As a result, we close too quickly and settle for conventional answers.

Narrow thinking. We lock our minds in small, circumscribed boxes based on past conditioning. Beliefs and biases keep us from questioning our own assumptions.

Fuzzy thinking. We become unclear and imprecise, making inaccurate distinctions, such as overgeneralizing or focusing on surface similarities instead of underlying differences.

Sprawling thinking. We wander all over the place, running from one connection to the next . . . and the next . . .

Alpha male strategists are most vulnerable to hasty thinking and narrow thinking: hasty because they've already figured everything out; narrow because their minds are so flawless there's no reason to consider other perspectives. Of course, when other people are narrow or hasty, it drives alpha strategists crazy. But what *really* makes them climb walls are fuzzy thinkers and sprawlers. Understanding these thought patterns will help you understand why people seem to fall short of your expectations. Instead of just writing them off as dumb, realize that (1) they actually have mental strengths you can harness, and (2) their shortcomings arise from common habits that can be overcome. If you invest in helping them improve their thinking skills, the effort can pay off big-time. In other words, don't complain; train. Figure 5-2 summarizes tips for avoiding these four thinking traps.

FIGURE 5-2

How to break free from thinking traps

If you're hasty:
- Learn to tolerate ambiguity and uncertainty.
- Avoid premature closure, especially with important issues.
- Actively solicit ideas and opinions from others.
- Stay open to new input as long as possible.

If you're narrow:
- Solicit ideas from people who think outside the box.
- Expand the range of information you draw upon.
- Partner with a sprawling thinker and help each other find balance.

If you're fuzzy:
- Conduct a dialogue with a crisp, clear thinker.
- Practice explaining your thoughts to people who know nothing about the subject.
- Before settling on a conclusion, ask, "Is there more to this?" many times.

If you're a sprawler:
- Partner with a systematic, structured thinker.
- Simplify and organize your space; cluttered surroundings clutter the mind.
- If you can't organize your thoughts, learn to organize how you communicate them.
- Jot down your three main points in numerical order before sharing your ideas in meetings.

Develop a Sense of Wonder

One of the reasons alpha strategists get pulled into defensive behavior is that they genuinely believe they have the right answer and they want their business groups to benefit from what they know. Their noble intention is to help others see things the right way. But the harder they push and the longer they persist, the more they come across as overly attached to their own point of view and closed to learning from others. The alpha leaders who are most successful at breaking loose from this self-defeating behavior are those who are willing to live with some uncertainty. They are willing to suspend their need for closure and give up the misperception that they and they alone have the best answer. Instead, they listen carefully to others and build on their ideas, seeking links between what they discover and what they already know.

Larry Lucchino, for example, uses what he calls the Martian Theory: he invites input from outsiders with no experience in the area he's concerned with, because they bring a fresh, innocent perspective. "I'd bring friends who knew nothing about the sports to basketball, football, and baseball games," he recalled. "They offered unique views of everything from why we only guarded in half the basketball court to why we chose some commonly used strategy in batting or fielding." As a baseball executive, he's learned the value of listening to cab drivers and fans as well as scouts and statisticians.

Just as important as seeking input is how you respond to what you receive. Larry learned only after years of experience that people need to feel that you genuinely want to hear them. Like other alpha male strategists, his impatience with imperfect data and belabored presentations often gave the opposite impression. Feeling dismissed or unappreciated, people would sometimes clam up, depriving him of the very information he craved.

In addition to drawing information from a variety of sources, you can benefit enormously by opening your mind to unexpected discoveries. Instead of settling for easy answers, ask what we call wonder questions. Here are some you might ask yourself:

- I wonder what this person is really trying to say.

- I wonder what I can learn from this situation.

- I wonder how I can achieve my goals in another way.

- I wonder how I can stop feeling misunderstood.

- I wonder what else I might not know.

How to Work with Alpha Strategists

Faced with a strategist know-it-all who shoots ideas like bullets, the natural reaction of most people is the familiar fight-or-flight response. Other alphas want to fight back. Those who are not alphas want to flee, but since they can't *literally* flee, they do the office equivalent: nod in agreement even if they haven't the faintest idea what they're agreeing to. Instead, learn to engage alpha male strategists on their own terms, by using these tips:

Shift into curiosity. Don't take the belligerent tone and condescending attitude personally. Instead, penetrate the nuances of the strategist's thought process. Try to discern his core message. Find the gaps between your thinking and his. Until you fully understand where he's coming from, you will not be able to help the alpha strategist understand where you're coming from.

Work with him one-on-one. The bigger the meeting, the more an alpha strategist will resort to dominance behavior; crowds trigger their primitive instinct to beat up on challengers. If you disagree with him, or seek to modify his ideas even slightly, try to see him alone. Alpha strategists are far more civilized in one-on-one situations, and they might even listen.

Align your thinking with his. Rather than simply disagreeing—which might trigger alpha defensive measures—dig into the data to fully understand the strategist's perspective; then actively link your ideas to his. Create alignment, not agreement, by building bridges between his perspective and yours.

Be prepared. The last thing you want to do with a clever, competitive alpha strategist is to enter a dialogue ill prepared. Do your homework. Gather facts, data, and documentation. Backing up your conclusions with solid, logical evidence will bolster your confidence and win the strategist's respect.

Write down your questions. To guard against forgetting key points when you're in the presence of an intimidating alpha male strategist, write down your questions in advance. Arrange them in a logical, sequential fashion. The more orderly you speak, the more you conform to the strategist style of thinking. He'll not only be impressed, he'll be better able to give you the information you need—and you'll help make him more successful.

In the next chapter, we'll complete our tour of the four alpha types with the executor—the alpha to call upon when you need to move a plan to completion with efficiency, discipline, and accountability.

ACTION STEPS

If you're an alpha strategist:

- Elevate your interpersonal skills to the level of your thinking skills.
- Use clear communication and effective teaching tools to create maximum support.
- Own up to doubt, fear, or confusion.
- Learn to point out flaws in others' thinking without making them feel stupid.
- Instead of writing people off as dumb, harness their mental strengths and help them overcome their thinking flaws.
- If others don't "get it," own it as your communication problem.
- Place team success above your need to be right.

- Learn to recognize when you're being defensive, and shift into learning.

- Use engaged listening and listen for accuracy, empathy, and intention.

If you work with or for an alpha strategist:

- Understand how the strategist mind works and address issues in a way that aligns with their thought process.

- Strive to be impeccably prepared by writing down questions and organizing your key points.

- Shore up your own thinking skills.

- Learn to disagree without making the strategist defensive.

- Listen to the strategist's criticism without taking it personally.

- Don't get competitive and don't be intimidated.

- Use the defensiveness-into-learning scale to recognize when you become defensive and train yourself to shift into learning.

- Work through disagreements with strategists one-on-one.

CHAPTER

The Alpha Executor

The Driver Who Can Drive
You Up the Wall

My early work at Dell focused on analytical approaches to our business challenges. As I moved into operational roles, first as president of the Americas and later as COO and then CEO, I became aware of my ability to zero in on issues at a very detailed level. This helps me spot near-term problems, target priorities, and drive execution through multiple levels of the company. Along the way, I learned that I could get so manically focused that I pushed people too hard. In driving others to success, I came across as too opinionated. I'd tell them how to fix things, and they'd feel overcontrolled and micromanaged. I realized I had to be more balanced in my approach.

In the last few years, I've worked hard to make sure people feel included and valued. I used to think that my biggest contribution was in knowing what to do and driving execution, but I came to see that strong people want to be led, not driven. My job is also to inspire people and help them reach higher levels of performance in their own way. I started taking the time to build closer relationships with people, to trust their expertise more, listen to their input, and point out what's working as well as what's not. I shifted from "Do this" to "What do you think we should do?"

Recently, when we were dealing with some major execution challenges, I became more directive to ensure that we'd get the important fixes in place. But I tried to continue feeding my personal connections with people, and to make sure they didn't think I was taking control and shutting them down. Overall, becoming more collaborative has not only made me a better manager but a much better leader.

— *Kevin Rollins, CEO of Dell Corporation, in interview with authors*

Executor Strengths

Highly disciplined, self-motivated, and doggedly persistent, alpha male executors are extraordinarily productive and efficient—the kind of people who pile up so many achievements in so little time they make jaws drop. Reaching the unreachable star is just another goal to them: define the coordinates, determine exactly how to get there, and drive relentlessly forward. Along the way, their eagle eyes stay wide open, spotting problems no one else sees, and they correct their course continuously, until they reach that star in record time.

Alpha executors believe in three things: results, results, and results. And time is of the essence: they'll mobilize every available resource and seize every opportunity to get to the finish line under the wire. Highly accountable, they can be depended on to do exactly what they say they will, and maybe more. As leaders, they get the same reliable follow-through from others as well. "He understands how to get the best from his people," said one teammate of an executor boss. "He expects you to say, 'Wow that's really hard, but here are the eighteen actions I'm going to do to get it done.'"[1] In the hands of a healthy alpha executor who energizes people with a sense of mission, "What have you done for me today?" creates huge positives for the company, and also for coworkers whose confidence and capacities expand in the productive furnace. Executors can be demanding, but they pull the best out of people and earn not only their respect but also their gratitude.

Like Sherlock Holmes, executor alphas are superb diagnosticians, only instead of solving crimes they solve the riddle of the underlying causes of business problems and how to surmount them. In a haystack of facts and figures, they'll find the needle that's making things difficult. Sometimes, long before anyone else even knows there's a problem, they identify some tiny flaw and fix it. "I see a problem, and I step through it: What needs to be done? How do I bring people along to get it solved?" Kevin Rollins explained. Having worked toward an engineering degree before veering into business, he still thinks of himself as an engineer. "I click ahead fifteen to twenty steps, and predict outcomes based on the data. Then I think through all the steps required to accomplish what needs to happen."

Where others see a hodgepodge of information, alpha executors decipher meaningful patterns, and what others resent as tedious they view as absolutely essential. For them, details represent vital steps in the trajectory of accomplishment. Each one that's checked off the to-do list brings them closer to the goal, and that applies not only to their own tasks but to those of their team members as well. Rollins compares it to taking out the garbage. "The fun stuff is the high-level strategy," he says. "But the reason they call it work and not play is that you have to take out the garbage sometimes, or you never execute your big vision." When managed well, this penchant for detail is an enormously powerful asset shared by top-notch leaders in all walks of life, from athletic coaches to heads of state. In an article for *Newsweek* on the traits of great U.S. presidents, historian Jon Meacham included "Know the details," explaining that "grasping the essence of what others do enables you to ask the right questions and can communicate a sense of security to others who may at times feel overwhelmed or anxious."[2]

By knowing the nuances of everyone's job, healthy alpha male executors can teach others how to deal with the key elements of their work and provide them with precise, unambiguous directions, whether it's working out a manufacturing and distribution process or designing kickoff returns that suit the strengths of their players. Bill Belichick, a recognized genius who has led the New England Patriots to three Super Bowl championships, is just such a master of minutiae. "He's got great attention to detail and he doesn't ever really let us get away with anything," quarterback Tom Brady told the *Los Angeles Times*.[3]

High-functioning alpha executors teach, mentor, and model both discipline and capability. Generous with their time and attention, they give people the feedback they need, accurately acknowledging their strengths and creating just the right level of performance anxiety to kick them into action without terrifying them. They let people know where they stand, and because they're impeccably accountable themselves, they can convincingly hold others to a high level of personal responsibility. Even when employees' work is criticized, they sense that the executor's motivation is to help them be the best they can be.

Healthy alpha executors model accountability. No scapegoating, blaming, or excuse-making for them. Every manager and executive at Dell, for example, is committed to spotting problems early, taking responsibility for finding solutions, and keeping their agreements, even with something as seemingly trivial as replying promptly to e-mail. The respect and trust this commitment brings enables those executors to wield power constructively. People want to succeed for them. And in this age of ethical breaches, alpha executors who live and breathe accountability keep their organizations grounded in integrity and higher purpose.

Most companies love having alpha executors around. What's not to love? They're pillars of responsibility, they're willing to give their all for good old Anything Inc., and they're among the most competent breeds on the planet. They blaze with such productive splendor, however, that their flaws often go undetected until there is a great deal of debris to clean up.

The Problem with Alpha Executors

After working for some years at a company with alpha executor leadership, a client of ours absorbed the corporate culture. "I learned to dig deep into the details to make sure all the small things got done," he said. "But in the process I became more critical of myself." Therein lies one of the executor's downside risks. In looking for problems like exterminators and diagnosing them like X-ray technicians, they often lose sight of what is working well. As table 6-1 illustrates, they become their own—and everyone else's—worst critic, and their incredible ability to drive success ends up driving people up a wall and their projects into dead ends. The box "The Data on Alpha Executors" summarizes our study's findings for this type.

TABLE 6-1

The executor syndrome: When strengths become liabilities

Alpha attribute	Value to organization	Risk to organization
Accountable and dependable	Tracks responsibilities; follows up to ensure commitments are kept; holds others accountable	Micromanages; doesn't create accountability in others
Results focused; high standards for output and completion	Energizes and actively helps team to reach aggressive goals; gets the most out of people	Expects the impossible; afraid to celebrate achievements; frequently disappointed in others; maintains life/work imbalance
Detail oriented, with a clear plan	Focuses on the steps that lead to success; understands the nuances of everyone's job	Gets overly involved in others' work; doesn't see big picture; doesn't explain priorities and rationale
Persistent; pushes for closure and action	Smashes obstacles to move organization forward; willing to take unpopular stand to get results	Drives self and others to exhaustion; gets impatient; stifles creativity and creates mistakes; finishes unnecessary projects; burns out early
Able to see what's missing	Proactively spots problems and adjusts; prevents things from getting worse	Criticizes and demeans people; fails to appreciate others' contributions; demotivates people
Disciplined and efficient; and expects that of others	Acknowledges accomplishments yet creates enough performance anxiety to drive results	Focuses more on punishment than appreciation; creates fear and self-protective behavior
Direct communication style	Makes sure everyone knows where they stand; team operates without hidden agendas	Comes across as biting, sarcastic, and personal; causes resentment and rebellion
Strong need for stimulation	Brings curiosity and sense of exploration to work; engages tasks with passion; gets a lot done in a short amount of time	Easily bored; finds problems where none exist; lashes out at minor infractions; makes everything urgent

The Data on Alpha Executors

O ur study found a strong link between executor strengths and executor risks. (See table B-1, appendix B.) Although there are many exceptions, the chances are that if you enjoy the assets of an alpha executor you also carry the weight of that type's liabilities—and if you're fortunate enough to score *low* in the risks, you're probably *un*fortunate enough to lack the advantages. It seems that the executor's endowment of detail-driven tenacity and high-energy dependability typically comes with side effects, like micromanaging, impatience, and burnout.

As expected, all three risk themes—competitiveness, impatience, and anger—correlated with executor risks. Of the three, anger and impatience had the strongest association. (See table B-3, appendix B.)

The High Cost of Executor Urgency

When executors are out of balance, they're critical, impatient, and unrelenting. Constantly in a state of urgency, they are never satisfied— not with their own success, their staff's performance, or their company's profits. Led by the noble intention to cross the finish line as quickly as possible, these Action Jacksons falsely equate speed with success. In their haste, they kill creativity, mix up priorities, and cause mistakes that lead to wheel-spinning and a pileup of incompletions. Dysfunctional alpha male executors can get so obsessed with checking items off their to-do lists that they don't think clearly about what's *on* the lists. Because they define their mission as getting everything finished, they end up finishing things that don't need to be done.

Naturally, their hard-driving manner and relentless oversight make unhealthy executors perfect villains in the alpha triangle. For example, a client of ours named Larry had a high-risk persona he named Speedo. Like many alpha male executors, he was constantly pushing the accelerator on his own schedule and insisting that everyone else keep pace.

He especially hated tedious presentations packed with nonessentials. You could practically hear his synapses firing away as he tuned out long-winded colleagues and fidgeted like a kid in a classroom who can't wait for the recess bell to ring. Sometimes he'd interrupt, or ostentatiously signal the person to hurry up, or even call out, "You have one minute to get to the point." Once he actually walked up to a presenter's computer, clicked past two dozen slides and said, "Start here."

In his mind, Larry was simply moving things along. But his impatience invariably diverted the group's focus from making important decisions to dealing with the villain. When we told him that people felt intimidated and were terrified of being embarrassed in front of the team, he responded defensively: "You think I should allow them to drone on about nothing and waste fifteen people's time? You want me to be soft on performance?" Paul Bell, a senior VP at Dell, calls the flaw in such reactions a problem of "false opposites." In an effort to justify an entrenched position, the person argues as if the other extreme were the only alternative. It's a common defense mechanism among dysfunctional alpha executors.

We made it clear that Larry had a choice: he could continue to drive people crazy, or he could take responsibility as a leader and train his team to make more effective presentations. Option one made him feel like a victim whom others saw as a villain. Option two gave him more influence and more control, which are advantages that alpha males normally seek. By choosing the second option, Larry opted out of the triangle. He replaced the Speedo persona with the patient wisdom of Yoda. Not every alpha male executor makes that choice, unfortunately, and some don't even know it's an option.

How Executors Become Accountability Cops

Healthy executors are accountability coaches; unhealthy executors who don't know how to coach or delegate are accountability *cops*—micromanagers who lurk over everyone's shoulder, ready to pounce on the slightest mistake. Instead of modeling rigorous oversight, they become some combination of FBI agent and smothering parent. Their insistent scrutiny can make the most confident person paranoid. See those peo-ple whispering while casting a wary eye around the office? They're probably whining about an out-of-control alpha male executor. The most dysfunctional executors hold everyone accountable but them-selves. They take pride in being straight shooters, convinced that their leatherneck bluntness is in the other person's best interest. "Someday they'll thank me for being tough on them," they'll say. But what they call constructive feedback comes across as biting, sarcastic, and pain-fully personal, sowing the seeds of resentment and rebellion among their triangle victims.

Often, when things go awry, alpha executors shift from villain to hero. Because of those slackers who are not willing to work late, and those myopic colleagues who fail to see the urgency of getting things done *now*, the poor executor has to cancel dinner with his wife or miss his kid's school play so he can get the job done single-handedly while microwaving pizza at his desk. Then, at the end of the day that he thinks he's saved, he feels like a victim. Executors can leap from villain to hero to victim so fast that the roles seem to blur.

Healthy alpha executors examine themselves with the same scrutiny they apply to others. The dysfunctional ones do not regard other people as worthy of the same respect they demand for themselves. They believe that most people lack their sterling qualities: drive, endurance, and a willing-ness to sacrifice; an uncanny ability to see into the heart of problems; and a knack for fashioning solutions out of whole cloth. Because alpha male ex-ecutors *are* exceptional in those ways, they struggle with their coworkers, like gifted athletes who become coaches and can't get ordinary players to see what they see. Here are three 360° assessments about an unhealthy alpha executor who gave himself the persona name Luke Rebuke:

> "Working for him is better than going to business school, but you don't want to let him down. When he gets frustrated, his tone gets edgy and his body language becomes threatening."

> "It would be a lot more bearable if he stroked you when you do something good, but all you get is a quick 'Nice work,' followed by a lecture on how to do it even better next time."

"I like working with someone who lets you know exactly what he thinks, but sometimes I want to crawl into a hole. He launches into tirades, piling one criticism on top of another. No matter how many times I've been on the receiving end, I still feel like a worthless failure. When people see this side of him, they clam up and conceal their problems."

The alpha executor's fatal managerial flaws are impatience, contempt for the less gifted, and the mistaken assumption that sticks motivate better than carrots. People often acquiesce to their demands out of sheer exhaustion. But "yes" is no guarantee of follow-through, so the executor ends up feeling unsupported, let down, or betrayed—a classic villain-to-victim two-step.

The pattern is often compounded by the alpha male's indifference to the personal touch. Friendliness and warmth seem beside the point, or even "soft," to many executors. Some can be so harsh they should be called alpha executioners, not executors. The same Bill Belichick whose penchant for detail we described earlier might be an example; he is said to be as cold toward the Patriots' players as their stadium in January. "He concluded as a beginning coach that it is a fatal error to become friends with his players," writes Robert Hogan of Hogan Assessment Systems in "Anomalous Leadership."[4] Hogan contends that Belichick blew his first opportunity as an NFL head coach because his players hated him for treating them harshly. "Belichick outperforms his competition because he is smarter and harder working than they are, and he appears to believe that treating his players with respect would give him no competitive advantage in that business." That's a typical alpha executor stance: creating a great system and executing a great plan are all that matter; relationships with people are a nonfactor.

Perhaps Belichick softened in his attitude before he started winning Super Bowls, or maybe running a football team is an exception to the rule, but in today's business world getting results is definitely related to treating people well. We've seen remarkable turnarounds among alpha male executors who are willing to come in from the cold and change how they behave toward coworkers at every level.

When Dell's Kevin Rollins saw that his impersonal treatment of others was impeding their output, he accepted the challenge. What convinced him were comments like these in his early 360s in 1996 and 1997:

> "Kevin is a steamroller. He constantly questions my judgment. It makes me start to question my worth."

> "He's too authoritarian. He ignores people who aren't equally strong, and he intimidates the junior people."

> "He doesn't get people on board. He needs to take the time to work the relationship."

> "He's so accusatory in driving accountability that people shut down and get defensive."

To his credit, Kevin acknowledged his downside in his own self-assessment: "People might feel that they have a cold, mechanical relationship with me, rather than a personal connection where they can confide in me and trust me to look out for them."

A few years later, his 360° reports were consistently like these:

> "He's moved the needle to the human side. He asks about my family, and he's genuinely interested in me. People are always impressed by Kevin's intellect. What he doesn't always get credit for is his warmth, and the way he invests himself at a personal level."

> "He dramatically changed his style. Because he no longer sounds sharp and irritated, people aren't so resistant to his astute content. Everyone always had deep regard for his knowledge of business, his strategic thinking, and his remarkable prowess in driving execution, but now he's widely respected for his leadership of people."

> "In the past, he would argue with you, no matter how valid your point. Today he listens, he asks questions to explore my thinking, then he builds on my ideas and works with me to improve my thinking. I feel like I'm more of a team member now, instead of just jumping to his orders."

"I used to go into a meeting thinking Kevin's going to hammer me about what I hadn't done. Now he gets his points across in a respectful way. We can have a positive interaction about the problems and what we're doing to fix them, without anyone feeling beat up on."

By moving from a Head Honcho persona to a Coach persona, Kevin was able to contribute even more to the Dell success story than he had before. Looking back, he says, "Some years ago I realized that I was a really nice guy at home and with my friends, and I decided to bring that same person to work. I wanted people to respect me, not to be afraid of me. It's paid off in much more satisfying and higher-quality relationships and a smoother road to the end results I want."

How Alpha Executors Cause Burnout

Add to the unhealthy alpha executor's control freak tendencies a pinch of unrealistic deadlines and a generous portion of reprimands for those who don't work at warp speed, and you get managers who become the butt of nicknames, jokes, and parodies. One was portrayed in an office skit as "Ol' Kick 'Em and Love 'Em," because he'd blast people and then try to soften the blow with ostentatious displays of caring.

When people don't feel supported, they don't grow, which is exactly the opposite of what executors have in mind. They *want* to coach excellence, but their noble intention gets thwarted by their propensity for being dissatisfied; their useful messages drown in a torrent of criticism. People can't sort the wheat from the chaff when they're chafing from blistering comments. As they work defensively, and perhaps work on their résumés as well, their performance stagnates—which only reinforces the alpha executor's mistrust. And dysfunctional executors make matters even worse by displaying contempt for those who can't handle their withering remarks.

Ironically, it's alpha male executors themselves who don't handle criticism well. Constructive feedback triggers a red alert from their internal Department of Homeland Security. Out come the first responders: long-winded explanations, lectures filled with facts and data, subtle blame shifting, and investigative action to ferret out the traitors. They have the typical alpha male attitude that anyone who complains about them is weak and defensive, but *they're* just telling the truth. Only when they realize that their own defensiveness interferes with the achievement of their goals can they begin to listen to well-meaning feedback.

For unhealthy alpha male executors, nothing is ever quite right and enough is never enough. Their remarkable persistence flips into obstinacy and obsession, and their admirable dedication turns into workaholism. They never even stop to celebrate achievements for fear of losing their edge. They might promise their spouses and doctors that they'll slow down, but when push comes to shove they'll offer themselves up on the altar of accomplishment. Because their motto is "I produce, therefore I am," they seek personal validation through their work. For many, even vacations are dominated by detailed checklists. The constant adrenalin rush makes them feel alive, but as we'll see in chapter 8, it's a serious health hazard.

When they realize they're about to hit the wall, alpha male executors slip into victim mode. Rather than recognize that their burdens are self-imposed, they blame the problem on the incompetence of those around them or the demands of higher-ups. Usually, though, they're moving so fast they can't see the warning signs of breakdown—until their star performers leave for greener pastures, or chest pain kicks in, or they come home to find their spouse packing a suitcase. Making matters worse, their behavior patterns can be so entrenched, and their self-esteem so dependent on constant achievement, that they're terrified of making the necessary changes.

Unfortunately for those who work with alpha male executors, their workaholic ways can be contagious. Because it's hard to say no to them, they often leave behind a trail of burnouts.

When Kate was vice president of human resources at KLA-Tencor, her top employee, an HR generalist named Kristen, resigned to take a position at another company. To Kate's astonishment, the new job was an hourly position as a benefits coordinator—the same job Kristen had three years earlier at KT, before her rapid series of promotions. Now, feeling burned out, she opted for less money, less status, and less stress. For Kate, it was a revelation. Because Kristen had been such a high performer, Kate had invested in her future, giving Kristen what she herself would have wanted: more responsibility and more opportunities to excel. But Kristen was not Kate. And that is exactly the misjudgment many alpha executors make: they think that everyone is as driven as they are.

Female Alpha Executors

Women who are alpha executors seem to be just as results driven and as detail oriented as the men. They are just as keen at spotting problems and finding amazing solutions. But we've observed a number of differences. Where alpha males issue detailed directives, women are more likely to drop hints and to give people license to create their own processes. Women might micromanage, but they generally try to cajole or persuade rather than to harass or threaten. They can be fault-finders too, but they're more likely to express their criticism in subtle, even silent ways. In *You Just Don't Understand*, linguist Deborah Tannen reports that female managers tactfully sugarcoat their negative feedback, while men usually dispense with niceties and deliver the blow directly.[5]

Because of that tendency to soften their messages, when alpha women intend to issue a clear directive the people on the receiving end—especially alpha males—often take it as a mere suggestion. When, as a result, that directive isn't followed, the female alpha executor is likely to respond by becoming more forceful and persistent. Depending on her communication style, that escalation can lead to her being labeled in stereotypical ways— as a nag, as pushy, or as having "sharp elbows."

These kinder, gentler differences in style can earn alpha executor women a great deal of loyalty and appreciation. When taken too far, however, the same traits make it harder for women to enforce standards. Conflict-avoidant male managers also have that problem, of course, but not many of them are alphas.

Executor Tools

The COO at a dot-com (we'll call him Doug) is a detail-oriented alpha executor who excels at processes, follow-up, tracking, and control. His ability to fully engage people in completing the massive number of steps required to complete a project complements the style of the company's CEO, a visionary alpha who is a master motivator and direction setter. When we conducted a 360° assessment for Doug, we heard admiring comments such as these:

> "He gets an incredible amount of work out of us with his tenacity and his 'can-do' attitude."

> "Doug is relentless, but he understands our limitations and is extremely fair and supportive in terms of resources."

> "He uses meticulous project management to run the infrastructure like a finely tuned watch."

Others called him trustworthy and principled. But even superstars have developmental needs, and Doug was no exception. Because he was so focused on his checklists, he got everything done without stopping to consider what was *worth* doing. And he was so focused on performance details that people were often fuzzy about the rationale behind their tasks. "We end up implementing without sufficient clarity about what we're doing and why," said one team member. Hence, priorities were often out of whack and the team was not properly aligned with Doug's intentions. Disconnects like that are typical in teams led by alpha male executors. Another common pattern was captured in this comment: "Doug believes he's the only one who can do things the right way, so he delegates tasks and then takes them back. We don't get to learn from our mistakes." Stingy with appreciation and recognition, he also had the classic alpha executor allergy to feedback; at the mere hint of constructive criticism, he would assume a defensive posture.

Over time, Doug altered his tasking and tracking techniques to give others more leeway and responsibility. He also learned to express positive feedback and to *receive* critical feedback from others. All of which enabled him to accomplish what he valued—accountability, efficiency, and process-driven results—without the negative side effects of the alpha male executor syndrome. The following sections will help you do the same.

Don't Bite Off More Than You Can Chew

Imagine that a baseball manager grabs the ball from a pitcher who's getting clobbered and takes over the mound himself. That's how alpha male executors try to make up for shortfalls in other people's performance. They take on more than their fair share, often driving themselves harder than they drive others. Here's the typical sequence: alpha executor pushes people too hard; his inflated expectations are not met; his people ask questions; he gets impatient and shames them for not doing a better job; he takes over and does it himself. In short, he becomes an alpha triangle unto himself—villain, victim, and hero all rolled into one.

Alpha male executors *love* to be heroes. Like lost drivers who refuse to stop and ask for directions, they won't ask for help, no matter how overworked they are, because they don't feel they can count on anyone to come through. Only *they* can be trusted to get the job done. Here are comments from Kevin Rollins's 360 in 1996:

> "He is turning into an 'iron man,' where he tries to do everything himself, even though he's worn out."

> "I don't know how he keeps up his pace. He's pushing very, very hard, and this frankly worries me. How long can he keep it up?"

According to Kevin, "If they couldn't do it, I would take over, because I liked solving problems, and with my level of authority I could get things to happen really fast. After a while I realized that this was killing me." Not only was it burning him out, it was damaging the confidence of the people whose tasks he took over. After recognizing this alpha executor liability, he learned it was more effective to work with people and to coach them to be more effective.

If you're an alpha executor, it is imperative to accept your limits, and equally imperative to learn the fine art of delegating. The first step is to recognize when your sense of responsibility exceeds 100 percent. The next step is to get others to take *their* full share of the load. Delegating properly might mean developing an entirely new set of influence skills: infusing others with a sense of mission, getting them fully aligned with your execution plan, and holding them accountable for achieving the desired results.

Create Accountability

On Friday, August 13, 2004, a headline in the *San Jose Mercury News* read, "HP Drops Profit Bombshell, Fires Execs."[6] At a time when some of its competitors were doing bang-up business, Hewlett-Packard announced a sharp decline in sales and profits for the preceding quarter. According to the article by Dean Takahashi, "Chief Executive Carly Fiorina blamed a series of internal missteps for the shortfall, which she called 'unacceptable.' She immediately fired three top executives." Fiorina also attributed some of the company's problems to "a slowing economy."

On that same day, as HP's stock plummeted by 13 percent, its chief rival, Dell, reported its highest revenues ever, with a quarterly increase in sales of 20 percent and a 29 percent leap in profits. Of course, when one company in the same industry soars as another sinks, the reasons are many and complex. One factor, however, was highlighted by Carly Fiorina's response to the crisis. She got angry, found people to blame, and made a public display of holding them accountable. That she herself might bear some of the responsibility was never acknowledged. Less than a year later, she was fired.

Compare that to what Michael Dell and Kevin Rollins called the "no-excuse culture" of Dell. At one point, Rollins announced that the company's total revenue for a particular quarter had fallen short of projections by a few hundred million dollars. As Gary Rivlin reported in the *New York Times*, there was no shortage of excuses and plausible explanations for Dell's leadership to draw upon: despite not meeting expectations, profits had actually risen 28 percent that quarter; industry-wide prices of personal computers had fallen in previous months; giant companies that dominate the market *always* find it challenging to increase revenues. Instead of falling back on those and other defenses, Kevin, who had been CEO for only a year, blamed himself. "We executed poorly on managing overall selling prices," he told analysts.[7] As consultants, we had witnessed a comparable moment in 2000, when the company reported its worst quarterly performance in many years. Instead of blaming the business unit presidents who'd failed to meet financial targets, Michael and Kevin claimed responsibility for having determined those targets erroneously. Their personal buck-stops-here attitude infuses the entire company with the spirit of accountability.

Accountability creates ownership, commitment, and determined action; nonaccountability leads to faultfinding, excuse making, confusion, and helplessness. And the best way to establish accountability in others is to model it yourself. How do you react to setbacks? Do you point fingers rather than asking, "How have I contributed to this?" Do you complain about things that are out of your control instead of working on what you *can* control? If so, you're falling into the alpha executor trap of looking outside yourself for the cause of problems. The slogan of truly accountable executives is "Claim, don't blame."

So, get into the habit of looking closely at how you may have contributed to whatever went wrong, and do it out loud. Ask your colleagues, "Could I have communicated my expectations more clearly? Could I have done more to help you understand the assignment?" (Figure 6-1 suggests other questions you can use to test your accountability.) Your staff might be so shocked at your questions that you'll have to wait until they get up off the floor, but once they realize you're sincere they'll follow your lead and become more open about their own mistakes. Accountability is contagious.

FIGURE 6-1

Questions that invite accountability

Ask yourself the following questions when results don't meet your expectations:

- Do I create this problem again and again?
- How does my attitude or behavior keep this going?
- Have I seen this pattern before?
- Do I have an unexamined personal agenda?
- Is there anything I'd like to communicate but haven't?
- Have I broken or missed any agreements?
- What about this situation feels familiar?
- What can I learn from this situation?

Use Proactive Accountability. The following steps will help you create accountability by infusing clarity and directness into your business relationships.

1. *Request, don't demand.*

   Requests encourage creativity and collaboration; demands foster compliance or defiance. To avoid miscommunication, make clear, straightforward requests. Here's how:

   - State exactly what you want the person to do: "Jane, will you take the lead on creating a project map?"

   - Describe the reasons for the request: "We need clear time lines to bring structure to this project."

   - Communicate the desired time frame for completion: "I'd like to have something on my desk by Friday."

2. *Make sure you get a clear response.*

   The response should fit into one of these categories:

   - *Accept:* "I'll be glad to do it for you."

   - *Decline:* "Sorry, but I can't do that for you."

   - *Counteroffer:* "I can complete this for you on time, but only if I reschedule a customer visit."

   - *Negotiated delivery:* "I can't get it done by Friday. How about next Monday?"

   It's imperative to allow people an honest "no" or a counteroffer when they don't think they can pull off what you're requesting. Putting into place a more realistic plan is preferable to a "yes" that's sure to create problems downstream.

3. *Make clear, unambiguous agreements.*

   Clear agreements foster integrity; integrity is central to commitment; and commitment is the cornerstone of execution. Here are the bare essentials:

- *Avoid compliance.* It's easier *not* to make an agreement than to get out of one you can't keep.

- *Establish clarity.* Don't assume everyone heard the same thing. State the terms of the agreement in precise, unmistakable language.

- *Put it in writing.* Send an e-mail that spells out exactly what you agreed to.

4. *If you can't keep it, renegotiate.*

   If you need to change an agreement, take a deep breath, tell the truth, and try to generate a win-win solution.

5. *Mend broken agreements quickly.*

   If you or someone else breaks an agreement, fully acknowledge what has occurred and immediately address the source of the breakdown.

Offer Straight Talk and Feedback

We've seen how vital it is to claim your share of responsibility. It's equally important to get other people to own *their* share. The key is feedback, and the key to feedback is direct, candid, but tactful communication. Alpha male executors are pretty good with the first two, but tact is often a foreign language to them. They tend to drive their point home so hard that people feel dominated and intimidated. Instead, try to describe your concerns in a way that stimulates change without damaging the person's confidence or undermining his trust in you. It's really quite simple. Figure 6-2 outlines the basics.

Giving feedback the right way is one thing. *What* you say and *when* you say it is another, and the key to that is consistency. In their book *Dog and Human Behavior*, C. W. Meisterfeld and Ernest Pecci describe an experiment in which a cage is divided into two equal sections, one empty and one housing lab mice. When given mild shocks, the mice quickly learn to cross into the safe zone. "So long as this is consistent, the mice appear to be minimally disturbed by the inconvenience," write

FIGURE 6-2

The art of feedback

1. **Ask the person if he is willing to hear your feedback.** This sets the stage for openness to learning, not mere compliance.

2. **State the bare facts.** Explain what happened as you see it, describing the specific behavior and results as nonjudgmentally as possible.

3. **Describe your reaction, using "I" statements.** Focus on *your* experience, separating your interpretations from the observed facts.

4. **Own your contribution.** Look at how you might have contributed to the problem and declare your willingness to take responsibility.

5. **Listen consciously as the other person reacts.** Don't try to convince him that your point of view is correct. The object is to learn together, not to win an argument. If he becomes defensive, make sure you stay curious and open, and don't respond by becoming defensive yourself.

6. **Make a request.** Clearly state what you'd like him to do in the future to prevent the situation from repeating itself.

7. **Get a clear response to your request.** If you don't get clear agreement, continue to work the issue until you reach agreement.

8. **Agree on changes.** Translate your input and insights into action.

---

the authors. "However, start administering the shocks randomly and inconsistently, and the mice will soon huddle helplessly in a corner, gradually ignoring the shocks."[8] Alpha male executors, who are notorious for giving inconsistent feedback, can drive people as crazy as those mice. Employees rely on knowing the rules. If you're inconsistent, they'll always be wondering how to make you happy, which is obviously not as productive as doing a great job based on clear performance standards.

Learn the Art of Positive Reinforcement

Modifying behavior is simple: if something we do leads to rewards, we do it again; if something produces pain or punishment, we avoid repeating it. Alpha male executors focus almost exclusively on the second form of reinforcement; they ferret out wrong behavior and attempt to eliminate it with punishment. Here are some 360° comments about one such executor:

> "It's hard for Martin to give a purely positive comment. He can never finish one without a 'but' at the end. Our running joke is that we get to feel good for thirty seconds."

"He's so insatiable about performance that he constantly raises the bar. This is the only job I've had where I've felt I can't meet the boss's expectations."

"It's great that he focuses on what's not working, and that we don't hide problems. But it would be nice if he could also acknowledge our progress."

"When I walk away from a meeting with Martin, I think differently about business problems. I feel challenged, but I don't feel good about myself."

Alpha executors not only take competence for granted, they also think that praise will cause people to lose their edge or rest on their laurels. In our estimation, more than 90 percent of their comments can be construed as criticism. The result is a double whammy to motivation, because (1) positive behavior is not reinforced and (2) people take the lack of acknowledgment as punishment. Instead of trying harder, they think, "Why bother?"

"Constructive criticism" can be downright *destructive*, as alpha executors often discover in the wreckage of their blame-fests. Consider the results of this study: tell a group of adults that they did poorly on a puzzle-solving test and their performance gets worse on the next try; tell them they did well, *even if they didn't*, and their performance improves significantly. Clearly, if improvement is your aim, appreciation should be your game. The cost-benefit ratio is impressive: How many things can you think of that take only a minute or two, make everyone involved feel great, produce a variety of positive results, and cost absolutely nothing?[9]

Alpha executors often tell us they *want* to balance their corrective feedback with positive validation, but they don't know *how*. The basic answer is: try anything, as long as it's sincere. If the person continues to perform well, it's a good bet that your reinforcement worked. If it doesn't, try a different reward. Just don't do *nothing*. Here are some specific tips:

Look for things to appreciate. Develop the habit of finding something to praise. Once you shift your focus, you'll be surprised at how much you find—and the effect it has on you and the people around you.

Appreciation should fit the behavior. While it's important to be generous with your praise, make sure it's commensurate with the actual achievement. If you celebrate routine competence the same way you celebrate spectacular achievements, you will only diminish the impact of both.

Don't mix messages. Alpha male executors are so used to correcting errors that they can't help themselves even when they're dispensing praise. Don't say "Nice job" only to add, "Next time, try to . . ." or "But you can do it even better if you . . ." The qualifiers are heard as criticism.

Be explicit. You might think you're sending appreciation signals when no such message is getting through. We had worked with one executive for nearly 40 hours over several months when we realized that we didn't know if he found our coaching useful. When we asked, he was dumbfounded. "Of course I'm getting benefit," he exclaimed. "Why else would I spend all this time with you?" What was obvious to him was not obvious to us. We pointed out that if we, as consultants, didn't know we were appreciated, his team probably felt even more uncertain. Don't wait for such a wake-up call. Face it, your employees are not thinking, "I haven't been fired, so he must appreciate me." They need to be told, and "Good job" is usually not enough.

Be systematic. Do what alpha executors do so well: create a system. Maintain an appreciation portfolio for everyone you work with. Each time you catch someone adding special value or improving on past performance, make a note in their file. Then, at an appropriate time, share what you noticed with the person. Update your portfolio regularly and refer to it often, so you're always prepared to express appreciation.

How to Work with Alpha Executors

When working with alpha executors, it is vital to make clear, unequivocal agreements. Ask pointed questions to make sure their expectations are unambiguous and the details they want you to deal with are spelled out explicitly. Leave nothing to the imagination, including *your* requests. Once you think an agreement has been made, communicate your understanding of it clearly, and always create a paper or e-mail trail, especially if the executor is too impatient to fully discuss these matters in person.

Above all, hold yourself to the highest level of personal accountability. It's very easy to slip into the victim role when you're being badgered by an impatient control freak. No matter how obsessive a dysfunctional alpha male executor is, or how much he hassles you with nitpicky corrections, don't turn him into a villain. The best way to get executors off your back is to get clear on what they want and take responsibility for doing your job with excellence. If you see alpha executors as your teachers, you can learn a great deal from them.

Those are the basic "do's" of working with alpha executors. Here's an important "don't": don't try to reassure them. They translate "Trust me" as "You better keep an eye on that person," and "Don't worry" means "Caution, danger ahead." If you want to drive an alpha male executor into paranoid, obsessive micromanagement, just let out a vague comment like, "I'll take care of that," without adding a clear plan, detailed notes, or any other way to indicate a strong commitment to follow up. The result will be the opposite of what you intend: instead of relaxing, the executor will become *more* vigilant.

Rather than give him empty reassurance, listen carefully to his concerns, ask detailed questions, and find out exactly why he's worried that you won't meet your commitments. Then give him concrete reasons why he *doesn't* need to worry. Provide specific details about your plan of action and your progress to date. And don't wait to be asked for updates; beat him to the punch and communicate regularly. Remember, alpha male executors don't necessarily want to control you; they want to know that you're in control.

This ends our survey of the four alpha types. By now you should know the strengths and risks of your dominant type and how your secondary traits factor in to your leadership style. You should also have a clearer understanding of the alphas with whom you work. In the next chapter, we'll examine what happens when alpha males are thrown together in teams.

ACTION STEPS

If you're an alpha executor:

- Claim, don't blame: be accountable and hold others accountable.

- Learn the art of creating—and modeling—accountability.

- Don't confuse bluntness with candor: state the truth without bludgeoning people.

- Ask, don't demand. Make clear, unambiguous requests.

- Make clear agreements, and follow up in writing.

- Balance constructive feedback with appreciation.

- Learn to coach: you'll get more out of people by teaching than by dictating.

If you work with or for an alpha executor:

- Stay out of the victim role.

- Take 100 percent responsibility for everything in your sphere of influence.

- Don't take criticism personally, and don't get defensive.

- Avoid explanations and reassurances; they provoke more policing behavior.

- Focus on what you can learn from his feedback, ignoring the way it's delivered.

- Take steps to protect yourself from burnout.

7

The Alpha Male Team

The Club Where Everyone
Wants to Be in Charge

If you want to see teamwork that's greater than the sum of its parts, watch a women's basketball game. If you want to see teams as they actually exist in alpha-driven organizations, watch *The Apprentice*. Like many real-life leaders, the TV program pays lip service to teamwork, but in reality seldom upholds the principle. What we see instead is the law of the jungle with Donald Trump as the dominant alpha male. The message is one that celebrates rugged individualism, cutthroat competition, and looking out for number one. Team members are encouraged to contend with each other for dominance, and conflict is not only tolerated but valued and sometimes even instigated. The show's winner-take-all philosophy produces good entertainment, but in today's matrixed environments, where collaboration and partnership are necessities, it makes for a dysfunctional workplace.[1]

In an article that concludes by giving Trump a D in leadership, Henry P. Sims Jr., of the University of Maryland's Robert H. Smith

School of Business, highlights what happened when an *Apprentice* contestant waived his immunity from being fired, a right he'd earned on the previous show by leading his team to victory.[2] He thought the gesture would enhance *esprit de corps*. Perhaps it did, but his team lost nonetheless. Was the candidate rewarded for his selfless deed? No way! "You're fired!" said Trump, who excoriated the young man for his "weakness." How would Trump's reaction play in real life? Sims said it would be "an act of madness" because "getting people to put the larger team above their own personal self-interest is one of the real keys to success for most any business."[3]

The Apprentice is a great example of what goes wrong with teams when alphas run amok. The syndrome boils down to these factors:

- Alpha males see themselves as high-impact players who influence others by driving and directing, not by collaborating and conferring. They fail to realize that their battlefield style might make sense during actual warfare, but that military *strategizing* is actually a model of collaboration, as it must be in business organizations.

- As youngsters, many alpha males were star players on sports teams, a heady experience that they try to recapture as adults. Healthy alphas learn that true stars shine even brighter on a winning team; others hog the ball and put themselves above the team.

- As team leaders, alpha males tend to overpower everyone else. Conversations flow from them to individuals, one person at a time, with very little interaction among the players.

- Many teams dominated by alpha males split in half, with talkers and influencers on one side and nontalkers and noninfluencers on the other. By monopolizing the group's energy, alphas diminish the contributions of less assertive members.

- Because of their brilliance and charisma, alpha males are often great at drawing people to their teams. But because they need to dominate, they find it difficult to join another leader's team and fit in.

Alpha Males as Team Players—or Not

Most companies haven't fully tapped the human potential in teams," Robert Shapiro, the former chairman and CEO of Monsanto once told us. "If you could get every person to be 30 percent more effective in performing their jobs, not by working harder and not by working smarter in ways that have already been tapped, but by becoming 30 percent more effective in working *together*, you'd be way ahead of your industry."[4]

As Shapiro indicated, a well-functioning team can produce far more than the sum of its individual parts. But, he added, "In all my years of working with people, I've noticed that they are often great individually, but if you put five of them together, you rarely end up with more than the sum of the parts. One plus one plus one plus one plus one doesn't even equal five. Instead, you end up with a sum of two and a half, or three if you're lucky. What's required isn't more effort, but a new way of working together."

Both the immense potential and the enormous challenges of teamwork are magnified when the players are alpha males. As every sports fan knows, a team of superstars whose primary ethic is selfless teamwork can be unbeatable, whereas one filled with me-firsters will collapse under the weight of its collective talent. Similarly, a collection of team-oriented alphas can produce business miracles, while a crew of dysfunctional alphas will tend toward self-destruction.

One of our clients, a VP in charge of a product services division at a high-tech firm, asked us for advice about a colleague who dominated every team interaction. "People are complaining," he told us. "Jim talks so much that no one else gets heard."

"What did he say when you talked to him about it?" we asked.

The VP was nonplussed. He had never even mentioned the problem to Jim. What's more, we learned, his own behavior in meetings had actually compounded the problem. He would pay close attention to Jim's comments, ask him questions, and laugh at his jokes—as did the rest of the group, when they weren't trying to get a word in edgewise. Without knowing it, the VP and the entire team had reinforced Jim's dominance at every turn.

Scenarios like that are very common in teams with strong alpha males. Alphas love to take control, and the other members play into their hands by paying more attention to them than to anyone else. Toss in a few more people like Jim and you get an alpha cacophony in which everyone else is drowned out, not just verbally but also in impact.

How Alpha Strengths Become Team Weaknesses

The take-charge energy of alpha males can ignite team members, enliven creative discussions, and drive productive action to new heights. But the same alphas can damage teams with impatient, judgmental, and self-serving behavior. Regardless of whether the team has a "tall structure," meaning there's an official leader, or a "flat structure" of peers, an unauthorized hierarchy often emerges, with the most aggressive alphas driving the agenda and setting the tone, even if they're not official team leaders. Taking control with their verbal weaponry, they silence other voices and never give a thought to what they're missing. They assume that those who don't speak up have nothing to say, when in fact they could be sitting on immensely valuable information and are too intimidated to open their mouths.

Alpha males who care about their teams and identify with the other members are the kind of people you want in the foxhole with you. They watch your back, they take personal risks for the common good, and they do whatever it takes for the team to win. Because they don't shrink from conflict, they make sure disagreements are aired and contrary views are expressed. When strife erupts, they move everyone toward a creative resolution. On the other hand, when alpha males put personal opportunism ahead of common objectives, the team's cohesion, trust, and unity of purpose fly out the window. Because alphas see their teammates as competitors, turf wars erupt in record time.

Healthy alpha male self-confidence makes it easy for others to embrace their recommendations and follow through gladly. But when it comes across as arrogant, that same quality alienates people. Unhealthy alphas get defensive, shut off debate prematurely, and refuse to explore ideas that contradict their own. When things go awry, they safeguard their reputations by blaming a teammate or another part of the organization. So strong is an alpha male's confidence that he can mislead an entire team by presenting his hunches as if they'd been published in a scientific journal. Kate once worked with an alpha male who was asked a question about a new technology. "I don't know a thing about it," he said, "but I have an opinion." He then delivered what sounded like a well-developed, logical position. When Kate asked him what factual evidence he had to back it up, he said with some pride, "None at all."

Alpha males with a strong team orientation respect the opinions of others even if they don't agree with them. To further the team's agenda, they air opposing views and courageously expose their own positions to scrutiny. On the other hand, self-serving alphas use their verbal skills to distort and disparage. Specializing in sarcastic zingers, they criticize excessively, draining the group's energy and silencing less aggressive members who might actually have the best ideas in the room.

The pluses and minuses of having alpha males on your team are summarized in table 7-1.

The Alpha Male Fight Club

Put a group of healthy alpha males together and stand back in awe while they pull fresh ingredients out of thin air and cook up gourmet ideas and mouthwatering visions. Put a dysfunctional combination together and witness *churn*. Instead of building on each other's ideas, they squabble over whose position should prevail. Instead of coalescing around solutions for the good of the organization, they close their minds and split into warring factions. Some alpha teams even battle over which issues require teaming in the first place. For some, the answer is essentially none. As a rule, unhealthy alpha males thrive on conflict. Whether it's a rugged boardroom debate or a friendly racquetball match, they love the adrenalin high of a good fight, and they always enter the ring believing they can score a knockout.

In business as in sports, internal sparring can have the paradoxical effect of solidifying the team against a common opponent. New York

TABLE 7-1

When alpha male strengths become team liabilities

Alpha attribute	Value to team	Risk to team
High achiever with sense of mission	Mobilizes energy; inspires every-one to march together and act in concert	Focuses on taking the hill and fails to get buy-in; drives self and others to exhaustion
Self-confident, takes charge	Takes command of meetings; stimulates bottom-line discus-sions; drives the team to action	Out-talks others; takes up too much space; gets impatient with brainstorming; criticizes leader if decisions are delayed
Strength of conviction	Comes across as believable; ar-gues convincingly; makes it easy to follow his recommendations	Gets defensive when challenged; creates churn in meetings by ar-guing his point too long
Persistent, tena-cious, determined, steadfast	Loves big challenges; over-comes obstacles; willing to take unpopular stand to get results	Pushes so hard he obliterates disagreement; thinks rules don't apply to him
Competitive, aggressive	Conveys a strong desire to win; pushes team to meet goals	Becomes overly competitive; causes internal conflict instead of focusing outward
Comfortable with conflict	Surfaces differences; ensures ideas are debated; drives resolu-tion and closure	Fuels arguments; sets up situa-tions with winners and losers; feeds distrust
Direct and forth-right	Presents authentic views and feelings; creates open relation-ships with team members	Criticizes aggressively and calls it candor; overshadows those who are less assertive
Smart, innovative thinker	Brings forth variety of different ideas	Generates more ideas than team can act on; generates compliance instead of creativity

Yankees owner George Steinbrenner, who once said winning was sec-ond in importance only to breathing, compared a tranquil team to a sailboat on a calm sea: "You never get anywhere." He prefers "a little bit of turmoil." Some might say that his franchise's unparalleled success proves Steinbrenner's point. Others might argue that (1) in professional sports an unmatched budget for talent goes a long way to make up for alpha male dysfunction, and (2) the Yankees' most successful periods came when "The Boss" butted out and let the experts do their jobs. Besides, conference rooms are not locker rooms; in business, excessive in-fighting destroys collaborative partnering and causes noncombatants to withhold their trust and respect.

Most important, excellent solutions become casualties in the battle for supremacy. With alphas defending their positions like goalies, creative interaction flies out the window. To many alpha males, win-win is so-so or a *no-no*. If they don't get their way, they either go along half-heartedly or withdraw. They fail to see the difference between compromise and collaboration. The former can certainly be a sellout, but the latter is a form of alchemy in which teammates build on each other's ideas and link together various options. What emerges from collaboration is something entirely different, and of far greater magnitude than simply selecting between two incomplete or inadequate options.

Groups of alpha males often begin in a spirit of healthy competition only to progressively lose perspective and turn a friendly scrimmage into a fight to the death. They go for the jugular in a debate that hardly merits an arm twist. Every team member needs to understand that both conflict seeking and conflict avoidance can create difficulties. Competition can be a great catalyst for learning and creativity, but it can also be an enormous waste of time and energy. Often, it leads to a buildup of team sludge that accumulates like crumbs at a breakfast meeting. (See the box "How Team Sludge Accumulates.") The symptoms include communication breakdowns, widespread mistrust, resistance to change, and chronic tension.

How Team Sludge Accumulates

In alpha-dominated teams, villains, victims, and heroes take the stage in various alpha triangles. Here are three typical scenarios:

Sludge Scenario 1. Glenn works hard to prepare a presentation, feeling confident that key team members agree with his approach. His presentation is interrupted by assertive alpha male villains, who pick his ideas apart like a Thanksgiving turkey. Feeling embarrassed, humiliated, and unsupported, Glenn the victim stops sharing his ideas. As resentment accumulates, his commitment to the team weakens, leaving various heroes to pick up the slack.

Sludge Scenario 2. During a meeting, Dave thinks Frank's approach is way off the mark. Since Frank is an alpha male who responds harshly to feedback, Dave holds back out of fear. Forgetting that he *chose* to withhold, he starts to feel as if he *had* to—a classic victim attitude. Eventually, the need to vent gets the best of him, so he complains behind Frank's back. Since the underlying problem is never resolved, the tension builds. To explain the situation, Frank makes up a story in which *he's* the victim and Dave is the villain. Their working relationship deteriorates further, and before long it spreads to others, who slip into the three positions in numerous alpha triangles.

Sludge Scenario 3. Matt disagrees with Al. But, fearing the wrath of alpha males who side with Al, he presents his case in a timid manner that conceals the strength of his conviction. The leader makes a decision with which Matt disagrees. Feeling like a victim after the meeting, he states his full case *privately* to the leader, who shifts in Matt's direction. At the next meeting, the new decision is announced. Feeling undermined and betrayed, Al—the new victim—sees villains everywhere and starts to watch his back. At one point, he slips into hero mode, maneuvering in stealth to save the day—as do other team members who suspect that deals were cut behind closed doors. The outcome? Time-wasting delays and reversals, costly inefficiencies in execution, and a growing atmosphere of distrust.

Unfortunately, a great many alpha male leaders find infighting so seductive that they send the game into overtime instead of blowing the whistle and leading their teams in a more productive direction.

How to Create High-Performance Teams

Getting alpha-dominated teams to work together at a high level of cohesiveness can be a formidable challenge, but the payoff is tremendous.

Table 7-2 describes the shift that takes place when leaders get alpha males to interact with their teams in a healthy, productive manner. The two left columns describe unhealthy alpha behaviors and their consequences; the two right columns describe healthy interactions using effective dialogue skills. As you read the chart, ask yourself the following questions:

- How does your team's current status compare with where you'd like it to be?

- What skills would enable you to move your team to a higher level?

- What measures will you take to develop those skills?

- How will you track your progress?

The following sections will help you move your team from the left side of the chart to the right by harnessing alpha male power for the good of your organization.

Put the Highest First

It's vital for everyone to place the good of the team before personal interest—and to hold them accountable for that commitment. This requires many alpha males to do things that go against their grain, like exposing their ideas to collective inquiry, sharing credit with people they see as adversaries, or treating strong performers as common resources rather than personal assets. But it can be done. Just as self-centered rogues can come together to win a ballgame, and scuffling soldiers can stand shoulder to shoulder against an enemy, fierce competitors in business suits can stop jostling for glory and build something none of them could accomplish on his own. The key is to keep team values and organizational goals constantly in sight as reference points. Here's how Kate described one such experience:

*On the Serengeti Plain, travelers come across the astonishing sight of
lions and zebras, antelopes and cheetahs drinking from a common
pool of water, having set aside their natural predator-prey relationships to quench their thirst. I was just as inspired by the sight of top
executives from six major semiconductor companies and their seven
major distributors working together to solve a mutual problem.*

*In the early 1990s, challenges facing the semiconductor industry,
chiefly from Japan, motivated these rivals to cooperate on reducing
costs and increasing productivity. The idea was to formulate industry
standards for exchanging data among suppliers and distributors. At
the time, some of the participants' companies were embroiled in contentious lawsuits. Others simply didn't like or trust each other. In the
first full-day meeting, one alpha male executive summed up the tense
atmosphere: "It's all well and good to try to collaborate, but the truth
is that tomorrow I'll want to kill some of you." Another equally strong
alpha put it in perspective: "People are people. Lawsuits are between
companies. We still have common goals."*

*These brilliant, highly competent leaders argued over what lan-
guage to use, what kind of data to generate, how to present it, and on
and on. But every point of contention was overridden by one central
factor: it was in the best interest of the industry to reach a conclusion
that every company could sign off on. In the end, they developed a
survey tool that fostered ongoing industrywide improvement.*

Get to Know Each Other

One reason teams fail to gel, or fall apart at the first appearance of difficulty, is that teammates don't really know each other. Teams with
dominant alpha males are especially prone to remaining strangers because many of them are interested in bonding only if they see an obvious personal benefit. They'll play golf with clients or have a beer with
someone who can help them advance, but they think hanging out with
peers is a waste of time or even a potential Achilles' heel. After all, being
buddy-buddy with a competitor might give the other guy a glimpse of
your weak spots.

TABLE 7-2

Unhealthy versus healthy alpha team leaders

Unhealthy alpha male leader	Resulting team behavior	Healthy alpha male leader	Resulting team behavior
Runs over others; impatient; creates excessive urgency	Team members are either competitive or passive	Drives hard, but delegates and creates personal and team accountability	Team is empowered; keeping agreements is highly valued
Issues commands and dictates solutions	Many team members are left out; leader operates from his agenda and talks to one individual at a time	Consults with team regarding problems and decisions; asks for and listens to input from whole group	Team dialogues openly, is innovative, solves problems efficiently and effectively
Dictates and controls every change	Team responds with passivity or resistance; lack of accountability prevents needed changes	Involves team in planning for change; fosters smooth collaboration	Team welcomes change; members engage fully and are flexible and adaptable
Has unrealistic expectations; opinionated, stubborn, and critical	Team members are defensive and offer limited input; individuals don't listen to each other	Gives constructive feedback and positive reinforcement; coaches and mentors team	Communication is direct; trust is high; people are receptive to development opportunities
Uses competition and conflict to see who comes out on top	Members compete with each other and manipulate behind the scenes; collaboration is low	Uses healthy debate to stimulate problem solving; encourages creativity	Team attacks issues, not each other; encourages people's best thinking
Conceals own vulnerabilities and weaknesses; doesn't admit mistakes	Team emulates leader, engaging in spinning and posturing; doesn't reveal the full truth	Owns mistakes and openly expresses developmental needs	Team communicates honestly, learns from mistakes, displays high level of trust
Hides own emotions and ignores feelings of others	Team discounts emotions; personal connection is superficial; cliques form	Pays attention to feelings; encourages fun that energizes the group	Members connect on a personal level to foster productive relationships

If you're truly interested in leading a Dream Team where victory transcends individual glory, trust the alchemy of human connection. We've seen it turn lead into gold countless times. On one memorable occasion, Kate was working with a team at Mentor Graphics at an offsite in the forests of Oregon. Housed in adjacent condos, the group spent the mornings working together on long-term business issues, then hiked together in the afternoons. Over dinner one night, the team discussed the next day's plan to ride Class V rapids on the Snake River. A man we'll call Ted remained stone silent as the others shared their excitement about the adventure. His face turned noticeably gray. Noticing his discomfort, Kate asked how he felt about the rafting trip. Ted took a big breath, then let it out with a gasp. "I nearly drowned when I was four years old," he said. "That's my very first memory, and it's terrifying to even think about it. Since that day, I've never been in the water."

Why hadn't he told anyone? "I was traveling when the decision was made to go rafting," he said. "I freaked out when I heard about it, but everyone was so excited I didn't say anything." He paused a moment, then added a stunner: "That's how I feel on this team: like I don't count."

His honesty had a powerful impact. To a person, the team agreed to cancel the river ride rather than leave Ted behind. But Ted insisted on moving forward. Kate had the group explore what it would take for Ted to feel safe. It was decided that the two best swimmers would stay close to him at every moment.

The next day, the group scaled the rapids together, landing on the riverbank safe, dry, and exhilarated. Because Ted had been courageous enough to open up about his fear instead of either backing off at the last minute or biting his tongue and toughing it out—in which case he might have caused a disaster by panicking at a crucial moment—the team came together in a deeply profound way. As a result, their work at the offsite rose to a markedly higher level. Subsequently, Ted became a strong player in the organization, and the team worked together productively for many years.

Get Aligned with Strong Agreements

On teams with powerful alpha males, perhaps no single act does more to enhance cohesion and trust than establishing governing principles for team interaction. The agreement serves as a reference point, reminding everyone of their highest intentions. They also provide a corrective mechanism when tensions arise; pointing out that someone has broken an agreement is far less likely to trigger defensiveness than saying you don't like what they did.

The following issues are important to address in formulating agreements:

Feedback and Learning

- Do we agree to be open to feedback and to learn from each other?

- Does everyone in the group have permission to offer feedback to anyone else?

- Do we place limits on the content, style, or timing of the feedback?

- What guidelines do we agree to follow when responding to critical feedback?

Healthy, Productive Debate

- How do we want to behave when differences of opinion arise?

- What guidelines for effective listening do we agree to follow?

Relationship Tension

- Should we establish procedures for conflict resolution?

- Are there any behaviors we wish to prohibit?

Accountability

- How should the group enforce these agreements?

- What will we do if someone is perceived to have broken one of them?

Give Them a 360° View

In a well-functioning team, each member fully owns how he or she affects the group and agrees to work on behavior that's having a negative impact. For alpha males, the key issues are their need to dominate and their tendency to compete with their peers. Other team members have to look at how they *react* to the strong alpha presence, particularly the tendency to withhold their contributions and to acquiesce. To foster the necessary self-awareness, we highly recommend garnering complete 360° assessments for everyone and sharing the results with the entire group. For many alpha males, the 360 is their first opportunity to see how their peers perceive them and how they impact their teams. Often, the epiphany is exactly what's needed to motivate change, and the positive results can reverberate throughout groups, divisions, and entire companies.

In the summer of 2004, Ken Schroeder announced that he would retire as the CEO of KLA-Tencor (KT) in about two years. When, a few months later, the presumptive heir left the company, Ken instituted a massive reorganization. One reason for the upheaval was to see how four particular executives would function in completely new roles. Ken explicitly declared it a competition to determine the next CEO, with the prime criterion being the candidate's team-building ability.

One of the contenders was Rick Wallace, an alpha who was a group VP at the time. Rick was not only put off by the contest, he was uneasy about his new assignment and displeased about leaving his previous team. He also believed that the next CEO would be an outside hire and not one of the presumed candidates. He agreed to stay on in what he described as *The Apprentice* meets *Survivor* because he felt his new responsibilities would be a useful building block for his next job. He focused on turning the customer group, which was now within his purview, into a high-performance team. To jump-start that effort, he scheduled an offsite, also inviting the services group, which was now led by John Kispert, the company's CFO and another candidate in the chief executive contest.

At Eddie's urging, Rick made a courageous decision: he would share with everyone at the offsite the results of his own 360 report, which included critical remarks by group members who had serious reservations about Rick's leadership. "I felt that if I wanted to build trust and show I was sincerely interested in building a team, I should be self-disclosing," said Rick. His openness and his commitment to his own growth as a leader transformed the group. "It turned out to be one of the most amazing things I've ever done," he said. "It really set the right tone and got things moving for me with the customer group. The team started to gel and I started to have fun again."

Rick's willingness to be vulnerable also fostered a strong connection between him and John Kispert. The two men had known each other peripherally for years but had never worked together. Their new bond not only paid off in teamwork between their groups, but had surprising and far-reaching implications. When the board interviewed each of the four candidates, they were impressed by the support that Rick and John showed for each other, and by their desire to work together. Many key employees had feared that either Rick or John would leave as a result of the succession decision. When it became clear that the two executives had compatible visions for the company's future and were eager to function as teammates, the succession issue was settled: Rick became the CEO and John the COO. As an added indication of how well the transition was handled, the other two contestants for the top position also remained with the company.

The team-building process that Rick and John started during the succession process became a building block for their future collaboration. One of the first activities of the new leadership team was to redefine corporate values, and building high-performance teams was one of the key features they added. Such is the power of 360s, particularly when they're shared openly and honestly with colleagues.

Because alpha males respond best to concrete data, we find that in-depth interviews packed with compelling verbatim statements carry much more weight than the usual 360s, which contain only high-level write-in comments added to online survey ratings. We interview as many of each person's colleagues as possible, including direct reports, peers, and other executives with whom they collaborate—or *should* collaborate. The goal is to determine what behavior works and what doesn't, and to back those findings with solid evidence.

In our experience coaching hundreds of influential alpha males, nothing ensures follow-through better than sharing their 360 results with everyone who participated in the process. This step can make alpha males feel extremely vulnerable, since they are not usually inclined to admit their shortcomings. Especially in corporate cultures where self-revealing candor is as foreign as Aramaic, the atmosphere can get so tense that people who are ordinarily talkative lose their tongues. It's essential that the team leaders acknowledge the challenge of self-disclosure and to do everything possible to make the person who's sharing feel at ease.

We begin these meetings by having the alpha thank everyone for the time they spent on their reports and let them know he appreciates their honesty. He then summarizes the content of the 360s—both the strengths reported and the areas that need improvement—and describes how he felt when he read them. Admitting that, for example, he was dismayed to discover that his style was confusing to teammates, or that he feels bad for having hurt people's feelings, can transform the audience from guarded to receptive. Even more powerful is when the alpha admits he's not sure how to fix the problem and asks for help. Such humble candor lets everyone know that it's safe to be honest. We then open the floor to dialogue. Following that vital phase, we encourage the focal person to reflect on what he's heard and to describe how he intends to address the most important items. Having committed to a specific developmental plan, he concludes by requesting ongoing feedback and support.

With rare exceptions, these 360 meetings catalyze a change in group dynamics. Participants feel the impact immediately and are stimulated by the possibility of future transformation. The alpha males on center stage emerge knowing that their teammates want to help them become better, stronger leaders, not cut them down to size. They also discover that being straightforward about their challenges is a powerful influence skill. By baring their necks and finding a comradely hand instead of a sharp blade, they come away with the exact opposite of what they feared: *more* respect, not less. The rest of the team invariably feels relieved and hopeful, and this, in itself, is a powerful predictor of positive growth.

In addition to whole-team meetings, we strongly encourage alpha males to meet one-on-one with their most important peers and their direct reports, to let them know how they plan to modify the behaviors that were singled out for development. By stating their intentions, they marshal support and derail cynicism—an especially important factor when the alpha's previous behavior has not inspired confidence in his ability to change.

Involve the Entire Team

The expression "It takes a village" applies to business teams as well as raising children. No matter how influential they are, alpha males are cells in a larger organism with a dynamic all its own. As a leader, you need to attend to the whole system, not just the troublesome individuals, or else the road to lasting change will be slow and bumpy, or even a dead end. Alphas sustain behavior changes only if those around them change too. No matter how much people may have complained about unhealthy alpha male behavior, they've adapted to it. If what they adapted to begins to change, they have to adapt again, and if they *can't* adapt, the team's progress will stall. It might even regress.

When Kate started working with Michael Dell in 1995, he was one of the purest thinkers she had ever seen, but he did not relate to people as emotional beings. Kate told him that his colleagues found him difficult to read, which left a lot of space for them to make up what they *thought* he felt. Sometimes, they'd think he was upset when in fact he simply disagreed. Because people didn't know where they stood, it was hard for them to align with Michael's thinking and get behind his ideas wholeheartedly. Kate encouraged him to be more transparent. "I'm really struggling with that part of our work," he told her. "I've spent my whole life making sure that feelings don't affect my decisions, and now you're saying I need to be aware of my emotions and even to communicate them to others."

Despite the difficulty, Michael saw the value in what Kate proposed and eagerly took up the challenge. As soon as he revealed more of what was going on inside him, other Dell executives followed suit. The result was a burst of creativity that helped fuel the company's remarkable performance in the last half of the 1990s.

A second tipping point occurred in 2001. At the time, the company was struggling as a result of the dot-com crash. With the stock price plunging and employment at Dell no longer seen as a guaranteed ticket to wealth, it became clear that only a more visible, emotionally connected, and inspiring leadership could build the sort of loyalty that keeps top performers from leaving. Kate advised Michael to share his 360° feedback, especially his leadership challenges, with his 14 senior VPs. To his credit, he did so.

That simple act boosted the level of cohesion at the top, triggering a profound shift in the executive team. A few months later, at the annual meeting of 150 to 200 vice presidents, Michael initiated an equally self-revealing discussion. In his speech, he said he knew that he needed to build stronger emotional connections with people. The task was awkward, he admitted, but he was committed to developing the capability. So powerful was Michael's candor that a video of the speech was used in training Dell managers worldwide, sending ripples of learning and self-awareness through the entire company. Starting in 2002, *all* the senior VPs shared their 360s with each other and with their teams. The results were so dramatic that the practice has continued ever since. In open forums, executive staff meetings, and training programs, company executives regularly talk about their strengths and weaknesses and describe what they're doing to improve. These comments from Dell senior vice presidents attest to the value of institutionalizing the candid discussion of leadership risks:

> "You have no idea the impact of Michael's openness. For a leader of his stature to openly address his personal challenges reassures people that it's OK to acknowledge their own."

> "The fact that both Michael Dell and Kevin Rollins are so committed to their own development breaks down walls and builds collegial, trusting relationships. The 360s are more responsible than anything else for the increased teamwork we now have."

> "They continue to get feedback and measure their own progress, and that commitment to development sets a great example. If they can change, we can change as well."

"They heard that we wanted them to make some changes, and they did. They could've said, 'I don't need to listen to this,' but by modeling growth they made personal development a way of life at our company."

Clear the Air

When we coach teams of executives, we follow the 360 process with a Clearing the Air exercise, in which team members speak candidly about their past challenges in working with each other. This powerful process roots out the interpersonal sludge that stifles working relationships, and also brings to light cliques and alliances that further gum up the works. It's particularly important when communication and collaboration have suffered because of mistrust, misunderstandings, or personal animosities. The process reduces tension and converts self-protection and fear into productive energy.

If you think that clearing the air is too touchy-feely for a team filled with high-powered alpha males, think again. It's been responsible for a great many breakthroughs. One of the many memorable examples we've witnessed took place at an offsite we conducted with the executive team at the Defense Logistics Agency. Vice Admiral Keith Lippert, DLA's director, had us conduct a two-day program to build trust and communication among top executives. At the beginning of the session, we asked the participants to write down issues that concerned or irritated them about their teammates, all of whom were present in the room. Their list encompassed pet peeves, grudges they'd held for 15 years or longer, and even derogatory nicknames they'd made up on the sly. Later, we had everyone mill about for an hour and a half, going from one person to another and sharing what was on their minds. Some revealed how angry they were with people who'd broken agreements. Others admitted their *own* failure to keep agreements. At the same time they expressed their grievances, people took responsibility for their own past actions. As a whole, the group took a giant step forward in eliminating blame, denial, and withholding. Two months later, DLA launched the first wave of a three-year project that transformed the agency.

Don't assume that built-up mistrust and tension will go away on their own. They won't, not with all the alpha triangles that block the exits. It's also vital to resolve new conflicts quickly, before they harden into granite obstacles to teamwork. Competitive alpha males seem to invite discord, and their battles can escalate into protracted donnybrooks, at a big cost to the team and the organization.

Act immediately: take full ownership of your own contribution to the problem, if any, and get everyone else to do the same, especially the alpha males who are busy blaming others. Use the following three-step process as a guide to ending conflicts between you and another individual—and to coach team members in resolving tensions that arise between them.

1. Complete these sentences, privately, to gain a fuller understanding of the situation:

    • What happened was

    _____.

    • The way I contributed to the situation was

    _____.

    • What I didn't do but could have was

    _____.

    • I felt

    _____.

    • I'm concerned that you thought

    _____.

    • I hope that you don't feel

    _____.

2. Hold yourself accountable:

    • Take full responsibility for finding a resolution.

    • Set your intention to communicate constructively, not to win an argument.

- Assume that the other person has an equally positive intention to resolve the conflict.

- Give up all your assumptions about how the other person will respond to you.

- Adopt an attitude of curiosity about the other person's perspective.

- Identify overlapping purposes that you and the other person might share.

3. Engage in genuine dialogue:

- Avoid interpreting the other person's behavior. Stay focused on the concrete facts.

- Avoid blame. Speak from your own experience, using "I" statements, rather than accusatory "you" statements.

- Stay aware of how your body feels (rising tension, tone of voice, etc.) and whether you find yourself getting "worked up."

- Use engaged listening. Notice whether you're preparing your next remarks while the other person is talking, and bring yourself back to listening.

- Keep in mind your most noble intention.

How to Meet the Meeting Challenge

Meetings are the business team's equivalent of the factory floor or the playing field—the place where crucial work gets done. By improving the quality of your meetings by even 20 percent you can astronomically boost your team's efficiency and productivity. The key is to harness the intelligence, vitality, and drive of alpha males without allowing them to stifle other voices or turn meetings into intramural bloodbaths.

Start by tuning your antenna to the ways alphas sabotage meetings. In addition to outtalking and outshouting other team members, they often dampen the group's energy with their impatience. They have extremely low tolerance for what they consider rambling presentations and off-the-point digressions. Depending on their authority level, they might shout, "Get to the point!" or gesture "Hurry up" by circling their finger in the air, or conspicuously multitask with their handhelds and Blackberries. Another way alpha males undermine meetings is with misguided humor. They see the foibles of others as weaknesses to exploit, and they're sharp enough to excel at rapid-fire repartee and sarcastic witticisms. When they start one-upping each other with clever put-downs, the conference room can quickly turn into a high school lunchroom with alpha comedians competing for center stage. All too often, the debilitating impact of this banter goes unnoticed even by team leaders because everyone is laughing—except for the targets.

Dysfunctional alpha males also sabotage meetings by being excessively image-conscious. They won't admit it, because they think they're all about results, but they have a need to be seen in a certain light by their colleagues. They try to display strength, control, intelligence, and power, like alpha animals that preen to let the pack know who the top dog is. By turning meetings into theaters for the Alpha Male Show they deceive themselves into thinking they were effective when all they accomplished was an attention-grabbing performance. We are often astonished by the difference between how alphas think a meeting came off and how others evaluate it.

If you let competitive, belligerent, or controlling alpha males dominate the room, your meetings will turn into a mess in which the true purpose gives way to the alphas' agenda. In time, the toxicity will infect everyone, and the following symptoms will break out:

- Meetings are used only for project updates and information sharing; very little problem solving and creative thinking takes place.

- People avoid taking on major issues; chronic problems that cut across businesses or functions don't get solved.

- Most interactions are between the manager and individuals; team members don't learn from each other or serve as resources for each other.

- Team members don't think for themselves or generate original ideas.

- Arguments are the rule; collaboration is the exception. Individuals present their positions strongly, then slug it out.

If you like your meetings flavored with creative energy, trust, and mutual respect, make sure that alpha bullies don't run over everyone else — and each other. Even contentious and incoherent meetings can be transformed into smooth, high-performing functions. This requires a serious commitment by a patient leader, along with a series of planned processes, activities, and interventions.

One key difference between ordinary meetings and extraordinary meetings is the number of people who take 100 percent responsibility for the quality of the experience. Everyone affects the chemistry of the room, and everyone can make a difference. As a leader, your job is to make sure every participant, from high-powered alpha managers to shy underlings, takes responsibility for making the meeting work. Especially in meetings filled with intimidating alpha males, it's important that all participants feel safe to express themselves. See to it that everyone is thoroughly informed about the issues to be discussed. Let them know you want to hear from them, and coach them in how to present their thoughts with the kind of clarity, intelligence, and fact-filled confidence that alphas respect.

At the same time, you have to coach self-serving alpha males to give up the need to be right, and to subordinate their natural tendency to compete for personal glory. Don't let them turn the meeting room into a combat zone. The tool shown in figure 7-1 has helped many of our clients raise the quality of meetings by making everyone accountable for their success. The rules are simple: each team member commits to checking in periodically, perhaps once every 30 minutes, to notice the quality of interaction in the room. Using the chart as a reference point, they score the meeting *at that moment* on a scale from 1 to 10. A score between 0 and 4 indicates the meeting is either mired in sludge or is fast becoming so. It then becomes their responsibility to ask themselves how

FIGURE 7-1

The meeting engagement scale

0   Committing to do something you don't have the time or resources to do

1   Accommodating—pretending to agree when you don't

2   Blaming people who aren't in the room

3   Aggressively grilling the presenter, judging and criticizing people

4   Complying while mentally judging and criticizing people

5   Polite disinterest—vacillating between engagement and zoning out

6   Turning complaints and criticism into requests about what you want

7   Expressing genuine curiosity about the issue and how you can contribute

8   Communicating your full truth in a self-disclosing way without blame

9   Actively and enthusiastically exploring problems and making decisions

10   Bringing issues to closure at the right time; creating a follow-up plan

they contributed to the low score and how they might shift the meeting to a higher level.

In the next chapter, we shift perspective from the team to the individual alpha. Don't make the mistake of thinking you can skip this portion; achieving mental and physical well-being is a crucial bottom-line issue.

ACTION STEPS

If you're an alpha:

- Commit to putting the needs of the team ahead of your personal ambition.

- Learn to collaborate instead of competing with your teammates.

- Use debates as a springboard for collective creativity rather than an arena for another contest.

- Honestly assess your impact on your teammates, especially in meetings.

- Encourage quieter members of the team to speak their minds.

- Open yourself to feedback and contrary opinions.

- Take responsibility for keeping meetings civil and productive.

- Harness the energy and intelligence of other alphas without letting them run roughshod over everyone.

- Recognize the value of revealing your imperfections and allow yourself to be vulnerable at appropriate times.

- Clear the air of anger, resentment, and hostility as quickly as possible, and learn to resolve conflicts in a way that satisfies every party.

If you work with or for alphas:

- Don't suppress your ideas; make sure anything you want to say gets heard.

- Don't succumb to feeling like a victim of your alpha teammates.

- Take responsibility for making meetings work effectively, regardless of your position on the team.

- Do everything you can to cultivate trust between you and each of your teammates.

- If you feel ignored or overshadowed by strong alpha personalities, instead of turning others into villains look inside for what's holding you back.

The Care and Feeding of the Alpha Male

Achieving High-Level Health and Wellness

When asked if he thought his high-pressure work was bad for his health, a great tycoon once said, "I don't get ulcers, I give them." A lot of contemporary alpha males would make the same boast, only now they'd say it about heart attacks. Most of them would be wrong. Alphas both give them and get them.

The excesses of all four alpha types wreak havoc not only on coworkers but on the alphas' own brains and vital organs. The consequences can be serious, not only on the medical front but on the bottom line. Executives whose physiology is buffeted by stress run out of energy more quickly, create tension and strife, and think with muddled brains, all of which can choke organizational productivity like high blood pressure constricts the coronary arteries. Alpha males like to think they're indispensable. Well, no one's all that valuable when he's throbbing with a tension headache, doubled over with colitis, groggy from insomnia, or recovering from bypass surgery. Neither are employees who are ravaged by the stress of dealing with rampaging alphas. And neither are businesses plagued by absenteeism, loss of productivity, and soaring medical expenses.

People often ask why Eddie gave up a highly successful career as a surgeon to do the work we do. His answer explains why we included this chapter in the book. Like most vascular surgeons, his focus was to cure atherosclerosis by either bypassing or replacing the blocked segments of arteries. He found it very satisfying to save lives and limbs, but he was also frustrated. Too many of the patients he treated would never have ended up in an operating room if only they'd adopted better health habits and changed their behavior. In many cases, surgical treatment was just a temporary stopgap; the patients reverted to their old ways and the disease continued to progress. Many of those patients were high-powered alpha males who were smart enough to know better.

Fighting and Fleeing

Alpha males tend to be hardy souls. They're wired to tolerate change, speed, and pressure with exceptional resiliency. They also have another medical advantage: their tremendous discipline, tenacity, and confidence can be put to excellent use in promoting health and well-being. Their can-do attitude and results-driven motivation help them to adopt and maintain healthy lifestyle habits. These assets also help them heal quickly from illness: medical research shows that patients with an "I can beat this" attitude do better than defeatists, and no one says "I can beat this" like an alpha.

That's the upside. The downside is, alpha males go pedal to metal much of the time, pushing their tachometers closer and closer to the red and sometimes into the danger zone. The fuel that drives their engine is adrenaline, and a high percentage of alpha males are as addicted to adrenaline as some people are to alcohol, caffeine, or nicotine. The stimulation they crave eventually takes its toll. And, as with all addicts, the toll includes the people around them. By now we're all familiar with the fight-or-flight response, the biological reaction that enabled our ancestors to battle wild animals and marauders—or to run from them. Chemicals such as adrenaline and cortisol flood the system like a SWAT team dashing to the rescue, mobilizing the body parts that are needed to handle the crisis. But, as we all learn one way or another, the proper response to ordinary business stress is not to throw a punch or sprint down the hall. Those adrenalized bodies in business suits are all dressed up with nowhere to go, like an athlete decked out in shoulder pads and helmet who's told he's in a ballroom dancing competition.

Continuous and prolonged mobilization weakens the mechanisms that keep us functioning at full capacity. The immune system becomes compromised, lowering the body's defense against disease; tissues, ligaments, and tendons become chronically inflamed; arterial walls become more vulnerable to blockage; insomnia, depression, and anxiety creep up insidiously. Acute stress also affects brain power. Blood is shunted to the action centers in the limbic system and brain stem at the expense of areas in the cortex involved in creativity, problem solving, and emotional intelligence. That's why excessive stress damages clarity of thought, decision making, and all the other complex mental processes that executives are paid to perform.

As the impact of sustained adrenaline secretion mounts, the likelihood of hypertension and strain on the heart muscle increases. Beta blockers, the chemicals widely used to treat hypertension, work at receptor sites on blood vessels and tissues, to keep them from responding to adrenaline. Unfortunately, this does not address the underlying cause; the brain continues to send fight-or-flight signals, and the flood of adrenaline can even *increase*. Excess adrenaline also elevates blood lipids, including the unhealthy form of cholesterol, and the buildup of fatty material and calcium hardens the arteries. Statins, another class of drugs, are commonly prescribed to block this effect. Unfortunately, a great many alpha males gulp down beta blockers and statins while doing nothing to change the behaviors that created the need for the drugs in the first place. To appreciate how absurd this is, imagine an emphysema patient on a respirator who still smokes cigarettes.

How the Alpha Brain Gets Hijacked

It's not just the arteries that get zapped by excess adrenaline; the brain suffers as well. Human emotions evolved as short-circuit organizers to speed up survival decisions. In emergencies, they override the cerebral cortex, where we do our rational thinking, in favor of more primitive brain functions in the limbic system and the brain stem, which are often referred to as the "crocodile brain." The survival purpose is to prevent the thinking process from interfering with our instinctive response to danger—or with opportunities to eat and reproduce, as anyone who's ever been hungry for food or sex can attest. But business alarms are not the same as jungle alarms: tragically, emotions like anger and frustration overwhelm the cortex, literally driving us out of our minds just when we need to do our best thinking. This "brain hijacking" is not just a health risk, it's a business risk, and it affects not only alpha males but everyone who works in the high- stress jungles that alphas create. Sometimes, entire alpha-led teams get their brains hijacked.

As we've seen, alphas tend to have sharp minds—in neurological terms, optimal or advanced cognitive abilities. Recent research has localized these capacities in the frontal cortex of the brain, which is responsible for intention and volition. In complicated, ambiguous situations requiring complex decision-making skills—in other words, typical business conditions—the cortex provides a cognitive structure for evaluating potential choices. However, the functioning of the cortex diminishes under stress. This shutdown shows up behaviorally in one of two ways: (1) by closing the mind to fresh thinking or (2) by doing the opposite— getting excessively attracted to new and different solutions. In the first scenario, alphas jump too quickly to closure and shoot from the hip (a particular risk for alpha executors). In the second case, people get caught in a loop of too many options, making them appear wishy-washy or indecisive (a particular risk for alpha visionaries).

Individuals tend to have default settings that draw them either to novelty or to routine. Among alpha males, visionaries and strategists are magnets for the new, while executors and commanders favor constancy, the former by sticking with their clipboard items and the latter by staying on message to keep the troops in line. In stressful conditions, these default settings get activated, and the person becomes even more resistant to different problem-solving styles. Either way, the result is an unfortunate restraint on creativity, self-awareness, and effective ways of thinking, just when those qualities are needed most.[1]

Blessed with composure, confidence, and neurological balance, healthy alpha males are the poster boys for "cool under fire." We turn to them in times of intense pressure because they can think clearly and creatively while others are losing their heads. Other alphas are at their *worst* under stress. Even under ideal conditions, they find it hard to collaborate, adapt to change, and listen to ideas that differ from their own, and when the pressure is on, those risk factors are magnified. When the going gets tough, tough alpha males get going. Healthy alphas make everyone glad they took charge. Dysfunctional alphas leave a trail of regret and disillusionment, perhaps even ruin.

Type A's and Hot Reactors

You've probably heard of the type A, that urgent, impatient, aggressive, hostile personality who is more prone to heart disease than the calmer, more patient type B. Not every alpha male is a type A, but in general alphas and type As share certain qualities. The most troublesome of those shared traits is hostility. We know from recent research that people with high levels of hostility have a 29 percent higher chance of dying of heart disease, and for hostile types under age 60 the rate is over 50 percent.[2] And it's not just hotheads and bullies who are susceptible. Recent research has identified a vulnerable personality type called the "hot reactor."[3] The hot reactor's physiologic responses are significantly exaggerated; a minor insult might set off the kind of sharp changes in blood pressure, pulse rate, and brain wave activity that most people record only during serious emergencies. The person might not *look* riled up, but inside he's a volcano.

Some hot reactors know they're hot reactors and look the part. Others neither fit the hothead image nor realize that they're hot reactors. All in all, there are four types:

1. *Know it and look like it.* Mad dogs and raging bulls. Under stress, they raise their voices, clench their fists, and chew people out.

2. *Don't know it but look like it.* Obvious mad dogs who are in denial about what's going on inside and don't realize how others see them. Their faces flush, their voices get sharp and clipped, their jaws tighten, and their spines stiffen.

3. *Know it but don't look like it.* Cool and collected on the outside, but seething inside and well aware of it. They have placid, hard-to-read poker faces; some seem to smile perpetually, but the smile doesn't feel genuine.

4. *Don't know it and don't look like it.* Seem cool, calm, and collected, with no discernible outward signs. But their heart rate and blood pressure are elevated, and their breathing is shallow. Everyone, including them, is stunned when they burn out, break down, or are rushed to a hospital.

Alpha males are found mainly in the first two categories; whether they realize it or not, their flare-ups, boardroom rage, and pugnacious bullying mark them as hot reactors. Some alphas, however, are in categories 3 and 4. Because their seething fury is well contained, people look at them and think, "I wish I could be that cool at crunch time." Then they get a physical exam and their risk factors are off the charts. Most category 4 hot reactors are not alphas, but they're likely to work in alpha-dominated environments. They might look as unperturbed as Cary Grant, but the fury, frustration, and fear inside makes them highly vulnerable to stress-related illness and brain hijacking. Because they don't know they have a problem, those in category four are the least motivated to take preventive measures.

The bottom line: alpha adrenaline junkies not only make themselves sick, they create a toxic environment for everyone else. That's why organizations dominated by dysfunctional alpha males are likely to have a higher incidence of illness, absenteeism, burnout, turnover, and early retirement than businesses run by healthy alphas and nonalphas.

Women are not immune to the ravages of stress, but their physiological responses are apt to be different. (See "Stress and the Alpha Female.")

Stress and the Alpha Female

Most of what we know about the stress response is based on nearly 50 years of biochemical studies on men. This gender imbalance, which was largely due to the research difficulties posed by the complex cyclical changes in the female neuroendocrine system, is now being corrected. In 2003, scientists working on a grant from the National Institute of Mental Health proposed that the female response to stress is significantly different from the male version.[a] They called it "tend-and-befriend" as opposed to "fight-or-flight."

The evolution of both sexes favored survival mechanisms appropriate to their roles in early societies, the scientists contend. Males protected themselves and their offspring by fighting or fleeing; females promoted survival by sheltering their children from harm (tending) and by fostering social groups to share resources and enhance mutual safety (befriending). Biologically, the male stress response activates the sympathetic nervous system, leading to the secretion of chemicals such as adrenaline and cortisol; the female response is mediated by the neurohormones oxytocin and prolactin, the upshot of which is to *deactivate* the sympathetic nervous system. The biochemical differences might help explain why men and women are likely to succumb to different categories of stress-related illnesses. Whereas men are prone to cardiovascular disorders, women are more vulnerable to disorders of the immune and musculoskeletal systems, such as chronic fatigue, arthritis, and autoimmune disorders such as lupus. Interestingly, this pattern changes after menopause, when women no longer have estrogen to protect them from artery disease and their risk of heart disease quickly catches up to that of men.

a. "UCLA Researchers Identify Key Biobehavioral Pattern Used By Women To Manage Stress," May 22, 2000, www.sciencedaily.com.

Becoming Aware

The first step to moving out of the hot-reacting, hyper-adrenaline lane is to realize you're in it. Ideally, that would happen long before the big wake-up call—the terrifying diagnosis, the midnight anxiety attacks, the broken relationship, the business bust. The first and most obvious clues are physical, but they can also be emotional, mental, or spiritual. Keep your radar tuned to the symptoms in table 8-1. They could be early signs of health problems in the making, or even conditions that warrant medical attention. The first stop might be a physician who's wise enough and patient enough to guide you in the use of self-help strategies rather than reaching for his prescription pad.

TABLE 8-1

Stress symptoms

Physical signs	Cognitive signs	Emotional signs
Headaches	Boredom	Anxiety
Digestive upsets	Confusion	Apathy
Heart palpitations	Dulled mind	Easily discouraged
Muscle aches	Flat energy	Crying spells
Back pain	Mental fog	Depression
Rashes	Forgetfulness	Feeling "no one cares"
Colds	Negative expectations	Cynicism
Change in appetite	Poor concentration	Frustration
Finger-drumming	Spacing out	Irritability
Foot-tapping	Mental churn	Lashing out
Fatigue	Replaying old scripts	Mood swings
Insomnia	Worrying	Nervous laugh
Accident-prone	Regret	Loneliness
Overuse of pharmaceuticals	Rationalizing	Restlessness
Alcohol abuse	Denial	Envy
Tobacco use	Blaming others	Distrust

Reset Strategies

A key factor in success—whether measured in health terms or business terms—is to build a repertoire of antistress tools, and to utilize them on a consistent basis. We call them *reset strategies* because they reset the physiological balance (what biologists call homeostasis) and restore integrity to systems that have been battered by stress. Just as regular maintenance keeps a car running smoothly and adjusting a thermostat keeps the temperature in the comfort zone, resets keep mind and body functioning at full capacity.

Resets are mediated by protein compounds called neuropeptides, which serve as chemical messengers, sending information from one area of the brain to another and between the brain and the body. Peptides connect in lock-and-key fashion to receptor sites on specific cells, triggering either an adrenaline response (the release of stress chemicals) or an endorphin response (chemicals that foster feelings of well-being). The two groups of chemicals work like fingers on a toggle switch: the adrenaline setting answers the alarm, mobilizing the body for crisis management; endorphins sound the "all clear," signaling the system to relax and recover. Simply put, adrenaline burns energy and endorphins restore energy.

Physically, resets can affect different systems depending on the individual, but the result is always a lower risk of disease. The changes we've observed in those who use reset strategies are both immediate and cumulative—not only medically but also in the way individuals respond to challenges on the job. Instead of reacting automatically and impulsively to events, they become conscious responders. Resets insert a space between stimulus and response, which can be filled with creative thought and calm reflection. Those who use them also tend to become more optimistic, approaching the demands of their work with confidence and inventive zest. The adrenaline-endorphin balancing act affects not only our bodies but also the quality of our thoughts and actions, dictating which areas of the brain are most active at any time. With resets, we can consciously adjust our internal pharmacy, lifting a hijacked brain to the higher ground of creativity and rational problem solving.

There are basically two types of reset processes:

Sustaining strategies. Like brushing your teeth, mowing your lawn, and other routine maintenance procedures, sustaining strategies are done on a regular basis to prevent breakdowns and keep the system functioning efficiently. They are most effective when they become routines and habits.

Acute phase strategies. Like flashlights, spare tires, and first-aid kits, acute strategies should be ready to implement in times of crisis and stress. Some resets require a certain amount of practice before they can be used in acute circumstances.

Acute strategies work best on a foundation of daily sustaining strategies. Ideally, everyone should have a personalized kit with resets in four compartments: cognitive, emotional, physical, and enhanced awareness. The sections that follow will guide you in developing your own repertoire. We urge you not to dismiss them under the false assumption that you don't have time for such nonproductive activities.

If each busy area of your life were a bucket of water, reset strategies would not eliminate a drop from any bucket. Instead, they would calm the waters in each one. What good is that? Think of it this way: What takes up more space, churning water or still water? Which is more likely to bubble over and make a mess of things? By calming the agitation, resets not only prevent the mess of overflow, they effectively create space in the buckets. This makes them an effortless time-management tool and a sound investment. They enable the mind to think more clearly and creatively; they revitalize the body and free up energy; they increase stamina; they help you stay cool in the midst of pressure. And they won't make you a wimp or a New Age lapdog. On the contrary, they'll allow you to move with the same speed and intensity but without the risk of breakdown or defective leadership. How can that *not* be a good investment?

Cognitive Resets

If Chicken Little were human, she'd be awash in adrenaline. Pollyanna, who saw sunshine everywhere, would be floating in endorphins.

Both would get themselves in trouble, however, because neither one saw the world accurately. Between those two extremes is a complex world where what we assume and what we perceive go a long way in determining our health and our bottom lines. That's why taking time to question our assumptions and reframe the way we look at a situation can be a vital weapon in the battle against stress.

Stuff happens, and when it does the body goes into alarm mode. A vital reset strategy is to catch yourself before you act on the emergency impulse. Pause. Rethink what's happening. What assumptions are you making? Are you distorting reality? These and other questions can broaden your vision and, if appropriate, replace your initial interpretation with a more accurate one. When we coach executives, we often address business problems by identifying the underlying beliefs that cause our clients to behave in particular ways. When we hit upon assumptions that have led to wreckage in the past, we help them reframe. Does your habitual way of seeing get you into trouble? Might there be more accurate interpretations? Would a shift in perspective suggest a different course of action? Reframing expands your perspective, allowing for a wider range of responses.

At one point in his career, George Nguyen, whom we met in chapter 5, persuaded his company's management to tap into the China market. George was asked to head up the expansion. He got off to a flying start, but he soon succumbed to classic alpha male behavior. Harsh toward anyone who questioned him, he alienated the coworkers he depended on to execute his strategies. Because he clutched every aspect of the project as if it were his prized possession and micromanaged excessively, he was seen as a lone wolf with a secret agenda. Ironically, his behavior was jeopardizing the China expansion that he himself had set in motion, and the pressure was mounting.

At a routine health exam, George learned that his cholesterol and blood pressure were sky high. He was a hot reactor of the category two type: he showed it but he didn't know it, even though everyone around him did. We told George he needed to reframe the way he perceived colleagues who questioned his decisions. Contrary to his assumptions, they weren't necessarily opposed to his strategy. Nor were they competing for power or criticizing his judgment. They were, in fact, trying to help him succeed. George learned to view their concerns as contributions that could help him meet his goals.

We also coached the people George had alienated. They had been thinking, "He doesn't respect me," "He's only out for himself," and the like. Then they learned about George's noble intention. Yes, he was motivated by personal glory, but there were other reasons he wanted so badly for the project to succeed: one was to boost the company's bottom line; the other was to revitalize certain regions of China—a higher purpose he'd never shared. A breakthrough came when we encouraged George to tell his colleagues about his childhood years in Asia. Uprooted by the Vietnam War, his family had moved from one foreign location to another. As an outsider, George learned to protect himself by becoming self-sufficient and highly independent. He also developed a burning compassion for victims of third world poverty. By sharing his deeper truths, George changed his coworkers' perception of him, and he was able to forge stronger connections to them. He also freed his physiology from a serious threat: within weeks his blood pressure normalized.

Physical Resets

Overwhelming data show that physiological fitness might do more for business success than any other leadership development strategy. By shifting the collective adrenaline-endorphin balance, regular exercise improves everything from attitude to creativity to teamwork, making the workforce more productive and more congenial. If you think you're too busy to waste time exercising, you really need an exercise break, because you're not thinking clearly.

In working with hundreds of executives to design personalized reset routines, we've learned to follow these basic principles:

Safety first. Ex-jocks often think they can jump into a fitness program no matter how long it's been since they laced up their sneakers. Such behavior is asking for trouble, and alpha males ask the loudest. Start modestly and work your way up. Before you begin, have a comprehensive health assessment.

Avoid competition. Full-court basketball and marathon squash duels might be your idea of fun, but scorekeeping can defeat the purpose of resetting. Driven alpha males, for whom every day is the seventh game of the playoffs, need to lower their adrenaline levels, not drive them higher with competitive stress and strain.

Commitment. The most important feature of a successful fitness program is regularity. The weekend warrior approach not only flops as a reset strategy, but it increases the risk of injury. If possible, work with a trainer to create a plan with specific goals and periodic reviews.

Consistency. Short programs, six or seven days a week, are ideal. We recommend 30- to 45-minute cycles with these components:

- *Stretching and breathing.* Open with a few deep belly breaths with accentuated movement of the back and spine coupled with a gentle shaking movement of all the joints. (See the instructions under "A Breath of Fresh Air" for a deep breathing exercise.) 3–5 minutes.

- *Aerobics.* Run, walk, spin on a stationary bike, jump rope, dance, skip, climb stairs—the possibilities are endless. To avoid competing with the ex-athlete of your glory years, choose an activity that you have not been good at in the past. 15–20 minutes.

- *Floor or table routine.* Choose a regimen that coordinates breathing and stretching, such as yoga or Pilates. Stored endorphins are released when we move our joints in different and creative ways. Dancing works as well! 5–10 minutes.

- *Relaxation/centering.* Conclude with a period of eyes-closed rest, ideally sitting erectly. This balances the oxygen, glucose, adrenaline, endorphins, and blood flow to the vital organs. 5–15 minutes.

Busy executives often find it easier to take several 5- to 10-minute breaks rather than one extended reset. Stand up and stretch; walk down the hall; put on a headset and dance; walk instead of driving for short distances; take the stairs instead of the elevator. Use every opportunity to move unused muscles and circulate stagnating fluids. And don't forget proper nutrition, hydration, and sleep. Make sure your meals contain a balance of protein, carbohydrates, and healthy fats (not trans fats), and reduce or eliminate refined sugar and highly processed foods. Ditto caffeine, which jacks up circulating adrenaline levels. Limit yourself to two cups of coffee per day, and beware the combination of sugar and caffeine in most soft drinks; it not only stimulates adrenaline but it adds pounds where you don't want them.

For the first three to six months of your fitness routine, we suggest keeping a daily log with metrics for energy level, sleep, weight, mood, and sense of productivity.

A Breath of Fresh Air. Sometimes the simplest strategies can be the most profound. What could be simpler than breathing? But what a powerful way to reset! To get the full value from this most essential bodily function, learn to puff out your belly like a balloon when you inhale. This motion pulls down the diaphragm, allowing for fuller, deeper oxygen intake. The multiple benefits include increased oxygenation, the balancing of pH and acid bases, reduced muscular tension, increased serotonin and other endorphins, decreased stress hormones, lower blood pressure, increased circulation to the heart muscle, and a shift of metabolic activity to the awareness centers of the brain. That's why "take a deep breath" should be a practice, not just an expression.

As a reset, we find the following steps to be extremely effective:

1. Breathe out completely, making an extra effort to expel all the air from your lungs. You'll find your belly tightening as you do.

2. When your lungs are empty, stop breathing and soften your belly. Just wait, relaxed and comfortable.

3. When you feel the need to breathe, relax and passively allow air to begin flowing through your nostrils and into your lungs.

4. Make it a complete breath by expanding your belly; lifting your chest, shoulders, and chin; and gently arching your back.

5. Transition smoothly into another full out-breath, again empty-ing your lungs completely. The full exhalations stimulate the endorphin response.

6. Again, wait with a soft belly until you need to breathe in.

7. Repeat three times.

You'd be surprised how something that takes a matter of seconds can radically shift your energy and settle your mind, opening space for clearer thinking. And this technique has the advantage of being inconspicuous: you can breathe deeply during meetings and phone calls, or when you're at your computer about to fire off an incendiary e-mail. You can even do it when driving or operating heavy machinery. Use it as a sustaining reset by taking a short breathing break once an hour during the workday. Use it also as an acute reset strategy: when you begin to feel irritated, upset, or anxious, and especially when a rage reaction is brewing, pause and take three deep breaths, holding the exhalation. This simple but profound physiological move will quickly trigger a calming reaction and divert en-ergy from the animal portion of the brain, which might urge you to pun-ish or pummel someone, to the higher centers of rational thought and creativity. You can then transform the energy of anger into productive ac-tion. The brief respite gives you time to reflect and to align your actions with your best intentions. What is your highest purpose at this moment? What's best for the team? The company? Your future as a leader?

One of our clients, an executive vice president in charge of a major business unit with over 12,000 employees, had an intense problem with anger. He had previously worked with two other coaches, with limited results. Eddie coached him to use this breathing technique whenever he felt a tantrum coming on. To the amazement of everyone who de-scribed his rants and raves in their 360s, his lifelong habit of explosive rage was ratcheted back to what seemed like normal irritability. A year later, his 360 follow-up contained enormously positive feedback from his team. When we asked what was most responsible for the change, he said that deep breathing made a bigger difference than all our psycho-logical and behavioral coaching. As a sustaining practice, it kept him steady and balanced; as an acute reset in times of stress, it not only fore-stalled rage reactions, it allowed him to see what lay beneath the anger, such as frustration with his team for not understanding his directions and disappointment in himself for not communicating better.

Take notice of an added benefit of acute resets: during the pause you might realize that your upset is actually a cover for other feelings. Perhaps you're upset because you feel you haven't helped your team grow into full accountability. Perhaps you're afraid that someone else will get the recognition you deserve. Whatever you uncover while you silently attend to your breathing or walk around the block, you will be better equipped to respond from an authentic state of awareness.

Emotional Resets

Emotions create a filter through which we interpret reality. If our interpretation causes us to respond with excessive fear or anxiety to events that are not major threats, we do serious damage to our health and productivity.

As you can see in figure 8-1, when confronted with a perceived threat, we defend ourselves with one of these four F's: fight, flight, freeze, or faint.

Generally speaking, alpha males go straight to fighting. Sometimes they begin with one of the other three and *then* escalate to fighting. In a

FIGURE 8-1

Four common defenses

These are the four common approaches we use to defend against threats, both real and imagined. Check the ones that most apply to you.

Fight	Faint	Flight	Freeze
• Attack	• Get confused or bored	• Get too busy	• Stonewall
• Blame	• Go blank	• Change the subject	• Get analysis-paralysis
• Criticize	• Get sleepy	• Deny there's a problem	• Focus on minute details
• Justify	• Get sick	• Dismiss issues as trivial	• Intellectualize
• Interrupt	• Eat or drink (stuff it)	• Make a joke	• Feel "above it all"

workplace dominated by unhealthy alpha males, you'll see battles playing out as power plays, intimidation, manipulation, and various forms of skulduggery. While the alpha males are going at it, those who are not alphas are stuck in different stages of freezing, fleeing, and fainting. Whatever your reactions might be, they're triggered by events you label as threats—and the perception of threat is heavily influenced by your emotions because the brain is wired to bypass the intellect in times of danger.

Resets create space in which to observe the underlying feelings that unconsciously steer your behavior. With the aid of this learnable habit, you'll be able to shift gears before your physiology runs amok. Each time you choose a different, less fear-oriented response without getting hammered by fate, you rewire your brain to react more appropriately in the future. Don't worry: if a *real* threat comes along, you'll still recognize it, and nature's fight-or-flight mechanism will come to the rescue.

Mapping the Emotional Body. When it comes to emotions, the biggest problem we have is that we can't recognize them in the first place; the voices in our heads drown out the quiet signals that tell us how we feel. In addition, we've been trained to hide unpleasant feelings where they can't be seen, like the bad sheep in a family. Alpha males are especially prone to concealing "weak" emotions such as fear and sadness. They let them fester and accumulate until they explode in the boardroom because someone has too many slides in his deck. The outburst surprises no one but the alpha. Emotional awareness is the one area where they're usually behind the curve.

Long before you consciously recognize that you're afraid or angry, your body has registered the emotion. By detecting the physical signals early, you can promptly reset. Mapping emotions in this way is remarkably healing in and of itself, as it allows feelings to dissipate rather than gather steam. We have, for example, referred several clients to a physician (John E. Sarno) who has had amazing success curing back pain—one of alpha males' most common stress-related symptoms—by helping patients get in touch with suppressed emotions, especially anger and fear.[4]

Each of us registers major emotions in specific body zones. When something like the slide deck incident occurs, pay attention to what goes on in your body. Do you feel a kind of itch or irritation under the skin? Tight shoulders or stiff neck? Tension in the chest? Similarly, where in your body do you notice fear? Frustration? Sadness? Anxiety? Chances are, you have at least some vague answers to those questions. Pay attention, and over time you'll raise your emotional awareness. By detecting negative feelings before they fully mature, you can prevent them from escalating to the troublesome stage.

According to our colleagues Gay and Kathlyn Hendricks, emotions can be grouped into four major categories: anger, fear, sadness, and joy.[5] Other feelings can be understood as subsets of these basic four. Also, each of the basic feelings is experienced at different levels of intensity. Table 8-2 describes where emotions are usually felt and how they escalate. Where do you find yourself most of the time? Where would you rather be?

Emotional awareness will help you liberate your formidable alpha strengths and neutralize your self-destructive tendencies. It just might give you a leg up on competitors who lack that awareness. What could be more practical?

TABLE 8-2

Emotional escalation and body awareness

Emotional intensity

```
1   2   3   4   5   6   7   8   9   10
Mild                           Strong
```

	Physical manifestation
Irritated ⟶ Frustrated ⟶ Angry	Tense shoulders and neck, clenched jaw, sore teeth
Worried ⟶ Anxious ⟶ Afraid	Fluttering in belly, tension in face, tightness in legs
Disappointed ⟶ Sad ⟶ Sorrowful	Tears, lump in throat, aching chest
Content ⟶ Happy ⟶ Joyful	Bubbling feeling in chest, watery eyes

Awareness Resets

In the late 1960s, when studies on the physiological effects of Transcendental Meditation were first published in scientific journals, the data were greeted with considerable skepticism. Now, hundreds of studies later, meditative practices are routinely prescribed as natural antidotes for hypertension, heart disease, anxiety, depression, and chronic stress disorders, and they're regarded by many business leaders as ways to enhance creativity, grace under fire, and overall productivity. Recent brain imaging studies have shown that mindfulness techniques shift brain activity to the left prefrontal lobe, which is held to be the center of awareness, allowing us to respond consciously to events rather than reacting automatically—to keep our wits instead of losing our minds.

Awareness resets encompass a number of practices, from mental techniques such as meditation and visualization, to movement disciplines such as yoga and T'ai Chi. Inner peace is a large room with many doorways into it. Regardless of their form, resets move the awareness from "continuous partial attention" to "continuous focused attention." In the initial stages, many people find this difficult and fleeting. Over time, however, our minds become trained, and the practices become easier. Awareness resets are valuable as both sustaining and acute strategies. Research clearly indicates that they produce immediate benefits—lowering heart rate and blood pressure, for example—and that regular practice over time solidifies the biochemical gains and helps the individual maintain equanimity in the midst of change and chaos.

We've refrained from including how-to material because awareness resets are best learned in the flesh from qualified teachers. Books can't individualize the instruction or answer specific questions. We urge you, therefore, in the name of results, to opt for quality over convenience. Shop around, sample the offerings in the marketplace, and commit to a promising practice for three months, after which you can submit to yourself a quarterly report and reevaluate your commitment.

To repeat: reset strategies are powerful executive leadership assets. They can be of enormous benefit to alpha males, who are often the last ones to acknowledge the need for them, and to everyone who has to work with alphas on a daily basis. The key to their success is the punch line to the old joke about how to get to Carnegie Hall: practice, practice, practice. As with any skill, reset muscles require use and reuse, or else they grow weak. If you find yourself resisting them, it's a good sign that you're a candidate to benefit from them.

The Alpha at Home

Why discuss home life in a business book? Because it impacts productivity and efficiency. Why is it in a chapter on health? Because your well-being depends on it. Home can be a reset or a stress trigger.

The work-home feedback loop is similar to the mind-body feedback loop: what happens in one affects the other in a continuous, unbreakable cycle. Yes, some people can compartmentalize, and alphas often do it exceptionally well. But we all know from experience that a good day at the office makes us a lot nicer to live with, and the joys and comforts of family life infuse the workday with extra clarity, calmness, and humanity. Similarly, a bad day at the office pollutes our home life, and a domestic argument, a crisis with a child, or any of a million upsets at home will carry into the workday, whether as a minor distraction, lingering fatigue, or a paralyzing preoccupation. Scientific evidence confirms that the physiological impact of workplace stress is either relieved or exacerbated by what happens at home.[6]

In short, to the degree that home is either a sanctuary or a stress factory, family life is a bottom-line issue. You may think you're a vastly different person when you enter the front door and take off your business attire, and in many ways you probably are. But you'd be surprised at how much you carry from one place to the other. The same alpha challenges that can make your office either a hellhole of stress or a smooth, happy engine of progress can make your home life either a prison or a sanctuary. Consider the impact on your family: if working for a micromanaging control freak is infuriating, try living with one; if having a demanding, workaholic boss is tough, try being married to one; if it's hard to work with a colleague who sees you as a rival instead of a collaborator, or who's constantly engaged in power struggles, try sharing a bed or a bank account with one; if it's a pain to have a know-it-all business partner whose idea of feedback is relentless criticism, try raising kids with one.

You get the picture. When alpha strengths turn into alpha risks at home, they can jeopardize your health, your family life, and, by extension, your career. Which is precisely why so many companies are helping employees achieve a sensible work-life balance.

Here's another reason why a supportive home life can be a career booster: your best coach and wisest adviser might be the person across the breakfast table. Take, for example, Dell senior VP Ro Parra and his wife, Cheryl, who is a physician. Like many high-powered couples, they have served as one another's champions on many occasions, and their insightful, honest give-and-take has been instrumental in forging two outstanding careers—Cheryl as a pathologist and Ro as the co-head of Dell's Americas business segment—and in raising four talented daughters. Here's how Ro describes a pivotal moment in his career, when Cheryl's guidance helped turn him around:

My life changed radically in April 1998, when Kate delivered the feedback from my first 360. My colleagues praised my business skills to the sky but ripped my ability to lead a team and coach people. What a wake-up call! I knew I was tough, but I didn't know I terrified people. Suddenly, I was forced to own up to part of me I'd always kept secret: The Wall. That's what I called the invisible barrier I built to keep others from getting too close. It made me feel invulnerable, and I needed that to feed my insatiable desire to win at all costs. It never dawned on me that The Wall prevented me from being a truly effective leader.

When I told Cheryl about this, I discovered something even more unsettling: The Wall had also kept me from being the husband and father I wanted to be. In fact, it warped all my relationships by keeping me from deeply connecting with people.

With Cheryl's support and prodding, I made a commitment to start letting people in, at home and at work. Over the next six months, I went from being anxious, irritable, and insecure to a far happier existence. Like everyone else, I still have personal challenges, but I'm a more open and communicative husband, I'm a better and more involved dad, and I'm a far better business leader, one who takes responsibility for the success of others. I learned to coach instead of criticize, and to listen instead of tearing down people's ideas.

Over time, Ro emerged from behind The Wall to become one of the industry's most respected leaders. We can't prove it, but it's obvious to us that his coach at home was the unsung hero of his transformation.

Bringing It All Back Home

The family bottom line is not calculated like a business bottom line. Success at home is not measured by efficiency, intensity of effort, or rate of productivity. If you're not careful, you'll bring home the overadrenalized condition we discussed earlier. Stress and strain build up, gradually and unconsciously, and eventually some vital piece of family life starts to break down, like a besieged bodily organ.

Over the course of 15 years, University of Washington professor John Gottman conducted seven separate studies involving 677 married couples, from newlyweds to partners of 20-plus years.[7] Eventually, Gottman was able to accurately predict the likelihood of divorce by watching a couple interact for only three minutes. How? By measuring the ratio of positive, appreciative behavior to critical, defensive behavior. According to Gottman's research, four types of negative behaviors are particularly destructive. He calls them the Four Horsemen of the Apocalypse: criticism, defensiveness, contempt, and stonewalling. Alpha males are masters of all four.

Criticism. Gottman found that marital success requires a much higher percentage of positive comments than negative ones. In fact, stable, happy marriages have at least a five to one ratio. That finding is bad news for alpha males, who deliver far more negative judgments than compliments. And if you really want to get under someone's skin, don't just hand out specific complaints; begin your critique with "You always" or "You never." Better yet, point to a permanent personality defect. "You made a costly mistake" is just a complaint. "You can't be counted on" is a scathing criticism, and a predictor of divorce. So is "You said supper would be ready at six. Why can't you ever keep your word?" Compare that to "It upsets me when I come home from work and supper is an hour late."[8]

Defensiveness. The second of Gottman's four horsemen, defensiveness, is defined as "any attempt to defend oneself from a perceived attack."[9] It's only natural for people who see the world as a competitive jungle to be on the lookout for attackers. Add to that the alpha male's tendency to see himself as a victim while everyone else sees him as a villain, and you have a recipe for defensiveness, complete with irrational blaming: "You should have reminded me that I had to pick up the dry cleaning!"[10]

Contempt. The third horseman could be the most devastating of all: contempt. Strong couples can withstand some healthy teasing and even enjoy making fun of one another's foibles. But the contemptuous mockery of a dominant alpha male is not mere teasing. It elevates the speaker and denigrates the target as inferior. No matter how much the alpha claims it's just some gentle ribbing and you're too darn sensitive—which is in itself another put-down—it strikes like a dagger to the heart. And it doesn't have to be verbal; contempt can be expressed with raised eyebrows, eye rolls, smirks, and other gestures.[11]

Stonewalling. This last version of Gottman's horsemen is a form of withdrawal. Not the obvious kind, like walking away, and not even the deceptive withdrawal of pretending to listen or faking concern while your mind is someplace else. Stonewalling is on another plane entirely. It's an in-your-face withdrawal that's meant to intimidate. "Stonewallers," says Gottman, "use brief monitoring glances, look away and down, maintain a stiff neck, vocalize hardly at all."[12]

Table 8-3 summarizes the signs of troubled and healthy relationships. How does yours measure up?

TABLE 8-3

Signs of strong versus unhealthy relationships

Relationship meltdowns	Strong relationships
Occur with a 1:1 ratio of positive and negative interactions	Need a 5:1 ratio of positive to negative interactions
• Blame	• Listen
• Criticize	• Be empathetic
• Complain	• Express appreciation
• Be defensive, a know-it-all	• Show you care
• Show disrespect and contempt	• Joke around
• Stonewall	• Share your joy

The Challenge of Change

Households featuring an unhealthy alpha male often get stuck in the alpha triangle, with the alpha as chief villain, the spouse as primary victim, and a supporting cast of children and extended family members who are either extra victims or heroes who step in to smooth things over. You can change the dynamic and drain your home of domestic sludge by taking steps similar to those we recommended for transforming your professional life, leveraging your alpha male strengths while avoiding the pitfalls of alpha male risks.

Learn to share responsibility. Needing to control everything and micromanaging everyone else's tasks is as destructive at home as it is at the office. Learn to treat your spouse and children as partners who can be trusted to get things done and make wise decisions.

Stop blaming. Blaming your partner for your own discontent might make you feel better, but it will change exactly nothing. Not blaming doesn't mean shutting up about things that ought to be improved; it simply means assuming that you helped to create or exacerbate the problem and holding yourself accountable.

Give up the need to be right. Being seen as flawless is even more destructive at home than at the office. You'll be respected more if you can admit when you're wrong. Studies indicate that if one partner always insists that he or she is right, disagreements last three times as long."[13]

Use positive reinforcement. If your home is like most others, the ratio of criticism to appreciation is about four to one. If you reverse that ratio, you'll find that it not only makes your spouse and kids feel better, it makes *you* feel better: positive perceptions boost endorphin levels and prevent brain hijacking.

Don't make marriage a power struggle. If the law of the jungle is antiquated in the business world, it's off the charts at home. Aggressively asserting your dominance and competing for authority will surely alienate everyone in your family.

Listen well to feedback. As with your coworkers, let family members know that you value their insights and wish to learn from them. No one knows you better or cares more about your well-being. When they point out areas that can stand improvement, shift out of defensiveness and into learning.

In *The 100 Simple Secrets of Happy People*, David Niven points out that "the difference between those who have happy personal relationships and those who have unhappy personal relationships is not the amount of conflicts they have."[14] What *does* make the difference? A mutual commitment to learning and growth. Dedicated couples who admit that they need to change and commit to following through have a 23 percent better chance of achieving marital happiness.[15]

Why not take the first step? Instead of waiting for your spouse and kids to snap out of it and change their ways, instead of blaming them for everything that goes wrong, instead of trying to mold them into your idea of a perfect family, take responsibility for the one thing you can control: your own behavior. Families are as interconnected as the legs on a chair: if one of you moves, the others will move, whether they know it or not. Do what alpha males do best: take the lead.

In the final chapter, we return to the workplace to encourage alpha males—and those who work with them—to move forward toward positive transformation by enlisting the services of a competent coach.

ACTION STEPS

If you're an alpha:

- Gain awareness of your stress response profile and the potential impact of stress on your health.

- Reflect on the cost of stress on your productivity and efficiency.

- Recognize the impact of your stress on those around you.

- Gather a repertoire of reset strategies, both sustaining and acute.

- Treat resets as you would any good investment: attend to them and monitor their progress. Make your home life a respite from stress, not another source of stress.

- Recognize that alpha traits have domestic risks as well as business risks.

- Work at applying alpha strengths at home while minimizing alpha risks.

If you work or live with alphas:

- Recognize your response to the stress created by alphas.

- Define the risk to your health and effectiveness.

- Adopt strategies to modulate your stress response in reaction to alphas.

- Acquire a battery of sustaining and acute reset strategies.

- Don't pander to the alpha's need for control at the cost of your self-respect.

- Learn to set clear boundaries.

- Accept that the problems are not all your fault.

- Be accountable for your fair share of responsibility.

Coaching for Alphas

Making Real Changes,
Making Changes Real

Having read this far, you have no doubt recognized the need to make some changes. But, if understanding the need to change were enough, America wouldn't have so many overweight, sedentary citizens, and no one would smoke. When we receive sound advice that seems hard to implement, or that requires effort we don't care to make, we resist—and we rationalize our resistance with illusory excuses, such as "It doesn't really apply to me" or "I don't have the time." We vow to get around to it in the future, when we meet our deadlines, when our kids are grown, or when we retire. But the changes that matter most should be made *now*, precisely when the pressure is on and time is at a premium. All it takes is commitment. You already know the importance of commitment; you ask it of your employees and teammates, and you demand it of yourself. Now it's time to apply to personal change the same do-or-die determination that you bring to your work-related duties.

The issues before you now are: Will you make a firm commitment to change? Will you hold yourself accountable for making those changes? Will you bring the same persistence to personal change as you do to your business objectives? Will you make the changes stick?

If you're an alpha male, you now know the many bottom-line reasons to build on your strengths and eliminate your risks. If you're not an alpha male, you've seen that there are ways to deal more effectively with the alpha males in your midst. In either case, to add focus, depth, and valuable assistance to your efforts, we strongly recommend that you consider working with a qualified coach.

If you're one of the many alpha leaders who would just as soon be seen with a coach as with an astrologer, please don't close the book just yet.

In our experience, alpha males who operate predominantly from their strengths welcome coaching. Like successful athletes, musicians, and others who are thankful for the help they've received along the way, they recognize the value of the process and continue to take full advantage of every opportunity to learn from a coach. On the other hand, a great many alpha males see coaching as a soft, touchy-feely fad with little substance, like aromatherapy, and they're about as eager to be coached as they are to cut their salaries. Even if they respect coaching, they think *they* don't need it, since the problems in their organizations are someone else's fault. Ironically, of course, the alpha males who are most hostile to the idea are the very ones who stand to benefit the most from a good coach.

Fortunately, they are often the ones who *do* benefit the most. Once they appreciate the bottom-line benefits of coaching, alphas can turn from a coach's nightmare into a coach's dream. They commit to the process fully, and follow through with such discipline and tenacity that the impact on them and their organizations is profound.

That's what happened with George Allen, the former deputy commander of the Defense Supply Center in Philadelphia, the largest business unit of the Defense Logistics Agency. When Vice Admiral Keith Lippert asked Kate to conduct in-depth 360s for his entire executive team at DLA, George was not interested. As a very successful executive who was close to retirement, he thought coaching would be a total waste of time—especially six months after 9/11, when DLA was under enormous pressure to get critical military supplies swiftly and efficiently to U.S. troops. What could a consultant who'd never run a business that size tell him about how to do his job? He marched into the room, ignored Kate's outstretched hand, and barked, "Let's not waste my time and yours. I've been like this for 30 years, and it's highly unlikely I'll change."

Instead of trying to convince him to sit down and talk, which was what George expected, Kate said, "Fine, you're busy and so am I. So, if you don't want to make any changes, I'm sure we can both use the four hours to do other work." She started to close the big binder that lay open on the table. "Wait!" George commanded. "What's that?" He pointed to a multicolored bar graph. Kate explained that it depicted his strengths and weaknesses in different competency areas, as reported by his colleagues in their 360s.

This was a critical moment in their coaching relationship: George had become curious. Scanning the graphics, he saw many of his strengths confirmed; clearly, he was held in high esteem as a leader. But he also saw that coworkers found his manner obnoxious and his attitude about his team parochial and closed-minded. What alarmed him most was the bright red bar labeled "ability to influence others, especially HQ." He was stunned to discover that he was seen as weak in an area he considered vital to his job: getting headquarters to see the importance of the Philadelphia business, and therefore the need to supply the resources George requested. Shocked to learn that his alpha tendencies were hampering his ability to support his team's best interests, he sat down and read the entire report.

"I was stunned," he says about reading the 360s. "I thought I had a likable personality, except perhaps when I got agitated and argumentative. I felt shocked to read statements like, 'He's overly dominating and not a team player' and 'He can be stubborn and myopic.' I'd been extremely effective in my career, but the data indicated that I was shooting myself in the foot over and over again. I was in serious danger of losing my ability to make an impact on others and to effectively represent my team."

In true alpha fashion, George saw the problem, accepted the challenge, and approached the task of changing his ways with the same determined effort that he brought to every other objective. By learning new ways to build coalitions and to influence people without bullying them, he found he actually had a greater impact. Within three months, his transformation to a team player was so noticeable that Admiral Lippert began to call him Corporate George. "Now I make sure everyone who reports to me has access to good coaching," he says.

How Coaching Can Help You Soar

In the Greek myth, a man named Icarus invents a method of flying. Donning a pair of wings secured with wax, he ascends into the air like a bird. But, intoxicated by his own power, he flies too close to the sun. The wings melt, and he falls to his death. Like Icarus, alpha males get so seduced by their strengths that they fail to recognize when those very strengths become tragic flaws. They resist changing what, in their view, has given them the wings to soar. Even if they've heard that their style upsets people, they shrug it off as a minor side effect of the medicine they dispense to cure business ailments. If you're in that category, let us assure you that: (1) you may be in danger of flying too close to the sun; (2) you don't need to clip your wings or retire them to the storage bin; and (3) if you strengthen your wings and lower your risks by modulating your altitude and speed, you'll fly a whole lot faster and further. Coaching can help you do that.

Many alpha males acknowledge that they stand to benefit from changing some of their ways, but they don't think they can. Their attitude mirrors that of their coworkers, who complain about alpha male behavior and sigh in resignation, "You can't teach an old dog new tricks" or "A leopard can't change its spots." Well, leopards may not be able to change their spots, but dogs—even top dogs—can learn new tricks. You're not being called upon to change the basic structure of your personality. Alpha risks such as poor listening, belligerence, and impatience are not wired into the genetic code; they're merely habits that can be modified or eliminated.

You not only can change, you *do* change. Like the rest of us, you make mistakes, you suffer setbacks, you earn victories—and in all those experiences you see what works and what doesn't. As a result of what you learn, you change—not always, and not in all the ways you *should*, but you do change. Everyone does, even when we don't know we're changing, and sometimes when we don't even want to change. And when we see the possibility of a significant payoff, we make a conscious, deliberate effort to change. It's called motivation.

If you were asked, "What kinds of problems keep you up at night?" how would you answer? Chances are you'd respond the way most of our alpha male clients do at first, by spouting a long stream of business issues, such as strategic challenges, margin encroachment, and competitive positioning—all areas of their work that they already handle exceptionally well. They rarely worry about things like how to get a fellow executive to buy into an initiative or how to coach their teams to improve their performance. They're so focused on quantifiable results that they don't think about their interpersonal behavior—until they realize that those two areas are closely related because leadership deficits have measurable business consequences.

In short, you might not give a hoot that your behavior upsets people, but you *should* care that it impedes performance and diminishes results. If drilling into people in meetings triggers performance anxiety, or insisting you're right even when you're wrong wastes time and stifles creativity, do you not stand to benefit from changing those behaviors?

That's where the potential payoff comes in—and it's huge. Like a baseball player who can clout balls out of the park but strikes out a lot and makes too many errors in the field, the chances are you've mastered a great many business skills but you've focused on some areas of learning at the expense of others. Perhaps you've focused on the long ball, not the subtle skills; or on systems and processes, not on yourself. A good coach can show you how to become a complete player. He or she can help you mobilize your copious energy, intelligence, and determination to change in the right ways at the right pace, so you'll be stationed perfectly for a big payoff.

Still not convinced? We've found that most alpha males who resist coaching are afraid that changing their behavior will limit their ability to drive high-level performance. It's a perfectly understandable concern, coming from people who value results above all else. They think that becoming more empathetic, listening better, and easing off on the whip will make them weak. They fear that acting nicer would be both inauthentic and ineffective, and they haul out stories about sweet, kind executives who are loved but not productive. We assure you—as we do our clients—that it's simply not in your nature to become too soft. As Eddie told one tough-as-nails leader with the steely bearing of a marine, who bluntly accused us of trying to turn him into a wimp, "You become a wimp? I'm not that good a coach."

Do You Need Coaching?

As you may have guessed, we believe that *everyone* stands to benefit from competent coaching, whether they're CEOs earning nine-figure salaries and adorning the cover of *Fortune* or ambitious entry-level youngsters looking for a leg up. That being said, you are surely an excellent candidate for coaching if you answer yes to any of the following questions:

- If you took the Alpha Assessment, did you score high on alpha risks?

- When you read about alpha risks in this book, did you feel as though you were looking in the mirror?

- Would you like to more fully leverage the alpha strengths that drive your success?

- Can you benefit from feedback on how your developmental areas impact your performance?

- Is there a consistent gap between your intentions and your results?

- Are you frequently surprised by broken agreements and miscommunications?

- Would you like your team to be more fully aligned around your goals and strategies?

- Is hallway venting and complaining undermining decisions already in place?

- Do you feel a conflict between your personal priorities and the demands of your job?

Choosing the Right Coach

In our experience, alpha male leaders are best served by coaches with the following characteristics:

- Strong, direct, and tenacious

- Quick thinking and smart

- Confident, bold, and courageous

- Analytical and logical

- Able to reduce complex changes to simple steps

- Emotionally intelligent and empathetic

- Nondefensive

While it's not necessary for coaches to be alphas themselves, it helps if they possess a number of alpha characteristics. It also helps if they have experience working with powerful and prominent clients. You need to know that they understand the rules by which alpha males play and the territory they occupy. Otherwise, it will be hard for them to empathize with your dilemmas. Make sure they also demonstrate personal strength and self-confidence. If they're dazzled by your stature or your strong presence, if they have a need to please you, if they get flustered, intimidated, overemotional, or defensive when you disagree with them or question their judgment, you'll quickly lose respect and the coaching relationship will be doomed.

There is also the subtle matter of chemistry. Since you're likely to be asked to do things that do not come easily to you, it's vital that you feel a personal resonance with the person you select as a coach. Not that you have to be best buddies, but you should have enough rapport to look forward to spending time together. A close, intimate bond is even better. Common interests such as sports come in handy, as does a shared sense of humor, but the best sign of genuine rapport is the ability to tell each other the straight, unvarnished truth without fear of being judged and found wanting. If you have that, you've built a foundation for real and lasting change; without it, the benefits of the coaching process will be more limited.

Perhaps the most important quality a coach of alpha males must have is a dynamic balance of grit and concern. You need to know that the coach has the courage to speak his or her mind and is strong enough to stand up to you when necessary. Coaches who are unwilling to express the hard truths can't possibly get the most out of those they coach. At the same time, you need to know they care. You have to feel confident that your coach will be there for you when your biggest faults and fears are laid bare. You also need to know that your sense of connection is strong enough to withstand any tension that might arise between you. Look for someone who's tough enough to tell it like it is, but also has a compassionate heart.

Once you make the right choice, be sure you're both committed to the long haul. Build time into your schedule for ongoing communication and follow-up. If you're a typical alpha male, it won't be long before things seem to be changing for the better and you think your style changes are completely under control. You'll be tempted to congratulate yourself for another job well done, thank your coach for his or her help, and move on. The danger, of course, is that you'll revert to your old ways at the first sign of stress or setback, and the new behavior you stepped into so boldly will be tossed aside like new running shoes that don't feel as comfortable as the old, worn-out pair. That is precisely when you want to call on your coach. One of the key functions of quality coaching is to help alphas apply the same tenacity to personal change as they do to their business pursuits. A good coach will remind you that you're in a marathon. Throughout the journey, the coach should perform ongoing follow-up to keep you committed and moving forward. The rest is up to you.

We encourage you to move ahead into your new future with boldness and confidence. But be prepared to falter. The question isn't whether you'll have setbacks, it's when and how often you'll have them. More important is this question: can you bounce back, recommit, and keep moving forward? When problems arise, you might find yourself slipping back into the alpha default position of blame. If you find yourself trying to fix other people, you might want to remind yourself—and have your coach remind you—to keep your focus on the one person you can control: *you*. Remember to always ask the question, "What can I learn from this challenge about my own thinking and behavior?" If you truly value accountability, make sure to hold yourself accountable first and foremost.

Above all, make a firm commitment to the process of ongoing growth. By constantly upgrading your awareness and your behavior, you'll be able to reverse the usual alpha dynamic: instead of having your strengths turn into liabilities, you'll transform your weak spots into additional alpha strengths. If you can rise to this challenge, you not only stand to benefit personally and professionally, you will bring enormous value to your family, your organization, and the larger society. The world can no longer afford the downside of alpha male behavior, but it needs the strengths of alpha males as much as it ever has.

A

Sample Alpha Assessment Report

The Alpha Assessment report outlines general behavioral patterns based on your survey responses, and should not be read as a concrete assessment of strengths and risks. This report can be used as a *guide* to help understand and modify your tendencies and risk areas. The key is to become interested in how you can develop yourself and to become aware of any tendencies you have toward defensiveness or resistance to learning.

Your results are divided into three different categories:

1. The first category discusses your general alpha characteristics, which are split into alpha strengths and alpha risks. These are your overall alpha scores, based on the entire assessment.

2. The second category, following your overall scores, contains four individual evaluations, in which your alpha qualities are analyzed for the four types: commander, visionary, strategist, and executor.

   • Commanders are natural leaders who know how to get people to do things.

- Visionaries see the big picture and dream the impossible dream.

- Strategists excel in abstract thinking, problem solving, and planning.

- Executors are dogged implementers who delve into details and drive accountability.

3. The third category contains information about three specific behavioral patterns—competitiveness, impatience, and anger— that often show up in alphas.

General Alpha Characteristics

In the graph on the left side of figure A-1, the red shaded bar above zero indexes your percentile score for general alpha strengths, and the red bar (progressing downward) indexes your percentile score for general alpha risks. The graph on the right follows a similar pattern with respect to each of the alpha types. In making sense of your scores, it is useful to compare your relative standing on each of the different categories, noting the categories in which your scores are highest and lowest.

Your Alpha Strengths and Risks Overall

You're likely to be a high achiever who is self-confident, dominant, and persistent. You're a "take-charge" kind of person with tenacity and persistence. You love a good challenge and the opportunity to break through barriers or jump over hurdles others might see as insurmountable. You tend to be courageous and are willing to take an unpopular stand if you believe it's best for the business. You are not necessarily a gambler in business and finances.

You have a strong results focus and drive for achievement. You come through for the business and typically accomplish your goals. You don't hesitate to make decisions; in fact, you move fast. You keep your vision of winning in mind at all times, and others tend to line up behind you in the effort to succeed. You very possibly operate from a place of per-

Sample alpha assessment

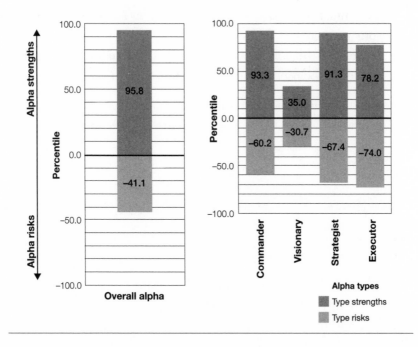

sonal vision, where you sense a noble calling that extends beyond your immediate work achievements.

You tend to be reasonably open to others' ideas and to changing your opinion based on new information. Unlike many alphas, you are also relatively relationship oriented, and enjoy accomplishing goals with your team.

Tips to Minimize Your Overall Alpha Risks

- Your results indicate that you possess many alpha strengths. Although your risks are more subtle, you should be conscious of their impact on others and seek to leverage your strengths.

- Be aware of how your tenacious and commanding leadership style impacts others. Get to know the personalities of your team and try to adapt your style accordingly in order to maximize productivity.

- Continue to develop relationships with your team and express your appreciation. By focusing on the positive achievements of others, you will continue to foster an environment where people challenge themselves and aim to achieve.

- If you do tend to push yourself too hard and experience stress, gain an awareness of the potential impact of stress on your health.

Alpha Types

Following are summaries of your strengths and risks for each alpha type, plus tips for areas of improvement.

Your Commander Strengths and Risks

Commanders are natural leaders who inspire respect and trust. As someone who is strong in commander strengths, you have a high level of energy and direct a lot of passion toward meeting your goals. You think big and aim high and are willing to run through brick walls to achieve your goals.

As a commander, you can generate a high level of performance in others. Your appetite for victory and accomplishment is infectious; your self-confidence motivates and excites others. While some commanders have better interpersonal skills than others, they all know how to light a fire under people and keep them moving toward the goal.

Your strengths are so overwhelming that your presence, especially if combined with a position of power, may be intimidating to some, even if you behave in very positive ways. You need to be aware of how people relate to you and spend more time engaging people and putting them at ease. As a result, they will be more open about their issues and potential problems.

As someone with moderately high commander risks, you sometimes hold strongly to your ideas and return to them again and again. When you push too hard for your perspective, you may appear unyielding and overbearing. Although people tend to comply with your directives, your style likely reduces productive debate and the level of alignment that creates loyalty and support. You often have great ideas, but you miss the input others could offer that would make your ideas phenomenal.

When your team fails to meet your expectations, you tend to get frustrated rather than wonder how you failed to communicate your intentions clearly enough. Your challenge is to round out your leadership style by becoming more aware of the impact you have on others.

Tips to Minimize Your Commander Risks

- Become more aware of your tendency to dictate to people. Ask more questions and find out how other people think problems should be solved, then add your ideas to theirs. People are more likely to support and follow through on ideas that they have played a role in creating.

- Become more collaborative by reaching out to peers and finding out what they want to accomplish and how they would like you to help.

- Practice giving constructive critical input or feedback in ways that encourage the receiver to benefit and learn. Offer specific feedback that affirms the person's value to you and the team.

Your Visionary Strengths and Risks

Your visionary scores suggest that you don't spend too much of your time generating long-term goals for your organization. You tend to apply your creativity to practical areas that allow you to leverage your own and your team's strengths. You may, however, imagine new possibilities and innovative ways of doing things, and you will speak up when you think there's an opening for people to hear your ideas. In other words, you're the realist with just a touch of the visionary.

When you are operating in a visionary or innovative way, you have learned to seek out people's input and to listen to their thinking, even if it's contrary to yours, possibly because you don't see this as a natural strength and therefore don't have such strongly held opinions.

Tips to Develop Your Visionary Strengths

- Look for ideas that challenge everyone's "comfort zone," including your own.

- Take time to solicit solutions from others. Stretch your thinking by collecting a wide variety of ideas from other people.

- It can be difficult to brainstorm new ideas and at the same time evaluate how well they will work. So, when brainstorming, focus on simply getting the ideas out, and then consider how to execute them as a second, separate step.

- Test your ideas on people who think differently from you, and use their input to ensure that your ideas are both expansive and doable.

- Focus on communicating your ideas broadly and developing alignment.

Your Strategist Strengths and Risks

As someone who scored high in strategist strengths, you excel in rational, analytic thinking. Strategists tend to be strong analysts with exceptionally high intellectual horsepower. They are insightful and creative in a linear and logical way. They might be described as both brilliant and methodical, and they're blessed with the ability to glide from premise to conclusion with ease. They're reflective by nature and can play out every permutation of a scenario to determine the best course of action.

You ask the right questions and can flesh out the important numbers and facts. You communicate your insights clearly to others in black-and-white terms. You're good at planning and envisioning breakthrough business models.

However, you also possess a moderate degree of strategist risks. Due to your many strengths, you may believe you have the best idea and most correct approach in almost any situation. You may tend to devalue the skills and talents of others and overvalue your own contributions.

Tips to Minimize Your Strategist Risks

- Shift into a style of curiosity and sound listening.

- Connect with people by meeting regularly and walking the floors. Gather ideas from people and listen thoughtfully to their perspectives. Build on their ideas to create the best thinking.

- Remember to welcome the ideas that other people bring to you, even if at first they seem overly obvious or not especially useful.

Your Executor Strengths and Risks

Executors are action oriented, results driven, self-disciplined, and persistent. As someone who scores relatively highly on executor strengths, you like structure, but you aren't obsessive about it. You're process oriented, but you don't track work as tightly as the most intense executors.

You have a keen eye for the needed details in projects and can easily spot what's missing. Sometimes, however, you offer unsolicited advice or micromanage people, even those who are consistently strong performers. At times you also revert to blaming other people for not understanding the task while failing to fully acknowledge your own responsibility for not communicating your ideas with enough clarity. Although your executor risk score is not extreme, it suggests that these are all areas in which your interaction style could be improved.

Tips to Minimize Your Executor Risks

- Take time to coach and mentor people—it's a strength you need to use more often.

- Be careful of your tendency to overcontrol. Focus on empowering people and letting go.

- Be aware of your high standards. Make an effort to turn your criticism into requests.

- Focus on also noticing what's working well and expressing your appreciation.

Alpha Behavioral Themes

The following feedback concerns three recurring themes: your ability to manage your anger, your level of competitiveness and zest for winning, and your tolerance and patience at work.

Anger

Your results on this assessment suggest that controlling your frustrations and anger at work is a moderate challenge for you. Although you probably keep your anger in check most of the time, there are definitely instances when your emotions get the best of you. For example, you may blurt out biting remarks that may seem funny to you in the moment, but that you later regret. Or you may become more irritated than you'd like when coworkers cannot see your point of view. In addition, you may feel your jaw and shoulders become quite tense in a frustrating meeting, or you may have other physical symptoms in response to setbacks or obstacles. While anger management may not be a primary issue for you, it is important to recognize that failing to handle your anger effectively is usually detrimental to your work; it takes up valuable time, inhibits rational thought, and alienates you from other people.

While anger management likely isn't a primary problem for you, it is probably something that you should work to improve. Given your results, it would be to your advantage to consider this issue and make changes that will benefit your work relationships, such as those listed here.

Tips to Better Manage Your Anger

- Differentiate real emergencies from other, less urgent matters. You may waste both your own and others' time and energy by responding urgently to issues without making clear distinctions about priority and importance.

- Although some people say they find it cathartic to express anger, research shows empirically that expressing anger induces stress and *additional* anger.

- Reflect upon a time when you have lost your temper at work, and then imagine how you could have dealt with the situation in a calmer and more rational manner. Consider the impact of this new behavior on the situation. How would it have influenced your coworkers and the decisions that were made? How would it have affected your team's impression of you? Once you can clearly see the benefits of more level-headed behavior, your motivation to make needed changes to your behavior will likely improve.

- Experiment with different strategies that help you let go of irritation and frustration, such as leaving the office and taking a walk, deep breathing, and clearing your mind by discontinuing what you are doing for a minute. Experiment with these different approaches, and identify which one works best for you.

Competitiveness

You scored in the third quartile in this category, suggesting that, on average, you are more competitive than others. Compared with other people, you are more likely to draw comparisons between yourself and your peers, to perceive new endeavors as games to win, and to separate the world into winners and losers. Nonetheless, you tend to measure the value of your work with your own personal standards and goals, and you are interested not just in outperforming others but also in achieving your own personal best. In general, your competitiveness is probably an asset more often than it is a liability.

Although your competitive nature is probably not a primary concern, it may be to your advantage to consider the following strategies. Doing so will likely create a healthier and more productive work environment.

Tips on Healthy Competitiveness

- Become aware of the subtle cues you notice in other people that suggest they feel somewhat intimidated or put off by your competitive statements or actions.

- Similarly, monitor situations for negative emotions. While you may approach new projects as a game and enjoy the prospect of winning, competition has a way of turning sour. You need to recognize when you have crossed the line and when the people who work with you feel uncomfortable with your competitiveness.

Impatience

You have a tendency to feel frustrated by the incompetence you notice in others, even though you may attempt to disguise how you feel. Although you tend to be somewhat impatient and think critically of people when they aren't on the mark, you generally react in a way that is appropriate. In an effort to maintain a congenial relationship with your peers and coworkers, you likely keep your frustration and critical opinions to yourself. Occasionally, however, these feelings and thoughts may manifest themselves in edgy or terse remarks that may be interpreted negatively by your team. Although you may frequently experience feelings of frustration and annoyance with the subpar performance of others, you are quite capable of empathizing with the fallibility of your team and behave in a manner that maintains a respectful work environment.

Your high standards may keep your own work on track and motivate some people to work hard for you. But when others fail to meet your high standards, your interpersonal style is likely to leave them feeling demoralized rather than motivated to improve. To help your team be more productive, you may need to become more accepting of the different ways in which people work and use encouragement more frequently as a way to motivate people.

Tips to Increase Your Tolerance and Sensitivity

- Make an effort to demonstrate more patience when dealing with others. While you may not agree with them or be interested in their ideas, you will forge better relationships with your team if you make an effort to acknowledge their input and communicate your own opinion in a respectful manner.

- Learn how to set realistic goals for other people. Instead of expecting people to achieve the highest of standards and then becoming disappointed when their performance falls short of the mark, set realistic goals that you are reasonably sure your team can accomplish. By doing so, you will spare yourself the disappointment and your team members will feel proud of their work. Although you may worry that success that comes too easily may make people lax in their work habits, research indicates that building a track record of success actually helps people improve their performance and sustain a positive track record.

- Make an active effort to recognize your team's strengths and achievements. By focusing more on the positives, you begin to create an environment where people challenge themselves and aim to achieve.

APPENDIX

The Alpha Scale

We developed the Alpha Assessment over the course of three separate testing sessions involving 1,646 research participants, each of whom responded to over 200 questions. The questions were designed to tap into ten constructs: strengths and risks for alphas overall, and strengths and risks for each of the four types: commander, visionary, strategist, and executor. Participants also completed a series of supplemental assessments, including measures of type A personality, dominance, need for closure, and anxiety.[1]

The final version of the questionnaire, based on these cumulative efforts, consists of 120 items and yields standardized scores for each of the ten categories. The supplemental data presented in this appendix are based on our third and final scale validation sample, which consisted of 1,523 readers of *Harvard Business Review*.

Table B-1 shows the degree to which each assessment subscale related to the others. More specifically, we show the correlation coefficients (Pearson's *r*'s) among the various subscales.[2] As shown in the table, there was a moderately strong positive relationship between the general strengths and general risks subscales. That is, the higher people scored on general strengths, the higher they tended to score on general risks. This pattern confirmed one of our basic premises: those who are gifted with alpha assets are also likely to be vulnerable to alpha liabilities.

Table B-1 also shows that general strengths were strongly positively correlated with commander, executor, strategist, and visionary strengths. Similarly, general risks were strongly positively correlated with commander, executor, strategist, and visionary risks. Thus, those who show relatively healthy traits overall tend to score high on the type strengths subscales, while those who show relatively unhealthy traits overall are prone to high scores on the type risks subscales.

Table B-2 shows respondents' mean scores for each of the ten subscales (all measured on scales of 1–5), as well as gender differences across each of the subscales. Males received slightly higher scores than females on both the general alpha strengths subscale and general alpha risks. Although these differences were small, they were also highly significant statistically.

Males also received higher scores on each of the four type (strengths and risks combined) subscales. Notably, the gender difference was highly significant statistically for the commander and strategist sub-

TABLE B-1

Inter-subscale correlations

Subscale	GS	GR	CS	CR	VS	VR	SS	SR	ES	ER
General strengths	1.0									
General risks	.40	1.0								
Commander strengths	.70	.07	1.0							
Commander risks	.42	.75	.17	1.0						
Visionary strengths	.50	.28	.37	.19	1.0					
Visionary risks	.17	.58	.07	.29	.49	1.0				
Strategist strengths	.70	.37	.25	.36	.12	.01	1.0			
Strategist risks	.28	.76	−.04	.50	.18	.32	.36	1.0		
Executor strengths	.67	.29	.31	.37	.03	−.10	.44	.16	1.0	
Executor risks	.39	.73	−.01	.49	.01	.24	.41	.53	.44	1.0

TABLE B-2

Means and standard deviations for alpha strengths and alpha risks, by gender

Factor	All participants			Males			Females		
	N	Mean	SD	N	Mean	SD	N	Mean	SD
Overall alpha*	1,523	3.24	.41	983	3.28	.40	539	3.17	.40
Overall alpha strengths*	1,523	3.58	.43	983	3.62	.42	539	3.50	.43
Overall alpha risks*	1,484	2.89	.53	959	2.93	.53	524	2.82	.53
Commander*	1,484	3.30	.53	959	3.34	.54	524	3.23	.51
Commander strengths	1,484	3.65	.65	959	3.65	.66	524	3.64	.65
Commander risks*	1,484	2.96	.73	959	3.03	.73	524	2.83	.71
Visionary	1,308	3.43	.54	848	3.44	.54	459	3.41	.54
Visionary strengths	1,308	3.59	.58	848	3.59	.58	459	3.57	.59
Visionary risks	1,307	3.27	.68	847	3.28	.68	459	3.24	.67
Strategist*	1,356	2.92	.61	878	2.99	.60	477	2.80	.60
Strategist strengths*	1,330	3.37	.72	861	3.46	.71	468	3.21	.73
Strategist risks*	1,356	2.49	.71	878	2.55	.72	477	2.40	.68
Executor	1,356	3.41	.53	878	3.43	.54	477	3.39	.52
Executor strengths	1,356	3.67	.62	878	3.67	.63	477	3.66	.60
Executor risks**	1,341	3.15	.64	870	3.18	.64	470	3.11	.63

Note: Sample sizes vary across subscale due to the fact that several study participants failed to complete any or all of the items within a given subscale (e.g., dropped out of the study midsurvey). The sample size ranged from 1,307 to 1,523 based on number of full scales completed—for males, from 847 to 983; for females, from 459 to 539. Throughout the analyses reported in this appendix, participants' subscale scores were considered only when they had completed all of the items within a given subscale.

Because one person did not indicate gender, the N for the "Males" and "Females" columns do not sum to the N for the "All participants" column.

*In an independent samples t-test, the gender difference was significant at the $p < .001$ level.

**In an independent samples t-test, the gender difference was marginally significant, with $p < .10$.

scales, but not for either the visionary or executive subscale. The strengths and risks type subscales told a similar story: males received higher scores across all of these subscales, but the male-female difference was statistically significant only about half of the time. Specifically, males scored significantly higher than females on commander risks and on both

250 Appendix B

TABLE B-3

Correlations between theme scores and type risk scores, for male and female respondents

Themes and types	All participants	Male only	Female only
Overall alpha risk			
Anger	.63*	.62*	.63*
Impatience	.43*	.43*	.42*
Competitiveness	.37*	.38*	.34*
Commander risk			
Anger	.55*	.54*	.54*
Impatience	.37*	.38*	.33*
Competitiveness	.34*	.35*	.31*
Visionary risk			
Anger	.23*	.24*	.23*
Impatience	.05**	.08**	−.01
Competitiveness	.20*	.18*	.23*
Strategist risk			
Anger	.51*	.46*	.59*
Impatience	.27*	.25*	.30*
Competitiveness	.24*	.21*	.29*
Executor risk			
Anger	.42*	.42*	.41*
Impatience	.42*	.42*	.42*
Competitiveness	.28*	.29*	.26*

*Correlation is significant at the $p < .001$ level.
**Correlation is significant at the $p < .05$ level.

strategist subscales, but the gender difference was nonsignificant in all other cases.

Table B-3 shows the correlation coefficients (Pearson's r's) between the various risk themes (anger, impatience, and competitiveness) and the type risks subscales. The three risk themes were, in general, highly associated with each of the type risks subscales. In almost every case, the correlations were highly significant. We found especially strong relationships between the anger subscale and general risks, commander risks, and strategist risks—patterns that held true for men and women alike. On the other hand, the clear *absence* of relationship between impatience and visionary risks was also notable. Thus, while table B-3 clearly shows that the risk themes were strongly associated with each of the type risks subscales, some of these associations were more powerful than others.

Table B-4 shows the correlation between these themes and gender.

TABLE B-4

Alpha risk themes and gender

Factor	All participants	Males	Females
Anger*			
Mean	2.98	3.04	2.86
N	1,484	959	524
SD	0.55	0.54	0.55
Competitiveness			
Mean	3.49	3.51	3.46
N	1,523	983	539
SD	0.49	0.48	0.51
Impatience*			
Mean	3.66	3.70	3.59
N	1,356	878	477
SD	0.57	0.57	0.57

Note: Because one person did not indicate gender, the N for the "Males" and "Females" columns, respectively, do not sum to the N for the "All participants" columns.

*In an independent samples t-test, the gender difference was significant at the $p < .001$ level.

Notes

Chapter 1

1. *Oxford English Dictionary*, online version, <http://www.oed.com>.

2. Jeanine Prime, "Women 'Take Care,' Men 'Take Charge': Stereotyping of U.S. Business Leaders Exposed," Catalyst report, October 19, 2005.

3. All of the stories in the book are real. In some cases, the identities of the actual individuals and companies are left out or disguised because they requested anonymity.

4. *The American Heritage Dictionary* (Boston: Houghton-Mifflin, 1992).

5. Thomas A. Stewart, private e-mail exchange with Louise O'Brien, January 2004.

6. Richard Farson, *Management of the Absurd* (New York: Simon & Schuster, 1996), 137.

7. Jerry Useem, "America's Most Admired Companies," *Fortune*, March 7, 2005, 67.

8. Chronicled in James B. Stewart, *Disney War* (New York: Simon & Schuster, 2005).

9. "Complaining About Bad Bosses Is a Big Time Drain," www.badbossology.com, posted October 4, 2005.

10. Uncited quotations in this chapter are from client interviews during 2005 and 2006, conducted by the authors, unless otherwise specified.

11. The type A personality is discussed in chapter 8.

12. Tension was assessed using the IPAT 16 personality factors.

13. These gender differences remained statistically significant even when stepwise regression analyses controlled for age, education, and whether or not respondents held supervisory positions.

14. For more on defensiveness and tools for overcoming it, see chapter 6.

15. Research findings on sex differences reflect generalities based on statistical averages. Among actual men and women there is huge variation; any individual's traits might be closer to the average of the opposite sex.

16. Hal R. Varian, "The Difference Between Men and Women, Revisited: It's About Competition," *New York Times*, Economic Section, March 9, 2006.

17. Prime, "Women 'Take Care,' Men 'Take Charge.'"

18. National Institute of Mental Health, "Gender Differences in Behavioral Responses to Stress: 'Fight or Flight' vs. 'Tend and Befriend,'" December 1, 2003, http://www.MedicalMoment.org.

19. Janet Guyon, "The Art of the Decision," *Fortune*, November 14, 2005.

20. Simon Baron-Cohen, *The Essential Difference* (New York: Basic Books, 2003), 38–42.

21. Jia Lynn Yang, "Alpha Females," *Fortune*, November 14, 2005, 91.

22. Patrick Dillon, "Peerless Leader," *Christian Science Monitor*, March 10, 2004.

23. Heather Clancy and Steven Burke in *CRN*, www.crn.com, November 11, 2004.

24. William Meyers, "Keeping a Gentle Grip on Power," *USNews.com*, October 31, 2005.

25. Dillon, "Peerless Leader."

26. Tiziana Casciaro and Miguel Sousa Lobo, "Competent Jerks, Lovable Fools, and the Formation of Social Networks," *Harvard Business Review*, June 2005, 94.

27. Kevin Voigt, "Malevolent Bosses Take a Huge Toll on Business," *Wall Street Journal*, March 15, 2002.

28. Michael Crom, "The New Key to Employee Retention," *Leader to Leader*, Fall 2000, 12.

29. Morgan W. McCall Jr. and George P. Hollenbeck, *Developing Global Executives: The Lessons of International Experience* (Boston: Harvard Business School Press, 2002), 162.

Chapter 2

1. Andy Serwer, "The Education of Michael Dell," *Fortune*, March 7, 2005, 72–82.

2. The alpha types are different from the types in the Myers-Briggs Type Indicator (MBTI), a well-established and widely used instrument. We find the MBTI especially valuable for team building, whereas our alpha typology is most useful in helping clients understand their personal style and make appropriate changes.

3. Uncited quotations in this chapter are from client interviews during 2005 and 2006, conducted by the authors, unless otherwise specified.

4. In our study, anger had a moderately high correlation with all four of the type risks.

5. William Shakespeare, *As You Like It*, act 2, scene 7 ("All the world's a stage, and all the men and women merely players").

6. See Gay Hendricks, *Conscious Living* (San Francisco: HarperCollins, 2000); www.Hendricks.com.

7. The interview process resulted from extensive field testing by Dr. Kathlyn Hendricks, who developed the tool and later taught us to apply it in corporate settings.

Chapter 3

1. Uncited quotations in this chapter are from client interviews during 2005 and 2006, conducted by the authors, unless otherwise specified.

2. This subscale had a normal distribution. Gender differences remained statistically significant even when stepwise regression analyses controlled for age, education, and supervisory positions.

3. "Workplace Dealbreakers," *Training and Development*, April 2006, 13–14, cited on www.badbossology.com.

4. "The Best and Worst Managers of 2004," *BusinessWeek*, January 10. 2005, 57.

Chapter 4

1. Desmond Morris, *The Human Zoo: A Zoologist's Classic Study of the Urban Animal* (New York: Kodansha America, 1996), 51–52.

2. Uncited quotations in this chapter are from client interviews during 2005 and 2006, conducted by the authors, unless otherwise specified.

3. Bill Burnham, "Just How Much Did VCs Pocket on Google?" *Burnham's Beat*, June 24, 2005.

4. Don Durfee, "Watch Your Back: As Companies Map Their Growth Strategies, They Should Pay More Attention to the Hazards They Entail," *CFO*, August 2000, 61.

5. Ibid.

6. Loren Fox, "Meg Whitman," *Salon.com*, November 27, 2001.

7. Roderick M. Kramer, "The Harder They Fall," *Harvard Business Review*, October 2003, 65.

8. Cited on http://www.thinkexist.com.

9. Brent Schlender, "Ballmer Unbound," *Fortune*, January 12, 2004.

Chapter 5

1. Uncited quotations in this chapter are from client interviews during 2005 and 2006, conducted by the authors, unless otherwise specified.

2. W. D. Crotty, "Eaton Trucking Along," *The Motley Fool*, October 17, 2005, www.fool.com.

3. John Kotter and Dan S. Cohen, *The Heart of Change: Real-Life Stories of How People Change Their Organizations* (Boston: Harvard Business School Press, 2002), 2.

4. Elkhonon Goldberg, *The Executive Brain: Frontal Lobes and the Civilized Mind* (New York: Oxford University Press, 2001), 95.

5. David Perkins, *Outsmarting IQ: The Emerging Science of Learnable Intelligence* (New York: The Free Press, 1995), 152–154.

Chapter 6

1. Uncited quotations in this chapter are from client interviews during 2005 and 2006, conducted by the authors, unless otherwise specified.

2. Jon Meacham, "A Road Map to Making History," *Newsweek*, January 24, 2005, 42–44.

3. Sam Farmer, "Bill Belichick," *Los Angeles Times*, January 24, 2005, D1.

4. Robert Hogan, "Anomalous Leadership," January 2006, www.hoganassessments .com.

5. Deborah Tannen, *You Just Don't Understand: Women and Men in Conversation* (San Francisco: HarperCollins Publishers, 2001).

6. Dean Takahashi, "HP Drops Profit Bombshell, Fires Execs," *San Jose Mercury News*, August 13, 2004.

7. Gary Rivlin, "He Naps. He Sings. And He Isn't Michael Dell," *New York Times*, September 11, 2005.

8. C. W. Meisterfeld and Ernest Pecci, *Dog and Human Behavior: Amazing Parallels/Similarities* (Petaluma, CA: MRK Publishing, 2000), 71.

9. Kate Ludeman, *The Worth Ethic* (New York: Dutton, 1989), 101.

Chapter 7

1. Uncited quotations in this chapter are from client interviews during 2005 and 2006, conducted by the authors, unless otherwise specified.

2. Henry P. Sims Jr., "Grading *The Apprentice*," *SMITH Business* 6, no. 2 (Spring 2005): 3.

3. Henry P. Sims Jr., "Trump Poor Model to His 'Apprentices,'" *Baltimore Sun*, January 23, 2005, 6F.

4. From a speech by Robert Shapiro to Monsanto executives, January 1997.

Chapter 8

1. Elkhonon Goldberg, *The Executive Brain: Frontal Lobes and the Civilized Mind* (New York: Oxford University Press, 2001), 69–71 and 89–91.

2. Anne Underwood, "The Good Heart," *Newsweek*, October 3, 2005. 51.

3. Robert Eliot, *From Stress to Strength: How to Lighten Your Load and Save Your Life* (New York: Bantam, 1994), 22–46.

4. John F. Sarno, *Healing Back Pain: The Mind-Body Connection* (New York: Warner Books, 1991), 29–58.

5. Gay Hendricks and Kathlyn Hendricks, *At the Speed of Life* (New York: Bantam Books, 1993), 34–35.

6. Robert S. Eliot, "Relationship of Emotional Stress to the Heart," *Heart Disease and Stroke* 2, no. 3 (1993): 243–46.

7. John Gottman, *Why Marriages Succeed or Fail: And How You Can Make Yours Last* (New York: Fireside, 1994).

8. John M. Gottman, *The Marriage Clinic* (New York: W.W. Norton, 1999), 26–30, 35.

9. Ibid., 41–44.

10. Ibid., 44–45.

11. Ibid., 45–46.

12. Ibid., 45–46.

13. David Niven, *The 100 Simple Secrets of Happy People: What Scientists Have Learned and How You Can Use It* (New York: HarperCollins, 2000), 33.

14. Ibid., 46.

15. Ibid.

Appendix B

1. Specifically, we used (a) the Framingham type A scale (S. G. Haynes, M. Feinleib, and W. B. Kannel, "The Relationship of Psychosocial Factors to Coronary Heart Disease in the Framingham Study: Eight-year Incidence of Coronary Heart Disease," *American Journal of Epidemiology* 11 [1980]: 37–58); (b) the dominance and anxiety subscales of the 16PF (R. B. Cattell, "Personality Structure and the New Fifth Edition of the 16PF," *Educational & Psychological Measurement* 55 [1995]: 926–937; R. B. Cattell, H. W. Eber, and M. M. Tatsuoka, *Handbook for the 16PF* [Champaign, IL: Institute for Personality and Ability Testing, Inc., 1970]); and (c) measure of need for cognitive closure (A. W. Kruglanski, D. M. Webster, and A. Klem, *Journal of Personality and Social Psychology* 65 [1993]: 861–876).

2. Note that positive correlation coefficients indicate positive relationships (as x increases, y increases), with a coefficient of .40, for example, indicating a stronger relationship than a coefficient of .30. Negative coefficients, on the other hand, indicate negative relationships (as x increases, y *decreases*), with a coefficient of −.40 reflecting a stronger (negative) relationship than a coefficient of −.30. Correlation coefficients that are close to zero—whether positive or negative—indicate a lack of relationship between subscales.

Index

Note: Page numbers in *italics* indicate figures; page numbers followed by *t* indicate tables.

on interpersonal relationships, 5,
37–38, 132–135
personas, 92
resistance to, 225–230
self-assessment of need for, 230–231
360° assessments, 226–228
value of, 228–230
for women who work with commanders, 91–93
"Coaching the Alpha Male" (Ludeman
and Erlandson), 7
cognitive effects of stress, 202–203, 206,
206t
cognitive resets, 208–210
collaboration
compromise contrasted with, 179
as major challenge for commanders,
72–73
team-building and, 186–187
collaborative style
in alpha females, 23
building, 149–150
developing, 239
combativeness. See aggression
command-and-control tactics, 19, 128
commander(s), 38, 65–93, 235
alliances with visionaries, 112–113
Alpha Assessment Report, 238–239
in alpha triangles, 106–108
anger in, 45–46, 47, 70, 73–75
anger management for, 84–88
balanced, example of, 68
behavioral traits of, 39, 238–239
behavior modification tools for, 79–88
bullying by, 71
coaching women who work with, 91–93
cognitive functioning, 202–203
conflicts with strategists, 132–135
demographics of, 70, 248t–250t
example of, 41–42
excessive competition of, 69, 69t,
70–73, 250t
female, 70, 77–79, 249t
intimidating presence of, 76–77, 238
methods for working with, 88–93

perspectives of tasks, 40
360° assessments of, 75, 76–77, 83–84
villain personas, 53, 59, 74, 75
commander risk factors, 43, 45t, 48–49,
69t, 69–77
achievement orientation, 69, 69t
aggression, 69t
anger, 45–46, 47, 70, 73–75
competitiveness, 69, 69t, 70–73, 250t
dominance, 69t, 71
frustration, 239
impatience, 70, 250t
tips to minimize, 239
work environment and, 71–72
commander risks scale, 78, 249t
commander strengths, 43, 45t, 48–49,
66–69
charisma and ethics, 68
personal responsibility, 67–68, 69t
sense of mission, 67
commander syndrome, 69t
commitment
to behavioral change, 225–228, 233
to growth, in home life, 223
to improve leadership, 124
to model accountability, 152
in physical fitness, 211
communication
avoiding miscommunication, 166
effective, personal responsibility for,
138–140
of expectations, 165
genuine dialogue, 193
linking data orientation to, 139–140
misguided humor, 194
ongoing, in coaching, 232
verbal weaponry, 176, 177
written, 171
communication skills
creating high-performance teams, 181
defusing anger and, 87
engaged listening, 140–142, 142t
improving, 77
strategist problems with, 127, 129, 132,
139

healthy versus dysfunctional leaders, 181, 182*t*

impact of alpha males on teams, 34

improving, 77

self-awareness, 27

strategic alliances, 112–114, 116–117

tenacity, 3

in alpha females, 5

of alpha males, 9, 39–40

of executors, 150, 153*t*, 160

rewards and risks of, 12*t*

teamwork and, 178*t*

"tend-and-befriend" response, 205

tension, agreements as corrective mechanism for, 184–185

thinking flaws, 143–144, *144*

thought patterns

innovative thinking of visionaries, 96, 100*t*, 178*t*

integrated versus linear thinking, 130

thinking flaws, 143–144, *144*

threats, common defenses against, *214*, 214–215

360° assessments

of alphas' colleagues, 13, 18, 55–56

in coaching, 226–228

of commander behavior, 75, 76–77, 83–84

defusing anger, 86, 87

of executor behavior, 156–159, 162, 163, 168–169

for high-performance teams, 186–189

on need for assertiveness, 91–92

of strategist behavior, 121–122, 124–125, 139

of visionary behavior, 102

Tierney, Tom, 23

time management tools, 208

tolerance, tips for increasing, 244–245

Transcendental Meditation, 217

Trump, Donald, 173–174

trust, establishing, 76–77

trust-building programs, 191

turf wars, 72–73

type A personalities, 14–15, 203

typology of alpha males, 34, 37–63

Alpha Assessment Report, 238–242

alpha triangle and (*see* alpha triangle)

anger and, 45–47, 47

commanders (*see* commander[s])

executors (*see* executor[s])

personality types, 2–3

personas, 58–63

self-analysis, 48–51

strategists (*see* strategist[s])

strengths and risks, 43–44, 45*t*

visionaries (*see* visionaries)

Tyson, Mike, 71

unhealthy alpha tendencies. *See also* dysfunctional alphas

in business world, 8, 8–9

healthy tendencies compared, 9–10

in team leaders, 181, 182*t*

USNews.com, 25

Vesterlund, Lise, 21

victims

in alpha triangle, 52, 52, 54, 56–57

avoiding role of, 90

executors as, 156, 160

in home life, 222

identifying personas, 60, *61*

team sludge and, 179–180

visionaries as, 106

villains

in alpha triangle, 52, 52, 53, 54

commander as, 53, 59, 74, 75

executors as, 54, 59, 154–155, 156

in home life, 222

identifying personas, 59, 59–60

strategists as, 53, 59, 123, 135

team sludge and, 179–180

visionaries as, 53, 59, 103, 106

visionaries, 38, 95–117, 100*t*, 236

Alpha Assessment Report, 239–240

About the Authors

Kate Ludeman, PhD, is a widely recognized executive coach who has worked with over a thousand CEOs and senior executives on every continent, in industries ranging from high tech to pharmaceuticals to consumer products. With her extensive experience and expertise, Kate offers innovative and practical skills to strong business leaders and those who work with them. Having trained in both engineering and psychology, she has a unique approach that helps leaders maximize performance by combining analytic skills with emotional intelligence.

Formerly the vice president of human resources for a high-tech company in Silicon Valley, she is the founder and CEO of Worth Ethic Corporation. Kate has been the featured speaker at numerous business forums, has appeared on more than a hundred television and radio programs, and has hosted a portion of ABC affiliate programs in Dallas and San Francisco. Her books include *The Worth Ethic, Earn What You're Worth, The Corporate Mystic* (with coauthor Gay Hendricks, now in its eleventh printing), and *Radical Change, Radical Results* (with coauthor Eddie Erlandson).

Eddie Erlandson, MD, an executive vice president at Worth Ethic Corporation, coaches executives to change their ineffective leadership habits to achieve greater personal, professional, and organizational impact. He has worked with executive teams in government and academia, and across a number of industries, including high tech, pharmaceuticals, hospitals, services, and professional sports.

Eddie taught and served in health care leadership roles at the University of Michigan, where he was associate professor of surgery and dean for student affairs. At St. Joseph Mercy Hospital in Ann Arbor, Michigan, he practiced vascular surgery for 20 years and codesigned and led Life Lessons, a pioneering wellness and executive fitness program that helped hundreds of patients reduce health risks, increase life satisfaction, and achieve greater sustainable results in business leadership.

With his expertise in the biological basis of change, leadership, and stress, Eddie employs unique strategies to help executives sustain peak performance while balancing their lives. A popular keynote speaker, he weaves medical science, endurance sports, and experience in coaching executives into a compelling and practical message.

Kate and Eddie are married, and live and work in Austin, Texas. Their company, Worth Ethic, offers individual executive coaching, intensive group programs for managers who seek to become more effective leaders, and certification programs for coaches who work with alphas. For information, see www.WorthEthic.com or call 512-493-2300.